*African Constitutionalism
and the Role of Islam*

African Constitutionalism and the Role of Islam

ABDULLAHI AHMED AN-NA'IM

PENN

University of Pennsylvania Press

Philadelphia

Published by
University of Pennsylvania Press
Philadelphia, Pennsylvania 19104-4112

Library of Congress Cataloging-in-Publication Data

An-Naʿim, ʿAbd Allah Ahmad, 1946–
    African constitutionalism and the role of Islam / Abdullahi Ahmed An-Naʿim
        p.   cm. — (Pennsylvania studies in human rights)
    ISBN-13: 978-0-8122-3962-1 (alk. paper)
    ISBN-10: 0-8122-3962-8 (alk. paper)
    Includes bibliographical references and index.
    1. Constitutional law—Africa. 2. Constitutional law—Africa—Philosophy
3. Constitutional law (Islamic law). 4. Islam and state. I. Title.   II. Series
KQC524 .N35   2006
342.6—dc22   2006042177

Contents

Preface

I began working on this book in 1995 under a grant from the American Council of Learned Societies (ACLS), but had to set it aside when I became the coordinator of a major study of legal protection of rights under the constitutions of sixteen African countries. That project was organized by the International Center for the Legal Protection of Human Rights (Interights) and Inter-Africa Network for Human Rights and Development (Afronet). All those studies were done by African researchers working on their respective countries according to the same terms of reference and uniform format. Ten of those country studies were in due course published in *Human Rights Under African Constitutions: Realizing the Promise for Ourselves* (University of Pennsylvania Press, 2003). I am pleased to acknowledge the initial grant of the ACLS, and the professional support of Interights and Afronet, but my special appreciation is for the rigorous scholarship and helpful insights of the researchers in that project. That project not only confirmed and helped define the concept of African constitutionalism that I am trying to further develop in this book, but also enabled me to test and revise some of my assumptions and initial thinking on the subject. This background is therefore important to note from the beginning because it relates to the genesis and objectives of this book.

I was already working on the cultural legitimacy of human rights and related ideas, with particular reference to Islamic and African societies, when I participated in a global comparative study of constitutionalism organized by the ACLS in 1988–89. Working on the Africa regional "institute" for that project contributed to shaping my understanding of issues of constitutionalism in a pan-African perspective, reaffirmed my commitment to this principle and my belief in the possibilities of its incremental success throughout the continent. The idea of writing a book about constitutionalism in Africa emerged at the end of that ACLS project.

However, it was my subsequent participation in the Interights/Afronet project that confirmed and helped me develop the proactive approach I am attempting to present in this book to emphasize the incremental success of constitutionalism in Africa. Those studies also provided me with a wealth of detailed information on the practical working of constitutional principles in a good cross-section of African countries. In particular, that experience affirmed my belief in the urgent need for socially engaged scholarship without sacrificing its quality. The implementation of that project made it clear to me that it is unacceptable for an African scholar to devote her or his whole attention to detached academic analysis without attempting to respond to the urgent needs and untold suffering of Africans throughout the continent. On the other hand, activist involvement with such issues raises risk of bias and lack of scholarly rigor. While appreciating and attempting to guard against this risk, I see no alternative to positively responding to the need for social engagement of the issues facing African societies.

From this perspective, I am seeking to promote constitutional governance in African societies, by developing ways of enhancing and consolidating the basis of the incremental success of constitutionalism, with due consideration of the difficulties and setbacks experienced by African societies in this regard. Moreover, I am suggesting that such difficulties and setbacks are to be expected as an integral part of the process of adaptation and indigenization of an essentially alien concept of the "nation-state" and its role in large scale political and social organization. As discussed later in this book, however, the assumption of "nation" in the nation-state concept can be very problematic in the postcolonial African context.

But my belief in the desirability and possibility of sustainable constitutionalism is based on a certain understanding of the concept, and a proactive approach to the conditions and processes of realizing it in the African context. This understanding and proactive approach should be seen as part of a universal project of constitutionalism that is to be conceived and pursued through global collaborations, but with due regard to the historical and current realities of international economic and political power relations.

A positive or negative outcome of these processes should neither be expected to automatically materialize, nor be assumed to be inevitable or permanent. Since adaptation and indigenization necessarily indicate that there are difficulties to be overcome, the success of these processes can only be incremental, through practical experience over time. This desired objective cannot be realized without critical analysis of experiences so far and pragmatic development and implementation of the necessary strategies in the future. African scholars have an important role to play in this regard, in addition to their personal engagement in political struggles within their respective countries. But scholars cannot play this role without meticulous verification of the factual basis of rigorous analysis. Otherwise, they would be doing a serious disservice to their societies if they compromise on the scholarly quality of their work. In other words, there is no conflict between rigorous scholarship and advocacy for social and political change because maintaining the highest standards of scholarly quality is the prerequisite condition for the role of socially engaged scholars.

The general progression of the analysis I am presenting in this book can be summarized as follows. The first chapter is devoted to a preliminary discussion of the problem of defining and implementing constitutionalism in general, and of the circumstances and assumptions associated with its introduction in late colonial and early postcolonial Africa. But for the concept to survive and thrive over time it has to be adapted and sustained through an indigenous rationale and dynamics of what might be called the dialectic of constitutionalism in Africa and African constitutionalism. This dialectic refers to the processes of progression from constitutionalism as an abstract concept or set of principles to the adaptation and indigenization of the concept or principles to local conditions and context. As I will emphasize later in this book, however, "progression" includes "regression."

Conceptual and practical issues associated with this process, as it is unfolding and evolving in the actual experiences of African countries, are discussed in the second chapter. In other words, I take the practical experience of African countries as being the primary source as well as practical method of adaptation and indigenization, but would emphasize the need for conceptual clarity and political leadership in drawing lessons and formulating and implementing strategies for future action. To this end, I examine in the third chapter the recent experience of some African countries along what I call a continuum of incremental success, including a variety and degrees of failure and setbacks. Chapters 4 and 5 are devoted to closer analysis of what I call the contingent role of Islam, as an application and illustration of the general thesis of the book as a whole. In conclusion, the last chapter offers some comparative reflections and assessment of the prospects of sustainable constitutionalism.

To avoid the risks of distortion or oversimplification, I will not attempt to summarize the content of these chapters. Instead, I wish to note some of the tensions that seem to be inherent to the sort of argument I am trying to make. There is first an underlying tension in the study of and policy reflection on such concepts as "constitutionalism" or "democracy," namely, how to apply principles that have received their present global articulation and development from the experiences of Western societies to African societies. In my view, such concepts can be accepted as viable philosophical, political, and analytic categories for evaluating the state of politics, society, culture, and so forth, in African societies, provided they are open to contestation and reconceptualization from the perspective of those societies. This can be done by drawing on indigenous and precolonial African traditions of political, social, and cultural thought and practice, as well as political and intellectual traditions of anti-colonial dissent and protest, in addition to concepts from European or Western social thought and disciplinary traditions, as relativized and reconceptualized in local context.

The deeply contextual approach to the incremental success of constitutionalism in present African countries that I am proposing in this book entails a tension between the requirement of assessing each experience on its own terms, and the need to have some verifiable standards for assessing the relative degree of success that is supposed to have been realized in any country at a given point in time. The way to mediate this tension is to identify elements of an emerging global consensus on some critical features of constitutional governance, and then apply them to assess the "performance" of each country in its own context. Critical assessment of the constitutional record of any African country is necessary and requisite for developing and implementing strategies for the promotion and consolidation of these principles in those countries. The question is how to do this in a deeply contextual manner, instead of applying a preconceived, linear approach to the assessment of success or failure, without due regard to the particular history and specific context of each society.

Another tension this book seeks to mediate relates to the paradoxical nature of the African postcolonial state, which is supposed to be sovereign from a legal point of view, though it is in fact incapable of exercising the full powers and responsibilities of sovereignty in practice. The question here is how to work with this reality while attempting to change it in the "real world" of power politics, collapsing economies and corruption at home, and persistent Western neocolonial hegemony abroad. Yet, the only way forward is through the practice of constitutionalism in order to empower civil society actors to hold governments legally and politically accountable to their own populations. The more effective this process is at home, the sooner will neocolonial international relations diminish over time. The main question for this book is how to make that happen in a sustainable manner throughout the continent. While I attempt to do that in broad theoretical terms in the first three chapters, it is the closer examination of the case of Islamic societies that I hope will clarify and illustrate the argument I am making for wider application.

My concern with the role of Islam in Islamic African societies raises another tension, namely, the conflict between traditional understandings of Shariʿa (the normative system of Islam) and modern principles of constitutionalism. The notion of the contingency of the role of Islam refers to a theoretical and political "space" within which the mediation of this tension can occur through a reinterpretation of Islamic texts to reformulate relevant principles of Shariʿa. The relationship between Islam and constitutionalism in Africa should be understood within the framework of the dialectic of Islam in Africa and African Islam, on the one hand, and the broader context of culture, religion and politics, on the other. Muslims are not only Muslims, nor do they behave all of the time as such, though Islam is fundamental to their cultural identity, social institutions and daily behavior. In particular, perhaps traditional forms of Africanized Islam might provide better prospects for reconciliation between the Islamic cultural identity of African Muslims, on the one hand, and the requirements of their daily lives in multicultural, multireligious states, on the other. The main idea here is that Africanized Islam, with its strong sufi (mystic) roots and practices, was inclusive and tolerant of diversity within Muslim communities and in their relationships with non-Muslim communities. But the regional and global nature of the cross-cultural and political interaction adds to the contingency of the role of Islam in relation to constitutionalism by bringing into Islamic African societies more "fundamentalist" interpretations of Shariʿa that are more exclusive and intolerant of diversity. This approach is hopefully clarified and illustrated by the comparative analysis of the contingent role of Islam in Sudan, Nigeria, and Senegal in Chapters 4 and 5.

Finally, I am also concerned about the current global context of a very destructive trend in the foreign policy of the United States in the aftermath of the 9/11 terrorist attacks. This primarily unilateral and aggressively militaristic response to the real and serious threat of terrorism, which has resulted in the illegal and counterproductive invasion and occupation of Iraq in March 2003, may have had two negative consequences for the objectives of this book. This global environment poses a most serious challenge to some of the most fundamental principles of international legality, and has seriously undermined the credibility of notions of universal standards of human rights and constitutionalism everywhere, especially among Islamic societies. This negative implication is compounded by the manner in which the United States is seeking to influence the domestic policies of African and Islamic governments that are vulnerable to American economic, political, and security pressure to adopt oppressive legislation and policies. Moreover, the combined effect of these negative developments have created or enhance a preexisting "siege mentality," especially among Islamic societies, which makes them more conservative and defensive about their religious and cultural identity. This would seem to indicate that these societies are now less likely to engage in internal transformation in favor of constitutional governance and the protection of human rights than they were a few years ago. The challenge is therefore how to maintain a positive and forward looking perspective on constitutionalism for Islamic societies in general, and those among them who are also African for the purposes of this book.

To conclude this brief Preface, I realize many tensions within my thesis and analysis are not resolved; indeed, may not be possible to resolve through any theoretical discussion, however developed or elaborate it may be. I am therefore painfully aware of the limitations of the scope of this book, and of the approach I am proposing to the promotion and consolidation of constitutionalism in African countries. Yet, I do believe that this thesis and analysis can make a useful contribution to the field on which others can build.

Finally, I wish to gratefully acknowledge the earlier support of the ACLS project, as well as the insights and wealth of detailed information I gathered from my colleagues in the Interights/Afronet project. But this book would not have been possible without the continuous support of Emory School of Law since I joined its faculty in 1995, and the able research assistance of too many students to mention here. But my most profound appreciation goes to Rohit Chopra, Ph.D. candidate at the Graduate Institute of Liberal Arts of Emory University and my most able research assistant, indeed colleague, for invaluable conceptual and methodological contributions to the final preparation of this manuscript.

Chapter 1
Toward an Inclusive Theory of Constitutionalism

Available evidence regarding the constitutional experiences of most African countries indicates repeated failure or at least a protracted crisis. I will argue in this book that these experiences can and should be seen as part of processes of incremental success. As explained later, the notion of incremental success indicates the accumulation of experiences that are conducive to better and more sustainable implementation of the principles, institutions and mechanisms of constitutionalism over time, even though some experiences may be negative in the short term. A critical question to be addressed at subsequent stages of my analysis is how to assess or evaluate any constitutional experience. The point to emphasize from the outset is that rejecting the application of a single standard of success or failure of these experiences everywhere does not mean that there are no standards at all. Rather, it is a matter of clarification and application of appropriate standards to each case in its own context.

The deliberately optimistic and positive reading I am proposing is necessary, in my view, for developing ways of enhancing and consolidating constitutional governance in these countries. That is, the apparent constitutional failures and serious setbacks of constitutionalism in various African countries are to be expected as integral to the necessary or unavoidable processes of adaptation and indigenization of this concept and its general principles and institutions. However, the success of this process of adaptation and indigenization should not be expected to happen as a matter of course over time. A sober and critical analysis of the experiences of each African country in light of a clearer understanding of the meaning and implications of constitutionalism is necessary for the development and implementation of practical strategies for the promotion of constitutional governance in that country.

Thus, a deeply contextual approach is necessary for understanding and appreciating the contributions of African societies to the concept and principles of constitutional governance, which might be called "African constitutionalism." This does not mean that African constitutionalism as such is inherently different or distinguishable from other experiences. The term is used to emphasize that the experiences of various countries in one part of the world should not be judged by criteria that are specific to another country or region. I am focusing here on the development of this approach to African countries because their experiences are often dismissed as necessarily negative or unworthy of serious consideration as legitimate contributions to the principles of constitutionalism and their implementation.

The thesis and analysis presented in this book are premised on a strong belief in the desirability and practical possibility of promoting constitutionalism in African countries. This premise concedes that the most significant development of this concept is closely associated with European notions of the nation-state and its relation to the actual civil society that existed in the historical context of those societies which are difficult to apply in most African countries today. From this perspective, I prefer to use the term "territorial state" instead of "nation state" in referring to the postcolonial state in Africa. The notion of "nation" on which European models of the state are premised tend to assume or presuppose that it consists of a single homogeneous ethnic group (Smith 1991, 2000). In this sense, individual African "tribes" as they existed before colonialism might qualify as "nations," but colonial boundaries often arbitrarily passed through such nations, or simply subsumed them under a broader, African "nation" state. In other words, African states were "granted" juridical sovereignty over their respective territories, as determined by colonial administrations, while their populations did not constitute "nations" in the European sense of the term. It is important to bear this commonly noted point here because of its implications for the possibilities of the sort of shared political culture and consensus that underlie "national" constitutional theory and practice in the European countries where these ideas became better established over the course of the last three centuries.

Such tensions in the recent history and current situation in almost all African countries should not be taken to diminish the paramount importance of constitutionalism as a necessary framework for protecting national sovereignty while respecting the human dignity and rights of all persons and communities or groups. On the contrary, such tensions emphasize the importance and relevance of constitutionalism in postcolonial states in Africa. An affirmative and positive approach to constitutionalism is particularly necessary in the present climate of persistent and profound skepticism about human rights and democracy. The legitimacy and relevance of these universal values are being undermined by their cynical and unprincipled manipulation by major powers, on the one hand, and opportunistic lip service being paid to them by African governments, on the other.

One critical aspect of the analysis that I will not attempt to address in this book is the relationship between constitutionalism and economic development simply because of my lack of sufficient expertise in that dimension of the subject, but also because that would require a significantly different type of methodology and information than is available to me. To concede that I am unable to do well enough is to emphasize the importance of the economic dimension, rather than underestimating the role of that relationship. Still, I hope that the sort of analysis and reflection I am able to offer can contribute to the field. As an African Muslim, I am particularly concerned about the struggle of African Islamic societies to reconcile their religious traditions with their commitment to constitutionalism in the present context. But first, here is an outline of the main elements of the proposed approach, subject to further clarification in subsequent chapters.

A Basic Understanding of Constitutionalism

The basic understanding of constitutionalism I am working with here is premised on two propositions. First, various conceptions of constitutionalism should be seen as complementary approaches to an ideal, to be adapted to different conditions of time and place, rather than as representing sharp dichotomies or categorical choices. Whether based on a written document or not, the objective must always be to uphold the rule of law, enforce effective limitations on government powers, and the protection of fundamental rights. In each case, the question should be about how the country's experience relates to the underlying rationale or purpose of constitutionalism as a general principle. Since any definition of this concept is necessarily the product of the experiences of certain societies in their various settings, it is neither reasonable nor desirable to insist on a single approach to the definition or implementation of constitutionalism, to the exclusion of all others. A more universally accepted understanding of the term may evolve over time, but that should be the outcome of comparative analysis of practical experiences, rather than an attempt to impose an exclusive definition based on one ideological or philosophical tradition or another.

Second, the construction of general principles (or universal features) of this concept should emphasize their role as means to the ends of successful and sustainable constitutional governance in country-specific contexts, while emphasizing the need for internal consistency of the relationship between ends and means. The ends of popular sovereignty and social justice, for instance, can only be achieved through the actual application of these principles, rather than by postponing application until "ideal" conditions for it have been established by some self-proclaimed ideological elite as has often happened in recent African experiences. Such conditions can only be realized through trial and error in the practical application of principles of popular sovereignty and social justice, provided society and its leaders are open to implementing the necessary correction of theory and modification of practice. Indeed, it is the practical pursuit of popular sovereignty and social justice that will provide opportunities for promoting an environment that is more conducive to successful and sustainable constitutionalism. In other words, the end of constitutional governance is realized through the means of empirical practical experience of constitutional principles in the specific context of each society.

The history of constitutionalism is often traced back to ancient Greece (Gordon 1999), but real sources of the modern concept are probably much more recent, including the Virginia Declaration of Rights of June 1776 in what came to be the United States of America, together with earlier documents like the English Bill of Rights of 1689. There were other constitutional documents in the context of the American revolution, such as those of New Hampshire (January 5, 1776) and South Carolina (March 26, 1776). But the Virginia Declaration of Rights became renowned for appealing to the sovereignty of the people, universal principles, and inherent human rights, and for proclaiming a written constitution "as the basis for the foundation of government" (Thorpe 1909: 3812). It also enumerated, for the first time, the responsibility and accountability of government, the separation of powers, and the idea that constitutional government should be a limited government. Subsequently, the concept of constitutional government was further refined in the French Declaration of Rights of Man and Citizen and in the American Constitution which has since been replicated many times all over the world. This emerging global consensus toward "world constitutionalism" (Ackerman 1997) lends credence to Dworkin's view that all members of the community ought to be treated with equal respect and concern (1977, 1996, 2000).

Put in elemental terms, therefore, constitutionalism is a framework for the mediation of certain unavoidable conflicts in the political, economic, and social fabric of every human society. This proposition assumes that conflict is a normal and permanent feature of human societies, and defines constitutionalism in terms of being a framework for mediation, rather than permanent or final resolution of such conflicts. But since struggles over power and resources cannot be practically mediated by all members of any society, there has to be some form of delegation from those who, as a practical matter, cannot be part of the daily and detailed processes of administration and adjudication. At the same time, however, those who have to delegate to others also need to ensure that their interests are served by this process by participating in the selection of delegates as well as in holding them accountable to ensure that they act according to the terms of delegation. These pragmatic considerations underlie the basic constitutional principles of representative government, including bureaucratic aspects of democratic administration of public affairs, which is fully accountable to its citizens. The above-mentioned premise of consistency of ends and means requires the constant verification of the validity of the structures and operation of the processes of representation and accountability, whereby the integrity and efficacy of these processes is conductive to the incremental success of constitutional governance over time.

For the appropriate processes to work properly in each setting, the general population must be able and willing to effectively exercise its powers of delegation as well as accountability of public officials, whether elected or appointed. There are many aspects to such ability and willingness, some relating to the population side while others pertain to the government and its organs, or the conditions of the interaction between the two. On the first count, for instance, the population at large must be capable of exercising intelligent, well-informed, and independent judgment about the ability of its representatives and officials to act on its behalf, and to verify that they do in fact act in accordance with the best interest of the population. The public must also have the capacity to challenge and replace those who fail to implement its mandate. To ensure and facilitate a wide range of operations and functions of democratic government, all citizens must enjoy certain individual and collective rights, like freedoms of expression and association, access to information and effective remedies against excess or abuse of power by official organs. But in the final analysis, the best principles and mechanisms of constitutional governance will not operate properly without sufficiently strong civic engagement by a critical mass of citizens.

Constitutional governance would therefore require respect for and protection of collective as well as individual rights not only because the two sets of rights are interdependent in that one cannot be effective without the other, but in the sense that the specific meaning of each one draws on the content of the other. For example, individual freedoms of opinion, belief, and association are necessary for the realization of collective freedoms of ethnic, religious, or professional/trade union associations, whereby the freedom of the individual person is meaningful within the context of the relevant group. However, since rights are ultimately tools for realizing the objectives of social justice, political stability, and economic development for all segments of the population, they should be perceived as dynamic processes rather than abstract legal rules. For instance, the content and rationale of a collective right to the use of language or protection of cultural resources of an ethnic group can shift and change in response to internal transformation within the group or challenge from outside.

However, such rights as freedom of expression and association are not useful without the institutional means for exercising the sort of judgment and continuous accountability of government officials envisaged by the principle of constitutionalism. To begin with in this regard, officials must not be able to obscure their activities or hide their excess or abuse of power, hence the general need for transparency of official action. Moreover, people are unlikely to invest energy and resources in holding officials accountable when there are no realistic prospects of effective remedy against officials who violate the obligations of their office or contrive to evade responsibility. Administrative and financial transparency is unlikely to lead to effective legal and political accountability without competent and independent institutions that can investigate possible violations and adjudicate on disputed issues and questions. This aspect of the process relates to various matters that cannot be discussed in detail here, ranging from technical questions of administrative law and tribunals to practical arrangements for securing the independence of the judiciary or political accountability of elected or appointed officials.

But what is probably the most critical aspect of constitutionalism relates to subtle and rather mysterious psychological and sociological aspects of what I referred to earlier as sufficiently strong civic engagement by a critical mass of citizens. These aspects are difficult to quantify or verify, except perhaps in terms of outcomes that indicate the success or failure of constitutionalism in a given context. They include the motivation of citizens to keep themselves well-informed in public affairs, and to organize themselves in nongovernmental organizations that can act on their behalf in effective and sustainable ways. People are unlikely to assert and pursue avenues of accountability and redress without the material and human resources as well the psychological and cultural orientation to do so. Public officials and the agencies and institutions they operate must not only enjoy the confidence of local communities, but also be familiar, friendly, and responsive when approached. This is the practical and most foundational meaning of popular sovereignty, whereby a people can govern themselves through their own public officials and elected representatives. Constitutionalism is ultimately concerned with realizing and regulating this ideal in the most sustainable and evolving manner possible, whereby the combination of theory and practice of this concept is capable of ensuring self-determination now and responding to changing circumstances in the future.

To illustrate some of the preceding features, take the need to mediate the tension between general principles and specific determinations in individual cases involving allocation of power or resources among social and political actors. Whereas general principles and policies tend to push for predictability and consistency of outcome in similar instances of conflict or when applied to issues that are likely to arise frequently, individual cases call for particularistic determinations that respond to claims of the specificity of the conflict at hand as distinguished from others. Since each type of function requires a different set of skills and institutional arrangements, it may be necessary for them to be performed by separate officials and organs, observing their distinctive procedures in accordance with the rationale of each function. This "separation of powers" is often taken to mean that legislative organs set public policy and enact laws of general application, executive organs implement those policies, and the judiciary interprets and applies the law in adjudicating disputes among or between organs of government, individual and groups of citizens.

But the lines of separation of powers are rarely categorical in theory or settled and neat in practice. The need for practical mechanisms to elect or appoint officials, including senior judges, and the institutional requirements of accountability in the daily operation of government agencies, create risks of either persistent deadlock or excessive accommodation among supposedly "separate" organs and functions of government. For instance, failure to limit or regulate the power of a supreme or high court to interpret constitutional provisions or adjudicate certain types of disputes may create risks of political manipulation or deadlock in the appointment of judges. The more serious or far reaching the consequences of judicial adjudication of controversial public policy or political issues, like the right to abortion or which candidate won the state of Florida in the 2000 presidential elections in the United States, the greater the risks for the independence of the judiciary in the future. Such risks can be diminished through the stronger development of the relevant institutions or more engaged public opinion, but that may not necessarily resolve the dilemmas of proper and appropriate separation of powers.

For example, a stronger judiciary may be tempted to tackle more controversial or politically sensitive issues, and it may be encouraged and supported in doing by a well-informed and active citizenry. But that may not in fact be wise or prudent for the judiciary—what may seem like a clear victory for one side of a controversy can turn into a defeat or create greater constitutional or political problems in the future. The judicial legalization of abortion, for instance, may provoke a political backlash, resulting in the appointment of ideologically driven judges who can then shift the whole political and social policy of the country in the opposite direction.

The preceding remarks emphasize the importance of such general constitutional principles as representative government, transparency and accountability, separation of powers and independence of the judiciary. But this is not to suggest that such features must all be present in particular models all at once for constitutionalism to be successfully implemented in a country. In fact, such principles and conditions can only emerge and develop in a variety of models through a process of trial and error over time (McHugh 2002; Franklin 1995; Rosenfeld 1994). The rationale and purpose of representative government, transparency, and accountability can be realized through different models, such as the parliamentary system of the United Kingdom or the presidential system in the French or American style. As I highlight in Chapter 6, these models achieve transparency of governmental practice and political and legal accountability in different ways. The principles of separation of powers and independence of the judiciary are implemented and safeguarded in various ways specific to each constitutional model. Each model of these successful constitutional experiences works in its totality, though not always, and is transformed or adapted in its own ways in times of crisis, as illustrated by the series of French constitutions adopted during the twentieth century.

From this perspective, constitutionalism is not only succeeding in African countries "incrementally" through practice, as I will attempt to show, but cannot succeed in any other way there or anywhere else in the world. The underlying rationale and objective of this book is to clarify and illustrate the application of this notion of "incremental success," in order to facilitate stronger and more sustainable success for African constitutionalism. But it may be helpful at this stage to introduce the other main theme of the book, namely, the contingent role of Islam in either promoting or obstructing this process. Including this perspective, however, is not intended to shift the focus of the book as a whole from African constitutionalism to an Islamic discourse around this principle. The former remains the primary subject, while the latter is only a way of clarifying and illustrating the application of the general, more inclusive theory of constitutionalism in African settings. This clarification and illustration begins here by contrasting traditional Islamic thought on the subject with the preceding outline of modern constitutional principles.

Islam and Constitutionalism

To begin with, I need to qualify the sense in which I am discussing the relationship between Islam, as an ancient and extremely diverse religious tradition, on the one hand, and constitutionalism as a modern secular doctrine of governance and rights, on the other. A straightforward comparison is of course out of the question in view of the fundamental differences in the nature, functions, and operation of these two paradigms. Moreover, in whatever terms the relationship between the two is conceived, it cannot be the same for all Muslims, who constitute one-fifth of the world's population today, living in every continent and region.

Indeed, as discussed in Chapters 4 and 5 below, I am counting on the diversity and contingency of this relationship for promoting constitutionalism in Islamic African societies. It is also clear, however, that some interpretations of Islam are seriously problematic from a constitutional point of view, while others are at least consistent with the principle, if not positively supportive of it.

The premise of highlighting the possibilities of positive as well as negative relationships is that the attitudes of Muslims regarding constitutionalism are partly shaped by their understanding of Islam. This does not mean that Islam completely or exclusively determines the constitutional behavior of Muslims, as that is also influenced by a wide range of economic, political, and other factors, which is also true of the role of religion in other human societies in general. Nevertheless, the role of Islam is probably a major issue in many Islamic societies because of its widely perceived impact on the legitimacy of constitutional theory and practice, though that tends to vary in intensity and implications. In other words, Muslims may take a negative view of constitutionalism, even one hostile to some aspects of it, to the extent that they believe it to be inconsistent with their religious obligation to observe Shari'a. This term is used here to refer to the totality of the normative system of Islam. The relevance of Islam to constitutionalism in Islamic societies is emphasized by the fact that Shari'a is believed to cover the political and social sphere, property and economic aspects, moral and ethic principles, in addition to matters of religious doctrine and ritual practices.

The following outline of some of the ideas and factors that are likely to influence the view Muslims may take of constitutionalism will necessarily be brief because it is not possible, or necessary for my purposes here, to attempt a comprehensive discussion of the subject. This overview will also be theoretical not only because the historical record is difficult to verify, or review in detail in this limited space, but also since it is the popular perception of the theory more than factual reality that resonates with the consciousness of Muslims today.

The predominant Islamic frame of reference is commonly taken to be the experience of the original Muslim community established by the Prophet in Medina, a town in Western Arabia, around 622, and believed to have been continued by the first generation of his followers (Faruki 1971). Patterns of individual and collective behavior, models of political and social relationships, and institutions commonly ascribed to or associated with that period continue to be held as the Islamic ideal by most Muslims today. To the Sunni majority, the Medina community of 622–660, the reign of the Prophet, and that of the four "rightly guided" Caliphs (successors of the Prophet) represent the most authoritative model of Islamic constitutional theory. The Shi'a minority (presently at about 10–12 percent of the total Muslim population of the world) hold a similar view for their own separate line of Imams, starting with Ali, the fourth Caliph in the Sunni sequence of succession (An-Na'im 1990: 29–31). Both sides uphold their respective model as the ideal, while constantly decrying deviations by subsequent generations, which are often justified as coerced by compelling circumstances such as internal strife or external invasion. As Anderson explains:

To a Muslim, it has always been a far more heinous sin to deny or question the divine revelation than to fail to obey it. So it seemed preferable to continue to pay lip-service to an inviolate Shari'a, as the only law of fundamental authority, and to excuse departure from much of it in practice by appealing to the doctrine of necessity (*darurua*), rather than to make any attempt to adapt that law to the circumstances and needs of contemporary life. (Anderson 1976: 36)

Thus, the common (or rather commonly assumed) view among Muslims today is that the Medina state was the original and perfect model of an "Islamic state," established and ruled by the Prophet who continued to receive Divine Revelation, according to Muslim belief, until his death in 632. In modern constitutional terms, the Prophet was the original and exclusive human sovereign and sole source of law and political authority. The subjects (as they could not be called "citizens" in the modern sense of the term) of that state are believed to have been the ideal model Muslims, both individually and collectively as a community of devout believers, the embodiment of Islamic values under the immediate instruction and supervision of the Prophet himself. By its own terms, therefore, this view of the Medina state and its population can never be replicated because Muslims do not accept the possibility of another Prophet after Muhammad and also believe the first generation of Muslims to have been the best possible embodiment of Islamic values and lifestyle. Yet the Medina state is supposed to forever provide Muslims with the most authoritative constitutional model of an Islamic government under Shari'a. In this light, it is instructive for our purposes here to analyze that model in constitutional terms because Muslims presumably continue to hold it as the standard by which a modern state is to be judged, if not actually implemented today.

The key constitutional features of the Medina state derive from the central role of the Prophet as the ultimate source of moral and political as well as "legal" authority, who as such enjoyed complete unfettered allegiance and obedience of the believers—those who believed him to be the final and conclusive Prophet. He combined ultimate legislative, executive, and judicial powers, declaring what the law was, interpreting and implementing it in practice, as well as adjudicating disputes. According to Muslim beliefs, it was simply inconceivable for the Prophet's political and legal powers to be restricted or challenged by any human agency. Moreover, the idea of formal or institutional limitation or separation of powers of rulers was itself totally unknown anywhere else in the world. We can consider the significance or implications of these and related issues after the following overview of the Medina state and its aftermath.

Upon the Prophet's death in 632, the first Caliph, Abu Bakr, was selected by a very small group of leading Muslims, the second, Umar was directly appointed by Abu Bakr before he died, and the third Usman, was selected by a small committee appointed by Umar as he was about to die. While Ali, the fourth Caliph, was not openly contested by any other contender, his appointment was indirectly challenged by some leading Muslims of the time for a variety of reasons. The ensuing civil war and the assassination of Ali resulted in the establishment of the Umayyad monarchy in 661, followed by the Abbasid monarchy that lasted in various forms and ways for several centuries. In all cases, however, the effectively final and conclusive selection or appointment of the Caliph was presumably confirmed by the general Muslim population through what was known as *bay'a*, public oath of allegiance. Although this may have been a fiction or mere formality, even during the Medina state, the notion of bay'a can have some paradoxical or ambiguous constitutional implications today, as explained below. In particular, while this notion of bay'a implied that the authority of the Caliph derives from the Muslim population at large, there was no way to hold him accountable or to terminate allegiance to a specific person in that office in practice.

Thus, Muslims have experienced a variety of methods for identifying rulers throughout history: from limited election, direct appointment, and limited selection in the city state of Medina to the hereditary monarchies of the imperial states that finally ended with the collapse of the Ottoman Empire after the First World War. From a modern constitutional point of view, and regardless of the method of selection or appointment, the Caliph enjoyed absolute powers for life because, once bay'a was given, there was no organized and peaceful mechanism for withdrawing or restricting it. Indeed, it is not clear at all that the Muslim population at large had a choice in declaring and upholding their allegiance once a candidate was selected or appointed by the leaders of the community. Withholding the oath of allegiance at the beginning or attempting to withdraw it subsequently was commonly perceived as tantamount to rebellion or treason, which may result in death if the person is thought likely to engage in military resistance.

In any case, there was simply no concept of or mechanism for organized peaceful political dissent, though the response may vary with the possibilities or likely outcome of other forms of political negotiations or mutual accommodation. Absolute monarchies were the standard and shared experience of all human societies in that premodern historical context. Such regimes were the invariable norm throughout the world until the modern era, and not only among Muslims, and those regimes often used religion as a legitimizing frame of reference. It can also be argued that premodern systems of governance also had appropriate mechanisms of accountability and did rely on the consent of the general population, though obviously not to the degree and in the manner required by modern constitutionalism. However, while one should not judge those experiences by today's standards, it is inappropriate to seek to implement those historical models in the present context. In other words, this constitutional critique of traditional Islamic political thought and practice is intended to challenge current calls for the reenactment of that historical model, rather than judging it as right or wrong for its own context.

Although the classical Caliphs did not enjoy the Prophet's religious authority, they did in fact exercise the full range of his political and legal powers, which were supposed to be limited and checked by moral and ethical constraints; the assumption that the Caliph and his officials would voluntarily abide by Shari'a. The limited and participatory nature of political leadership is often said to have been ensured by the notion of *shura*, whereby the ruler is expected to consult with the community about public affairs. Verse 159 of chapter 3 of the Qur'an instructs the Prophet to consult (*shawirhum*) with the believers, but once he made up his mind, he should act accordingly. The obvious meaning of the Arabic term shura in that context at most indicated a requirement to seek advice, without necessarily being bound by it. The actual practice of the Prophet and of the Caliphs of Medina also confirmed this understanding, which became the norm for the monarchies of the Umayyad and Abbasid empires and other states throughout the premodern history of Islamic societies. Another verse often cited in this context is verse 38 of chapter 42, which describes the believers as a community who decide matters in consultation, but it does not explain how that might be done in practice or what happens in case of disagreement (Coulson 1957: 55–56).

This limited and historically conditioned understanding of the concept of shura does not mean that it cannot be used today as a basis for institutionalized constitutional principles of democratic government that are legally and politically accountable to the population at large. In fact, that is the sort of evolution and development of Islamic principles that I am calling for, but that possibility would be better facilitated by a clear understanding of what the notion of shura and its historical practice used to be. To pretend that that notion has already been understood and practiced as "constitutional democratic government" in the modern sense will be counterproductive because that would confirm and validate unconstitutional practices. In any case, that claim still has to account for the lack of practical institutional arrangements for peaceful political dissent and orderly transfer of power throughout Islamic history up to the postcolonial era. As briefly explained later, these concepts and institutions have only evolved very gradually and tentatively since the eighteenth century in some Western countries, and are only beginning to emerge and take root in most parts of the world.

Another dimension of this historical conditionality of principles of constitutional and democratic governance in relation to historical Islamic principles and practice relates to what is commonly known in present constitutional discourse as "civil rights," also confirmed now as "human rights" under international law. I now highlight the main features of this dimension and then offer a general approach to mediating the tension between these problematic aspects of the historical understanding of Islam and modern constitutionalism, as background for further discussion in Chapters 4 and 5.

It must be first emphasized that, like the English Common Law and other legal systems, the general rule of Shari'a is that people are guaranteed freedom of action (or inaction) unless, and only to the extent that, action (or inaction) is expressly prohibited or restricted. In this sense, there are no theoretical limitations on civil rights under Shari'a except in specific cases, as highlighted below. But the practical application of this general principle is complicated by the diffused nature of Shari'a in a wide range of schools of thought, and the strong disagreements among Islamic scholars (*ulama*) on almost every conceivable subject. Muslims are therefore often uncertain about whether under Shari'a they have the right to act or refrain from actions, that open the door for political manipulation by rulers and the scholars who support them. Such manipulation not only is more likely in civil rights matters because that tends to serve the political interest of rulers, but is also more effective because of a traditional emphasis on the duty of the "subject" to obey the ruler in order to avoid political upheaval, especially when rulers express their commitment to Shari'a.

Besides the generally inhibiting effect of this traditional political culture on the civil rights of all citizens in the modern context, women and non-Muslims are subjected to further restrictions under historical formulations of Shari'a. For example, verse 34 of chapter 4 of the Qur'an has been taken to establish a general principle of men's guardianship (*qawama*) over women, thereby denying them the right to hold any public office involving the exercise of authority over men. While jurists differ in their views on the subject, none of them would grant women equality to men in this regard. This general principle is applied in interpreting, and is reinforced by, various specific verses that apparently grant women unequal rights to those of men in marriage, divorce, inheritance, and related matters. The same principle of interpretation is applied to other verses, like verse 31.of chapter 24 and verses 33, 53, and 59 of chapter 33, to restrict the right of women to appear and speak in public or associate with men, thereby limiting their ability to participate in the government of their country. Thus, although Muslim women have the same freedom of belief and opinion enjoyed by men, their opportunity to exercise this right is greatly inhibited by restrictions on their access to the public domain. The same type of combination of general and specific verses has been used in traditional formulations of Shari'a to restrict the rights of non-Muslims in various categories of People of the Book (mainly Christians and Jews) and unbelievers. But none of those categories qualify for full and equal citizenship under traditional interpretations of Shari'a (An-Na'im 1990: 88–91).

Other examples of inequality and discrimination can be cited, and I will return to these issues later in this book, but my main point for now is that there are specific civil rights problems in addition to the broader constitutional concerns outlined above. Some proponents of the application of Shari'a tend to cite a few examples of the high level political role played by a few women or the role of non-Muslims in the administration, as evidence of equality and nondiscrimination in practice, despite discriminatory principles in theory. Besides being few and far between, which confirms the realities of exclusion and discrimination, those examples were the product of political expediency and not institutionalized principles of equal citizenship for women and non-Muslims as a matter of Shari'a or general Islamic political thought.

In my view, whatever political or sociological justifications may have existed in the past for these aspects of Shari'a are no longer valid in the context of the modern Islamic societies. This view appears to be shared by the majority of Muslims today, as evidenced by the fact that the national constitutions of most Islamic states now provide for equality and prohibit discrimination on grounds of sex or religion. Many Islamic countries are also parties to international human rights treaties that require equality and nondiscrimination. It is true that Islamic countries rarely live up to the level of their constitutional or civil rights commitment, but that is a common problem among all countries. While emphasizing the need to understand and combat the underlying causes of this common failure, I find it significant that many Muslims around the world express commitment to the values of constitutionalism and civil rights. To assist these Muslims in honoring that commitment, I suggest the implementation of internal Islamic law reform in order to address the general constitutional concerns raised earlier mandating complete equality for women and non-Muslims as a matter of Shari'a. Such reform, I suggest, will contribute to the process of legitimizing and indigenizing the values of political participation, accountability, and equality before the law, thereby enhancing the prospects of constitutionalism in Islamic societies (An-Na'im 1990: 97–100).

One of the critical questions from this perspective in particular is how to apply constitutional concepts and institutions developed centuries after the model of the Prophet's state in Medina in analyzing the nature, powers and operation of that state. The first step in this process is to argue that the fact that these concepts and institutions evolved much later does not make them inherently "un-Islamic." On the contrary, the recent drastic transformation of Islamic societies and their local and international environments makes the patterns of political participation and power relations of the early Islamic era irrelevant and counterproductive. By the same token, the present context strongly indicates the need to incorporate constitutional principles and institutions into the Islamic political thought. Instead of continuing with traditional ideals that are neither workable nor desirable today, it is better to seek to understand the underlying rationale of the early principles and practice and reformulate their substance into more relevant and practicable principles.

For instance, as suggested earlier, the traditional bay'a (oath of allegiance) should now be seen in terms of mutual contract between the government and the population at large, whereby the former assumes responsibility for the protection of the rights and general well-being of the latter in exchange for their acceptance of the authority of the state and compliance with its laws and public policy. A modern Islamic constitutional theory would also require the development of adequate mechanisms and institutions for the election and accountability of government, and other features of modern constitutionalism, as necessary means for achieving the rationale and content of the notion of bay'a. This can be done through the development of the notion of shura into a binding principle of representative government rather than merely discretionary consultation. Civil rights are necessary not only in order to evolve and elaborate this modern concept of shura, but also for the proper implementation of the ensuing constitutional theory which must be inclusive of all the citizens of the state, men and women, Muslims and non-Muslims alike.

As indicated at the beginning of this section, however, this focus on issues of Islamic constitutional and civil rights theory should not be taken to imply that Islam is the only or decisive ideology in the Muslim world. Muslims in fact subscribe to a wide range of ideological orientations, and their constitutional and legal systems must respond to issues and concerns shared by other developing countries. Moreover, in view of the vast range of perceptions and practices of Islam among Muslims, one cannot speak of Islamic discourse except at a very high level of abstraction and generalization. The role of Islam in the political, constitutional, and legal systems of Islamic countries should be seen as integral to the role of culture as the local setting for theory and practice in this field. Although I believe that the sort of debates and reformulations suggested above are critically important in predominantly Islamic societies, many other considerations must be taken into account. This variety of factors and considerations can be examined in terms of what I call the dialectic of the global and local, the universal and relative.

Dialectic of Universality and Relativity of Constitutionalism

In light of the preceding two sections, it may be useful to reflect on the philosophical and political assumptions of the concept of constitutionalism and its application in different parts of the world. For example, one can inquire into the sort of economic, social, and other conditions and circumstances under which the concept is most likely to work in a satisfactory manner. In relation to the particular thesis of incremental success proposed in this book, one can examine whether and how the essential elements of this concept can be reproduced under apparently unfavorable circumstances. Comparative reflection is therefore necessary for both constructing a general theory of constitutionalism from various "national" experiences, as well as for understanding how it works in different settings. How does it become established and consolidated in some places, or undermined and eroded in others?

An underlying tension regarding concepts like "constitutionalism," "democracy," or "human rights," relates to the relationship between their formulations in Western societies, where they developed and were applied earlier, and their more recent application elsewhere, as to African societies for our purposes here. That is, do such concepts, as defined by the experiences of societies where they were first developed and established, have universal applicability so that they can be "transplanted" into other settings? In my view, such concepts can be accepted as viable philosophical, political, and analytic categories for evaluating the experiences of African societies, provided they are open to contestation and reconceptualization from the perspective of those societies. It may therefore be useful to clarify this dimension of the ambivalence and contingency of the application of such concepts in different settings.

To being with, one should avoid asserting a categorical dichotomy between Western and non-Western societies. There is no uniformity among so-called Western or non-Western societies to justify lumping them into mutually exclusive categories. As tragically illustrated by the rise of fascism in Spain and Italy, Nazism in Germany, and Soviet totalitarianism in Russia during the twentieth century, Western societies are as vulnerable to regression into despotic authoritarianism as any other human society. It is also clear to me that there is no such uniformity even within the same society at any given point of its history. Indeed, the permanent and profound diversity within and among different constitutional, philosophical and religious experiences and perspectives is most conducive for cross-fertilization and mutual influence. In referring to "Western," "non-Western," or "African" as shorthand terms, I am neither implying total uniformity among or within any of these broad categories, nor suggesting permanent differences in their constitutional experiences.

From this perspective, I hold that the universal validity and applicability of concepts like constitutionalism is a pragmatic necessity in view of the universalization of the European model of the nation-state through colonialism and postcolonial relations. This model is likely to continue as the dominant form of political organization in national politics and international relations for the foreseeable future. Even globalizing trends and transnational integration, like the European Union, still evolve and operate through the agency of the territorial state, often facing strong resistance from the proponents of traditional notions of 'national' sovereignty. The persistence of these realities require the development and implementation of concepts like "constitutionalism," "democracy," and "human rights," which have been found to be necessary for regulating the powers of the state, and organizing its relationship to individuals and communities who are subject to its jurisdiction.

Accordingly, it would be desirable to articulate some "universal" principles around each of these concepts as political and philosophical parameters for domestic territorial and international practice. In other words, the commonality of tensions in state-society and state-individual relations recommends giving notions like constitutionalism and democracy broader applicability by expanding their meaning to include the experiences of other societies now seeking to adapt the same notion to their own respective contexts. However, as I have argued elsewhere regarding human rights (An-Na'im 1992), this process should be premised on mediating the generality of purportedly universal principles and the cultural/contextual specificity of the particular situation. The claim about the actual universality of a specific "content" of such concepts can be realized only through a coherent framework for deliberate processes of consultation and consensus-building. Thus, regarding the thesis and analysis of this book, the genuine universality of some principles of constitutionalism requires a framework that can substantively incorporate the contributions of African as well as Western societies.

Whatever level of development or degree of clarity may be achieved through that process of theoretical universalization, concepts such as constitutionalism must still be specified and adapted for local application in a given setting. That is, any candidates for "universal" principles of constitutionalism will need to satisfactorily answer the questions and concerns arising from the socioeconomic and political context, and cultural traditions of each time and place. It logically follows from this requirement of adaptation of universal principles to local context that some of them may or may not work in relation to a specific place at a given point in time. Moreover, this failure of adaptation may be at any point in a continuum, from one or two minor differences regarding practical arrangements, to incompatibility on fundamental or substantial aspects of constitutionalism. Differences or variations in practical arrangements for such matters as separation of powers or judicial review may be expected and acceptable, while failure to acknowledge the need for separation of powers or judicial review may be tantamount to repudiation of the core of constitutionalism. A failure to adapt such universal principles to local conditions can also be temporary or continue for a long period of time.

As a practical matter, at what point in an analysis can one judge that the local adaptations of universal principles of constitutionalism have failed, and what does that mean? For instance, can one declare that constitutionalism itself has failed in Sudan, which has been ruled by military and single party regimes since independence in 1956, except for a total of eight years of quasi-constitutional democratic governance? To what extent would it be a failure of the concept of constitutionalism itself to provide for, or be sufficiently adaptable to, such situations? Which criteria or indicators is one applying in evaluating the success or failure of the experiences of various countries? Should it be the same for all, or devised according to the context and experience of each country? Does responsibility for the failure lie with various groups of ruling elites, or with the people of the country? Whoever is responsible for the failure of constitutionalism in a country, where and how can it begin to recover or improve its standing in this regard?

I propose to address these and related questions at various stages of this study, but the underlying question for most of them is whether the dialectic of universal principles and local adaptations has already been set by Western countries once and for all, or is this relationship open to other contributions? That is, are Western experiences to remain the ultimate norm or standard by which constitutionalism is judged or assessed everywhere, or do the local experiences of African countries still have an opportunity to influence the content and future development of the general theory of constitutionalism? Assuming that process remains open, who is going to "organize" or "adjudicate" disputes that arise in practice? For instance, when and how would the constitutional experiences of an African country be acknowledged as having made a contribution to relevant universal principles of constitutionalism, how are such determinations made, and by which criteria?

For instance, how are the experiences of African countries regarding customary law and traditional systems of administration to be assessed in relation to state law, courts, and administration systems? Are these indigenous elements of law and administration to be deemed inconsistent with the principles of constitutional governance, and as such to be eliminated as soon as practically possible, or should they be incorporated into the concept on their own terms. This question has always been present, at various levels of visibility among officials during the colonial period, and in public policy debates since independence in many African countries. As recently illustrated by the application of the traditional Gacaca process of accountability and reconciliation in the aftermath of the genocide in Rwanda (Eltringham 2004; Lattimer 2003), the issues include the appropriateness and legitimacy of applying traditional or customary law principles under drastically transformed situations, as well as the risks of deviation from established modern constitutional safeguards of fair trial, separation of powers, and so forth.

Part of the problem of standards to be applied in assessing the success or failure of African constitutional experiences, by whom such standards should be applied, and how, is the marginalization of African scholars in the global academy, and/or their failure to take the initiative. The reasons for either are too complex and controversial to be fully explained or discussed here, but it seems to me that they include the following factors. Since the educational systems of postcolonial African states are typically continuations of colonial education systems, Western academic disciplinary traditions of political science, history, sociology, anthropology, and so on continue to dominate. The same intellectual figures, theories, and methods that are prevalent in the Western academy are automatically adopted by African scholars and opinion leaders. These dynamics of academic and intellectual dependency are being perpetuated by the fact that African scholars tend to obtain their advanced training in Western institutions, under the supervision of Western academics. African scholars therefore continue to follow the concepts and methodologies they learned in Western universities when they return to their home countries and institutions.

Such realities of complex and multifaceted dependency persist despite the significant contributions of African and Asian scholars to knowledge, not just about their own societies but also in broader terms. These contributions have not been incorporated into the dominant scholarly frameworks of the global academy. In contrast to the foundational significance of Plato, Marx, or Vico as theorists of society, politics, or history in general and not just of or in the West, this level of recognition is not given to Ibn Khaldun as a philosopher of history and Gandhi as a theorist of society in general. Instead, to the few who know his work at all in the global academy, Ibn Khaldun is seen as a sociologist of the Arab world, and Gandhi is still largely categorized as an Indian social thinker. Neither of these categorizations is inaccurate in itself, but compared to the mode in which a Plato or Marx is "canonized" in the global academy, the regional or cultural qualifiers for Ibn Khaldun or Gandhi effectively operate as a denial of the universal value of their thought. While it may be true that many scholars in the global academy would not dispute the claim that the thought of Ibn Khaldun or Gandhi is as "universal" as that of Marx or Vico, there is no indication of such acknowledgment in the syllabi, courses, and training, indeed the pedagogy in general, of the global academy.

To highlight these issues is neither to suggest that the global academy deliberately works according to an exclusivist agenda, nor to imply that scholars in the academy (whether in the West or non-West) are not aware of and sensitive to these concerns. Rather, it is simply to note that the primary disciplines and epistemology of the Western academy continue to dominate at the institutional level as foundational frameworks for research, to the exclusion of all other contenders. It is therefore necessary, in my view, for African scholars, policy makers, and other opinion leaders to strive to diminish these dependencies and minimizing the distortion or loss associated with the postcolonial political economy of the global academy.

The thesis and analysis I am proposing in this book raise philosophical, ethical, and methodological challenges for African as well as Western scholarship in this field. At the philosophical level, there is need for formulating and developing a positive relationship among African, Islamic, and Western epistemological frameworks relevant to constitutionalism. Ethical concerns include responsibility to fairly and adequately represent the societies being studied, to recognize the autonomy of a variety of actors, how they might understand accountability or exercise political participation on their own terms. For my purposes here, the challenge includes how to critically apply a concept like constitutionalism, without reifying it into simplistic polarities of so-called African/Islamic versus Western models or experiences.

The Postcolonial Condition

The thesis and analysis presented in this book are deeply rooted in what might be called the postcolonial condition, which signifies a complex web of power relations, institutional arrangements, socioeconomic structures both within formerly colonized societies and in their relationship to former colonial European powers and the postcolonial world at large. This perspective is of course a familiar theme in a wide range of studies, especially in relation to African and Asian societies, politics, cultural studies, and law (Davis 2004; Slater 2004; Thieme 2003; Kloppenberg 1999). It can be applied to individual formerly colonized countries long after they have achieved formal political independence, and also as a broader principle that affects all of them collectively. While this condition can be elaborated and illustrated in relation to different parts of the world, I am primarily concerned here with its nature and manifestations in Africa today.

In the case of Africa, the term postcolonial does not mean "after independence." Rather it is a concept which takes into account the historical realities of the European imperial incursions into the continent from the fifteenth century onwards. These incursions manifested themselves in the transatlantic slave trade. The violent conquest of the continent in the nineteenth and twentieth centuries, in what may be described as the "scramble for Africa", formally lasted until the decolonisation processes were complete. These processes began in the 1950s and culminated in the 1990s with the liberation of South Africa. Nevertheless, the enduring legacy of colonialism continues to be characterised by its neo-colonial policies. (Ahluwalia 2001: 14)

By the postcolonial condition in Africa I am therefore referring to a predicament whereby the colonial legacy endures in former colonies through the persistence of the inherited apparatus of colonialism and its political, social, economic, and legal consequences. This legacy continues to strongly influence structural and institutional developments in African countries long after independence. Another aspect of the postcolonial predicament relates to the ways in which colonial exploitation and postcolonial hegemony are perpetuating conditions of dependency by former colonies on their respective European colonial states and other developed countries in general.

The postcolonial predicament sustains a sense of profound ambiguity among former colonies who are struggling to incorporate and reconcile contradictory histories and political visions. On the one hand, the postcolonial state is shaped by the colonial vision that subjugated and exploited its population, without sufficiently preparing them for the responsibilities of sovereign independent statehood. On the other hand, the postcolonial state is also shaped by the visions that have resisted the colonial apparatus and still sustain the intellectual and political legacies of anticolonial resistance and struggle. The postcolonial state is therefore being contested among competing constituencies of leaders and populations at large by the pull of colonialism and the push of liberation. This profound ambiguity also relates to an underlying paradox of the postcolonial state as a legal fiction, in contrast to empirical realities on the ground.

As elaborated further in this book, the African postcolonial state is a legal fiction in the sense that it is neither quite in control of its own territory, nor sufficiently sovereign in dealing with other entities, including the major transnational corporations that continue to exploit the human and material resources of the country. Yet, at the same time, the state does affect the life of people in a wide variety of serious and far reaching ways. As far as its own populations are concerned, however weak and artificial it may be, the state is a fundamental and effective reality through its monopoly of the use of force, its legal institutions, its ability to enforce its will in a range of fields, from taxation to education and economic policies, as the only means for private persons to engage in international trade, and so forth. Indeed, one of the urgent tasks at hand is how to bring this awareness of the far-reaching and all-pervasive power of the state to the consciousness of African populations.

The approach to understanding and engaging notions of constitutionalism in African contexts presented in this book attempts to contribute to the mediation of the paradoxical nature of the African postcolonial state. As the means by which the power of the state is defined and mapped, both enabled and constrained, constitutional governance can be seen as the mechanism for bridging the gap between the fiction and reality of the postcolonial state. It can also be the medium for re-vesting the sovereignty of the state in the people, which can result in a transformation of the nature of the state, from a tool of hegemony and exploitation to an agent of positive social change and development that enjoys popular legitimacy and credibility. As a broader concept, constitutionalism can be the means by which various segments of each society can contribute to designing and implementing the kind of state they wish to represent them and regulate their existence. Even when this notion has been deployed by authoritarian or corrupt elites, the idea of constitutional governance has been an integral part of the postcolonial history of the continent because that indicates an acknowledgment of its popular appeal and legitimizing power.

An aspect of the postcolonial condition that is relevant here is the persistence of the view that African constitutionalism must be judged by European standards. The underlying assumption here, which was used to rationalize colonialism in the first place, is that Europe is always the origin of the history and culture of the world, the center that is dynamic, modern, and the source of innovation. In contrast, the peripheral world is "traditional," characterized by stasis or lethargy, and merely imitates the West (Blaut 1993: 1). From this perspective, since concepts like constitutionalism and democracy are reflections of a self-contained "Europeanness," derived entirely from an inherent ability that is lacking elsewhere in the world, then they are simply unattainable outside Europe (and by extension the Americas and other parts of the world populated by people of European descent) in their fully developed form and substance. The non-European world is condemned to failure in whatever reaction it has to the imposition or transplantation of such notions in their exact and detailed European forms. If a non-European society resists or rejects the imposition of a European model of constitutionalism, this is perceived as proof of its inherent incapability to embrace progressive modernity. Any alternative to the European model will always fall short of the "authentic or genuine" variety precisely because it is not European enough. Yet, to adopt and accept a fully European model is by implication accepting the claim that Europe stands for a more evolved stage of progress in human history.

The colonial European stereotypes of Africa and Africans continued to hold sway in scholarship well into the twentieth century. For instance, the dominance of "ethnographic" modes of analysis of "tradition" in Western scholarship leads to an excessive particularism or exceptionalism of African societies and politics, as if they defy understanding in broader comparative terms. Such conceptions of Africans in academic and nonacademic discourse have not gone uncontested (Falola 2002). African scholars have debated issues such as the representation of Africa in Western discourse, the relationship between African philosophy and Western philosophy, African philosophical and epistemological perspectives, and the role of traditional African thought in philosophy (Eze 1997; Mudimbe 1994; Serequeberhan 1994).

The question often raised in these debates that is particularly relevant to the subject of this book is how we use the tools and concepts of a European discourse that has systematically and consistently excluded and devalued African or Asian histories and societies? What is at issue here, it seems to me, is the relationship between concepts and history in understanding terms such as "constitutionalism." Writing or speaking in English, for instance, such terms would necessarily evoke some sense of "Europeanness," but does that mean that the term itself cannot transcend its Western historicity? In my view, as indicated earlier, such terms can be viewed as useful diagnostic and analytic tools for the study of African societies, provided they are conceived in transregional, "universal" terms beyond their Western relativity. The challenge is how to reconstitute African histories and concepts deemed in the postcolonial discourse to be provincial and affirm them as part of the more genuinely universal histories and conceptual formulations of humanity at large. For my thesis and analysis of constitutionalism in Africa in particular, and the implications for politics, policy, and advocacy, challenging Eurocentric perspectives is only one step in the right direction that must be followed by constructing universal concepts that are inclusive of non-European experiences and histories.

Process/Practice-Based Approach to Constitutionalism

The view of constitutionalism as a contested concept and the contingent outcome of the experiences of African countries in the postcolonial context will be further explained and discussed in the following chapters. By representing and examining this concept as a site and product of the contestation and mediation of power, I am emphasizing that it should be seen and understood as a living and evolving process, as *practice*. As both the site and symbol of popular legitimacy, this concept can be a productive medium for transforming and transcending the postcolonial condition, a means as well as an end of self-determination and political independence. From this broader and deeper historical-political perspective, the success or failure of various constitutional experiences should be assessed as an incremental process, affected by external as well as internal factors and actors that have shaped the political history of postcolonial Africa.

To briefly clarify this fundamental aspect of my whole thesis and approach, I will briefly recall earlier aspects of this chapter through the useful framework suggested by Rajeev Bhargava regarding the relationship of Indian secularism to its Western counterparts:

a widespread misconception exists in India that a unique uncomplicated separation of religion from the state is a feature of all modern, Western societies, and that this separation is conceived in the same manner everywhere, and because consensus on the precise relation between religion and state practice is an incontrovertible fact, the secularity of the state is a settled, stable feature in all Western politics. . . . *Western secularism too, is essentially contested, with no agreement on what it entails, the values it seeks to promote, or how best to pursue it* . . . each country in the West has worked out a particular political compromise rather than implementing a solution uniquely required by the configuration of values embodied in secularism. The separation thesis means different things in the US, in France, in Germany, and is interpreted differently at different times in each place. (Bhargava 1999: 2–3, emphasis added)

This is clearly true of constitutionalism in general, as it is for the contingent role of Islam to be discussed later. If taken as the limitation of the powers of the state by law, we find that in Western countries like Britain, France, and the United States, discussed in Chapter 6, this function operates in deeply contextual ways in which the different structure and operation of power and law are structured uniquely in each setting. The same is true of attributes and values commonly associated with this concept, such as democracy, sovereignty of the people, or mechanisms like judicial review of the constitutionality of law or state policies. Indeed, one can even argue that there is no single common historical fact or attribute that can be found in all three societies that can yield a monolithic definition of constitutionalism. There is no uniform philosophy of governance that underlies political structures, dominant vision of the society or nation-state, or the sociocultural basis for respect for law.

For example, the purported strong correlation between democracy and the constitution in the United States neither precluded slavery until the second half of the nineteenth century, nor included women until well into the twentieth century. A correlation of democracy and constitutionalism is even less true of most of the history of the Britain and France cases, although these concepts eventually converge after a protracted struggle between secular and monarchical authority. The viability of French constitutionalism derives from the fact that the constitution is subsumed under the law; in Britain there is no constitutional text that can legally limit the will of any parliament, while the constitution is paramount law in the United States. Thus, these three Western models differ significantly on this fundamental matter.

In addition to its inherent relativity, the success of constitutionalism in Western societies cannot be traced to any single historical moment or turning point. No single event or series of events, like the Revolution of 1688 in Britain, or the French or American Revolutions, can be said to have guaranteed or secured the sustainable achievement of constitutional governance in that country. Indeed, subsequent moments of regression or ambivalence could have resulted in a totally different line of development. Conversely, no single failure or series of setbacks necessarily signaled the end of constitutionalism in those countries. For example, the Vichy government in France of 1940–1944 collaborated with the Nazi occupation and adopted antiparliamentary and antidemocratic policies that were reversed after liberation in 1944. Yet, one cannot categorically reject any possibility of the recurrence of such regressions in any country. In other words, the establishment of constitutional governance is always contingent as well as being *relative* to the context and history of the country in question, whether so-called Western or not.

The unavoidable relativity and contingency of constitutionalism everywhere, as illustrated by these Western cases, mean that this concept cannot be viewed as a single ideal principle that various societies have systematically and progressively realized on the basis of a blueprint or master plan. Any understanding of this concept is necessarily abstracted from the *cumulative* experiences of various societies, rather than a fixed preconceived notion of what it has to be. This clearly indicates to me the possibility of expanding the scope and applicability of constitutionalism to a much wider range of non-European, postcolonial societies, while recognizing that the concept was initially reflective of certain Western experiences. The specific constitutional experiences of Western societies can also point to fruitful insights and strategies for promoting the concept and its related institutions and processes in African countries, provided each experience is understood in its own context.

A key directive that follows from this perspective is to look closely at the internal dynamics and processes by which constitutionalism is effectively consolidated and established in *any* society. This requires combining a historical imagination with political and sociological analysis in assessing the relative "failure" or "success" of the concept in each setting. In other words, the failures or setbacks are as much a part of the evolution and establishment of the concept as are apparent successes in this regard. Instead of thinking of constitutionalism as an end that has either been achieved or not achieved, it is more useful to view it as a *process* that emerges through *practice.*

This approach is critically important because focusing on constitutionalism as an end that is judged by a "success/failure" standard tempts one to seek overriding causal or structural reasons for such assessments. Thus, a "verdict of failure" on a society tends to slide into simplistic judgments and assertions about the society as a whole, such as that the people are not "ready" for democracy, are fundamentally incapable of grasping the value of the accountability of government, or that identification with particular ethnic or religious identities represents primordial attachments that are incompatible with notions of citizenship. Indeed, this line of thinking typically results in precisely the kind of rationalization used by European powers to justify colonialism in Africa and elsewhere.

In contrast, the process and practice-based approach I am proposing in this book allows for a richer and deeper analysis by requiring one to address the complex social, cultural, and political dynamics within which a range of state and non-state actors, individuals, and communities, ethnic, social, and religious groups understand and relate to constitutional governance. Instead of taking an apparent "failure" as indicative of an inherent "defect" in a society, one should also consider the possibility that such an outcome may in fact reflect a "blind spot" of the concept as understood or implemented within a specific time-frame. That is, a negative outcome may simply indicate the inability of the concept, as formulated or applied, to contain and organize the actual circumstances or experiences of a particular society. In my view, it is unwarranted to assume that any normative conceptual or theoretical framework is so definitive that there must be something wrong with the facts if they fail to fit the proposed theory. I would therefore prefer a process-and-practice based approach that takes a broader and deeply contextual view of specific developments in the longer term in order to keep the possibility open for the "half full" glass to get more full, over time.

As emphasized earlier, the postcolonial condition must be taken into account in any analysis of the territorial state in a postcolonial society, without of course blaming colonialism for all the problems of African societies today. In particular, and drawing on the specific experiences of diverse postcolonial societies, a normative understanding of the post-colonial state should be incorporated into normative definitions of the state itself. No postcolonial state can be viewed simply as an individual case study or as variation on a European theme. The implication that anticolonial nationalism must replicate the modes of Western national-ism denies and effaces the agency of anticolonial nationalist movements. If the assumption that Europe provides the world with the paradigm for nationalism, which underlies European conceptions of constitutional-ism, is taken as axiomatic, the resultant conception of constitutionalism cannot even "recognize" the character of anticolonial nationalism, let alone account for it.

This emphasizes that the postcolonial condition, outlined earlier and to be discussed later, should be integral to the process/practice based approach I am proposing in this book. To reiterate, the object is simply that this broad and complex condition should be integrated into analy-sis of the process/practice of constitutionalism in each African context, without implying that colonialism as such is "the causal explanation" of an assessment of success or failure in one case or another.

Toward an Inclusive Theory of Constitutionalism

I conclude this chapter by revisiting the above-mentioned philosophical question, whether normative conceptualization of constitutionalism can transcend its Western historicity. The preceding analysis of the relativity and contingency of that European historicity represents one aspect of the theoretical framework and approach of this book. Another aspect is the need to incorporate the historical, social, and political experiences of African societies in the normative definition of the concept as well as in assessing its development in a specific context. Without attempting to be exhaustive, I am proposing to do this by drawing on indigenous and precolonial African traditions of political, social, and cultural thought and practice, as well as political and intellectual traditions of anticolonial dissent and protest, in addition to concepts from European or Western social thought and disciplinary traditions, as relativized and reconceptualized in the manner described above.

The overview of some traditional African constitutional values, as well as related experiences under colonialism presented in Chapter 2, is that the legitimacy and sustainability of African constitutionalism somehow need to tap the consciousness of African peoples, including recollections of relevant precolonial conceptions and historical experiences. Among the obvious conceptual and theoretical obstacles facing such an objective

is the fact that the understanding of precolonial African history is itself
shaped by notions of European history and its epistemological frameworks according to which knowledge of societies is gathered, analyzed,
and applied. While overcoming these conceptual difficulties involves what
may be called retrieving the irretrievable, achieving African objectives
despite structural limitations requires imagining the unimaginable.

These ideas and processes will be discussed in more detail later, but I
wish to note here that this proposition involves a relationship between
recollections of the past and ways of imagining the future that can, in
turn, provide a blueprint for action in the present. If what some may
view as irretrievable is to be retrieved, it must be recuperated with a view
to the future that African peoples and societies envision for themselves.
Kwame Anthony Appiah, it seems to me, is arguing for such a view of
African philosophy, when he says:

> there are reasons for developing a notion of African philosophy, not as
> Hountondji's philosophy "by Africans themselves"; nor simply, as others have
> proposed, as philosophy *in* Africa, either, but rather as philosophy *for* Africa.
> And to make sense of [this] idea we must inquire into what it is that Africa now
> needs of her intellectuals (which is to say intellectuals who are *for* her); and what
> parts of that need a training in "philosophy" can supply. (Appiah 1992: 228)

Similarly, I call for recuperating relevant indigenous traditions with a
view to what constitutionalism should be for Africa today. To avoid
a common confusion, I am not suggesting that Africans should strive
to retrieve an "imaginary" history of complete and perfect sovereign
accountability to the highest standards of human dignity and rights in a
golden age of the precolonial past. That was neither the case anywhere,
nor is it capable of being reconstituted in the present postcolonial condition of African societies. Rather, I am suggesting that Africans must
imaginatively reclaim the agency which was denied to them during colonialism. If communities are "imagined" and traditions are "invented,"
then Africans can imagine and reimagine and invent and reinvent their
societies unfettered by the hegemony and constraints of European experience and epistemology. European discourse does not have an authority or monopoly on the past of all other people. It can neither propose
a European past as a more "authentic blueprint" for the development of
African constitutionalism, nor dictate *what* and *how* African societies
can or cannot retrieve from their own histories.

The notion of retrieving the irretrievable is to indicate that contemporary discourse on constitutionalism must incorporate the legacy of a
relatively autonomous realm of "civil society" during the colonial period.
This legacy of both everyday and organized political resistance, I argue,
can be envisioned as a separate constitutional realm in contrast to the

constitutionalism of the state. Part of that legacy, I suggest, has to account for the relationship between Islam and constitutional governance in different African contexts, as discussed in chapters 4 and 5. For African Islamic societies, the role of Islam in politics, culture, and society has always been, and will continue to be, contingent on context and circumstance. Instead of taking an unrealistic view of Islam as inherently or necessarily antagonistic or conducive to constitutionalism, I propose viewing this relationship in terms of competing currents of Islamic thinking and practices, or visions of Islamic identities and their political, constitutional and legal consequences. By indicating possibilities of alternative initiatives and outcomes of the politics of Islamic identity, and emphasizing that the impact of Islam on political and cultural institutions is negotiable, I am arguing that this dimension of the legacy of African societies can provide a basis of legitimacy for constitutionalism.

Accounting for the Islamic dimension of the legacies of some African societies is not to say it is the sole or even primary determinant of the status of this concept in Islamic countries (that is, those where Muslims constitute the majority of the population). Rather, I am questioning whether secularism can or should only be conceptualized in opposition to religion, or be viewed as hierarchically prior to it. I am also calling for deeply contextual understandings of secularism, including a religious discourse about its meaning and implications, as a product of the broadest and most inclusive negotiation.

In this regard, I resonate with Akeel Bilgrami's critique of Indian Nehruvian secularism, which can be applied to constitutionalism here:

[Constitutionalism should be] emergent rather than assumed, sees itself as one amongst other doctrines such as Islam and Hinduism; a doctrine that its proponents must persuade all others (including Hindus and Muslims . . .) to agree to as an outcome of negotiation. Thus, secularists [constitutionalism for us here] must start *in* the political arena with its *substantive* commitments to its secular [constitutional] principles, facing up to other substantive doctrinal and political commitments of the communities, and working towards the adoption of their secular [constitutional] principles—by democraticizing these communities and thereby giving them the confidence to embrace, from elements within their own evaluative framework and point of view, arguments in favor of these principles. (Bilgrami 1999: 400)

I am not in full agreement with Bilgrami regarding the dialectic relationship of religion and politics (1999: 401). The point for me is that constitutionalism, as well as related notions like secularism and democracy, requires legitimacy and credibility in terms of the frameworks that challenge an exclusively secular view of constitutionalism, in the sense that religion is necessarily and permanently problematic in this regard. In that part of the argument I am neither saying that constitutionalism cannot or should not be secular, nor suggesting that Islam is the communities and individuals whose existence it regulates. Like European notions of secularism or democracy, constitutionalism has predominantly come to African societies as an *external* colonial imposition. Without necessarily accepting Bilgrami's view of the relationship between secularism and religion, I am simply emphasizing that there are different ways of imagining relationships between religion and constitutionalism, and they should all be open to negotiation within and among present and future African societies.

Mazrui defines "*Afrennaisance* as living evidence of Africa's self-renewal, living testimony that the human spirit is reasserting itself among the African people" (2003: 163). He assesses the considerable odds that this rejuvenated spirit has to overcome, and concludes that "An African capacity for self-participation needs to be married to self-democraticiza-tion. Against the background of such a marriage, African swords may be turned into ploughshares, African spears transformed into elongated spades. The continent's self-renewal has gotten underway" (2003: 176). From my perspective, constitutionalism can be a mechanism for both self-participation and self-democratization in Africa; it can embody a productive commingling and encounter between traditional notions of selfhood, human dignity, and political values of consensus and community building along with notions of human rights, sovereignty, and the nation-state (as distinguished earlier from the postcolonial "territorial" state in Africa). It can reflect a rich and valuable engagement between religious and secular discourses, and hopefully, ultimately reflect a productive outcome of a fusion of European and African thoughts, experiences, and traditions.

Chapter 2

Elements of African Constitutionalism

In speaking of "African constitutionalism" throughout this book, I am neither implying that there is a specific type of constitutionalism that is peculiarly African, nor suggesting that the experience or feature I am discussing is true or applicable for the whole continent. In particular, the elements of precolonial and colonial experiences to be highlighted below, and the notion of "retrieval and imagining" proposed there, are not intended to suggest or imply a blanket application of these ideas in the same way throughout Africa. Rather, the adjective "African" is used to refer to a regional context, without minimizing the diversity within the region, or underestimating similarities and connections to the constitutional experiences of other parts of the world. That is, the reference is to constitutional experiences, or elements of constitutionalism, that are associated with Africa on such grounds as geography, culture, and politics. To emphasize the point, such usage does not mean that the point I am making is definitive or applicable to Africa as a whole, or any other parts of it than the one being discussed.

Subject to this caveat, I attempt in this chapter to generally highlight aspects of what might be called African constitutional values, institutions, and experiences, examine some relevant features of the traditional values and institutions of certain parts of the continent that can be reclaimed as antecedents of constitutionalism in each society or subregion. I also outline some of the constitutional experiences of African societies during the colonial and postcolonial periods, as integral parts of the same process of incremental success through practice for each society. Against this background, I then examine some aspects of sovereignty, accountability, human rights, and dignity as key concepts in the evolution of constitutionalism in Africa.

But first, it may be helpful to begin by briefly clarifying some of the conceptual and methodological difficulties and possibilities of what I call the "retrieval" of precolonial antecedents and colonial experiences, and "imagining" how they can contribute to the present and future development of constitutionalism in various African societies. The rest of this introduction is devoted to an attempt to clarify some theoretical and methodological questions about the incremental success thesis in general, though the process itself would always be deeply contextual and specific to each society.

One of the themes I am developing in this book is the notion that the legitimacy and sustainability of constitutionalism need somehow to tap the consciousness of a particular people, which in the case of African societies would include the recollections of relevant precolonial ideas and historical experiences of each society. Part of the difficulty is that recollections of ideas, values, and the meaning of institutions and relationships in the precolonial past are filtered through the lenses of European historicity. The question is how to avoid or transcend postcolonial perceptions of what "counts" as history and how to interpret it, as discussed in Chapter 1. A related problem is that policies emerging out of such recollections are likely to be inhibited by the present realities of postcolonial hegemony and global capitalism.

To achieve continuity of historical experiences in the process of building constitutionalism over time, Africans need to reconnect to their precolonial past on their own terms, as if colonialism and its aftermath never happened. One aspect of the challenge is therefore how to retrieve what appears to be irretrievable, namely, to recover some of the moral and philosophical resources of the precolonial past of African societies into a present that has been totally transformed by colonial and postcolonial conditions. Another aspect of the challenge is how to imagine what appears to be unimaginable, which is the ability to integrate those resources into a theory and practice of constitutional principles that were developed in Western societies, while retaining the new acculturated outcome within recognizable parameters of constitutionalism.

I am not suggesting that Africans should strive to retrieve an "imaginary" history of complete and perfect sovereign accountability to the highest standards of human dignity and rights in a golden age of precolonial past. I do not think there is an original, virgin African constitutionalism waiting to be retrieved from the depth of an imagined memory. The idea of traditional society may be a "benchmark against which to measure the imperial impact and to trace the continuities of precolonial time" (Hodder-Williams 1984: 11), not an ideal experience. My point is simply that different Africans should seek to clarify, adapt, and implement what they "remember" of their indigenous conceptions and institutions regarding such constitutional principles as sovereignty, accountability, human dignity, and rights. The basic idea that Africans should be able to seek to retrieve, rejuvenate, and develop such conceptions and institutions, regardless of whether or not they can verify and validate such recollections in terms of Eurocentric historiography and epistemology. But equally important is that such retrieval includes a critical examination of that historical experience, instead of blind sentimental assertion of ideas and institutions. This project should also include the adaptation of historical notions of sovereignty and accountability to present day realities by imagining how they might have evolved if they had never been interrupted by the colonial intrusion.

African intellectuals have been struggling with the conceptual and practical difficulties of developing and implementing indigenous models for several decades now, and linking to scholars engaged in similar projects in other parts of the world, like those of "subaltern studies." The term "subaltern" refers to someone who is of inferior rank, or something that is particular and not universal, but as a school of thought or approach to critical studies, it signifies the perspectives of nonelite or marginalized segments of the population. Emerging in India as a critique of both nationalist and Marxist criticisms of colonialism, this approach is critical of the way postcolonial nationalism sought to reverse colonialist assumptions by attributing agency and history to the subjected nation, on the same assumptions about Reason and Progress instituted by colonialism. Scholars adopting this approach are also critical of the Marxist critique of colonial exploitation that was framed by a historical analysis of capital and class struggle that universalized Europe's historical experience.

Subaltern studies scholars object to both nationalist and Marxist critiques of colonialism as themselves Eurocentric, constrained by what they seek to criticize (Prakash 1994: 1475). As one of these scholars made the point, to nationalist and Marxist critiques of colonialism, "Europe remains the sovereign, theoretical subject of all histories, including the ones we call Indian, Chinese, Kenyan, and so on. There is a peculiar way in which all these other histories tend to become variations on a master narrative that could be called 'the history of Europe.' In this sense, 'Indian' history itself is in a position of subalternity" (Chakrabarty 1992: 1). In addition, this group of scholars also criticizes an internal subalternity within postcolonial societies and regions, and affirms that "the subalterns had acted history on their own, that is, independently of the elite; their politics constituted an autonomous domain, for it neither originated from elite nor did its existence depend on the latter" (Prakash 1994: 1447–48).

Even when we take this objection to applying the assumptions and methodology of Eurocentric historiography to African societies, the question may still be raised whether these societies have achieved the necessary level of development and culture to be able to implement constitutional or democratic governance. The answer that seems to be implied in the question is always in the negative. As a consequence, a "sense of failure overwhelms the representation of the history of these societies. Such images of aborted transitions reinforce the subalternity of non-Western [African] histories and the dominance of Europe as History" (Prakash 1994: 1484–85). The criticism of anti-colonial nationalism for having adopted colonial frameworks for its own indigenous elite project is expressed as follows. The very conception of the country as a national community seeks to pit nationalism against communalism which is accused of being unable to recognize religious, cultural, social, and local community as a political form. For our purposes in this book, Eurocentric ideas about "public life" and "free access to information" do not account for the realities of how knowledge is conceived and transmitted in African societies, how it belongs to and circulates in the numerous and particularistic networks of kinship, community and socially constructed spaces and structures. If this is the case, how then can one assume the universality of the canons of history writing, and on whose terms are such universals constructed? (Prakash 1994: 1482, 1485; Chakrabarty 1992: 100)

The value of the subaltern studies approach is that it reinforces the self-confidence of African scholars and policy makers in the validity and relevance of their own recollections of their history and understanding of current experience. Still, the challenge remains how to avoid reproducing the dichotomies of colonial ideologies of the civilized colonizer and the primitive colonized into new variations of modern versus traditional, or by inversion in the destructive imperialist versus the sustaining community of the victim. "The difficulty is to confront the power behind European expansion without assuming it was all-determining and to probe the clash of different forms of social organization without treating them as self-contained and autonomous" (Cooper 1994: 1517). For the subaltern studies insight to really be helpful, one must open both precolonial and colonial experiences of African societies to less dichotomous and less polarized analysis, even in terms of the colonial and subaltern. One should not escape postcolonial discourse by replicating it in sharp dichotomies between European colonial domination (appropriated by the nationalist project after independence) and African subaltern resistance.

Maintaining a dichotomous and polarized analysis of dominant and dominated leads to the paradox of wanting the subalterns to have a rich and complex consciousness, to exercise autonomous agency, and yet to remain in the category of subaltern. Instead, one should appreciate the contradictions of the colonial (or any other oppressive) project—how the oppressor may have to concede to the oppressed what might undermine the basis of dominance (Cooper 1994: 1532). As Cooper concludes:

Africa's crisis derives from a complex history that demands a complex analysis: a simultaneous awareness of how colonial regimes exercised power and the limits of that power, an appreciation of the intensity with which that power was confronted and the diversity of futures that people sought for themselves, an understanding of how and why some of those futures were excluded from the realm of the politically feasible, and an openness to possibilities for the future that can be imagined today. (Cooper 1994: 1545)

The main point of these theoretical reflections for our purposes here is that the retrieval projects of various African societies need not and should not be expected to conform to predetermined specifications, least of all externally defined ones. There is no preconceived script or blueprint for the constitutional course of any African society, no prescribed goals of transition from one point to another that must be achieved. Each society is constructing its constitutional development on its own terms, and that includes its own retrieval and adaptation projects, as well as internally generated responses to current challenges and concerns. The outcomes of these processes may be analyzed by observers as stages in the development of each society, but such analysis should not attempt to anticipate or constrain the visions and direction of any African society regarding its own development.

Precolonial Antecedents

To elaborate on some of the preceding reflections, I will highlight some ideas and institutions of precolonial African societies on which present societies can draw in developing their respective constitutional experience. This view of historical evolution does not preclude a broader cultural influence for such ideas and institutions beyond the particular region of Africa where they emerged or evolved. Recalling the caveat I stated at the beginning of this chapter, such antecedents are not applicable to any other part of the continent simply because they are "African" in some generic, decontextual sense. But this does not mean that relevant antecedents should be rejected for the same reason either. Neither claim would be consistent with the thesis and analysis of this book. It is also important to emphasize here that an inquiry into possible antecedents for constitutionalism in any African society should be done in a realistic and critical manner, avoiding unproductive apologia or sentimental exaggeration. The purpose of reviewing such traditional resources is not to suggest that the particular African society enjoyed well-developed and functioning constitutionalism simply because the concept itself was unknown then in its present sense. Nevertheless, it can be appropriate to consider the constitutional potential of traditional values and institutions that may inspire the confidence of the particular African society in its ability to reclaim those values in the modern context. This combination of a positive yet critical view of traditional African constitutional ideas and experiences can be illustrated by a brief review of a debate among some African scholars in relation to a specific region.

Wiredu, a Ghanaian philosopher, centers his analysis of decision-making by consensus in the traditional political system of the Ashanti, a matrilineal group in West Africa where lineage is the basic political unit, but he also cautions against sweeping generalizations about consensus in traditional African life (Wiredu 1997: 303). He emphasizes that consensus as a staple of decision-making in African life "is not a peculiarly political phenomenon" but is "a manifestation of an immanent approach to social interaction." The prevalence of consensual relations in social and political life does not mean that "African society was a realm of unbroken harmony" (303) or that there was no conflict among different social groups. Rather, the goal of negotiation was understood as "the attainment of reconciliation rather than the mere abstention from further recriminations or collisions" (304). According to another Ghanaian philosopher who wrote about the larger Akan, of which the Ashanti are a part, the "time to express one's eccentricity was in the period of deliberation. To persist in one's individual opinion, when this deviated from the public opinion deliberately arrived at and publicized, was a piece of malice" (Abraham 1962: 75–76).

According to Wiredu, Ashanti decision-making by consensus can achieve "substantive representation," in contrast to the will of the majority rule where the minority viewpoint may be formally represented but will lack a "substantive correlate." (Wiredu 1997: 307) He seems to find what he describes as the "consensual democracy" of the non-party variety, as exemplified by the Ashanti political system, superior to the majoritarian democracy of the multi-party system. In his view, the multi-party system has not invariably or necessarily promoted democracy, though it has some benefits. But he also concedes that transformed social and political conditions mean that the "kinship networks that provided the mainstay of the consensual politics of traditional times are simply incapable of serving the same purpose in modern Africa" (309). Another limitation of the traditional consensus approach is that it worked within the internal politics of ethnic groups, while "historically, inter-ethnic relations involving those same groups have by nature been marked, or more strictly, marred by frequent wars, the most extreme negation of consensus" (309). But as can be seen in other parts of Africa, inter-ethnic wars were themselves constrained by imperatives of interdependence and coexistence. In precolonial Kenya, for instance, warriors of the nomadic Maasai and the agricultural Kikuyu often fought while their women traded amicably a short distance away. During drought periods,

Maasai women and children sought refuge among the Kikuyu, and returned to their community when the rains fell (Muriuki 1974). Such overlapping of hostility and interdependence indicate notions of sovereignty and dispute resolution mechanisms that could be retrieved in promoting the legitimacy of African constitutionalism in local settings.

The point Wiredu draws from traditions of consensual politics is in the possibilities of dialogue between different ethnic groups within African states. In the many African states where some ethnic groups are numerical and political minorities, the multi-party democracy system marginalizes and excludes them from the ambit of power. He perceives the non-party alternative as "a dispensation under which governments are formed not by parties but by the consensus of elected representatives" (1997: 310). Such a system does not in any way prohibit political associations that may be devoted to particular ideological agendas. However, affiliation would not be a criterion for positions of political authority. In this model, a minority that may disagree with a decision will still have their concerns addressed—the politics of consensus will require that the minority be convinced through dialogue to provide their assent even if they have reservations. The minority cannot, in terms of the structures of political power, be ignored (310–11).

Eze questions Wiredu's emphasis on a contrast between consensual democracy as belonging to a traditional precolonial African heritage and "adversarial democracy," and sees contemporary political practices in Africa as being characterized by a complex combination of such "traditional" and external sources (Eze 1997: 314). For Eze consensus cannot be seen as a more fundamental value than democracy, but rather as one "moment of its outcomes . . . the only consensus primary to democracy—democracy's most privileged moment, if any—is the initial, formal, agreement to play by a set of rules that allows the institutions and respect of dissent as much as its opposite" (321). He suggests that the same kinds of traditional cultural metaphors in which Wiredu reads consensus can also be understood as implying the principle of democracy, in their emphasis on multiple perspectives and voices. The critical question for Eze is which political framework is of more value for present day Africa: democracy that is dependent on consensus or democracy as the framework of competing (and not only consenting) interests. Asserting that neither conception can be classified as inherently "African" or "Western," he suggests that the ideal form of democracy is one that "culturally reconciles" tendencies that are "centripetal," that is, oriented toward consensus and agreement, as well as "centrifugal," that is, oriented towards competing perspectives.

Gyekye emphasizes several of the same aspects that Wiredu highlights among the Ashanti, but in relation to Akan of which the Ashanti are a subgroup. He maintains that "the Akan people institutionally express, in their own fashion, certain basic ideas of democracy" (Gyekye 1997: 129). Such mechanisms include the requirement of popular support for election and rule by the chief, the possibility of free expression of opinion, and the emphasis on consensus which provides space for dissenting views and opposition. However, in affirming that "there is a need to urge that traditional values and ideas be brought to bear on modern political life" (135), Gyekye also stipulates that such an application must take into account the complexities of contemporary political settings. Toward this end, certain traditional political practices might be amenable to an appropriate "translation" while others, like the notion of a hereditary political authority, would not be feasible. He offers a list of institutions that would promote democracy (136), and argues that "the political values of consultation and consensus—thus of inclusion—must be given institutional expression" (139) in contemporary politics. While different procedures have their respective benefits and drawbacks,

the democratic principle of popular sovereignty requires a stronger consensus than the simple majority method of reaching political decisions can offer, even though consensus formation is not easy to obtain . . . [the consequent] political inclusion evokes in every individual citizen (or representative) a sense of belonging and being a member of the political community, a virtue essential in all political settings, whether multinational or not. (1997: 140)

As indicated earlier, the point of reporting the analysis of these scholars is not to draw a direct line of development from such limited and rudimentary ideas and institutions to full-fledged constitutionalism, even within the same region, present-day Ghana or West Africa generally. Rather, it is simply to affirm that some of the basic ideas and institutions of modern constitutionalism are indeed part of the historical experience of African societies. The same point is made more broadly by Young in his analysis of what he calls the "precolonial precursors" to the range of contemporary notions of freedom in Africa (2002: 14). Various precolonial understandings of freedom can be discerned in customary and ritualized structures of governance, in the decentralized character of political authority across much of the continent, and the nature of social and economic life in precolonial Africa. Like the other scholars cited above, Young points to the "framework of customary restraint· which imposed important limits on capricious exercise of authority" (16). He draws attention to "unarticulated notions of freedom that were implicit in the highly decentralized nature of political structures in large parts of the continent. A wide range of freedom for those unencumbered by servile status in these regions, although not reflected in doctrine, was embedded in everyday practice" (16). The diffuse nature of political authority and the lack of an apparatus to enforce state power contributed to the forms in which such lived notions of freedom were manifested. Even where states were centralized, their authority tapered off beyond a certain area. Past this territory, "rule was limited to sporadic extraction of tribute" (17).

According to Young, one difference between Western and African perspectives is the latter's lack of "joining of property to life and liberty as constitutive elements in personal freedom" (2002: 17). While the sanctity of property was a critical bulwark against the expanding claims of the early modern state in Europe, land did not play the same role in precolonial Africa for various reasons. First, land was abundant and labor was the commodity in short supply, which meant that control over labor and not land was essential for production. Another reason is that land was a communal good, and land use was easily accessible to all those in a community. Young argues that the pattern of land use suggests another aspect of "embryonic notions of freedom" (18), the idea that freedom was vested not in the individual but derived from the community.

Young also points out that "the spread of universal religions contained yet another notion of freedom" (2002: 18). With deep historical roots in Africa, both Islam and Christianity were spreading into new regions in the century before colonialism. Both offered the "concept of a community of believers, ultimately equal in their submission to or faith in God, as *umma* or *res christiana*. Unfree status was reserved to the unbeliever. Conversion, for many, was thus a personal act of liberation" (2002: 19). Religion also offered entry into a community, "as entire local units followed their leaders into the new faith," and "scriptural sources became a privileged library for political language of protest, and subsequently liberation" (19). At the same time, however, religion brought with it "subordination to its prescriptions and its authorities, not all of which advanced the idea of freedom" (19).

It is also relevant here to note that there is evidence that toward the end of the nineteenth century, before the colonial encounter, some African societies were engaged in constitutional experiments that sought to address the impact of social and political developments of previous decades. There appears to have been ongoing centralization of power, using indigenous technologies of war, among various African communities, like the Zulu and the Baganda, in the period leading up to colonialism. Boahen points out that the nineteenth century was a time of dynamic change in Africa: "these internal dynamics . . . were not only economic and political but above all social and intellectual [among autonomous communities whose] rulers were in full control of their own affairs and destinies" (Boahen 1987: 1). The abolition of the slave trade and its replacement by trade in natural products led to the end of the wars for slaves and to a more just distribution of wealth, especially across rural regions.

In the political sphere, state-building was characterized by greater centralization. Technology transfer enabled by European capitalism led to the establishment of processes of industrial and military modernization in several states. Boahen suggests that at that point, Africa "was in a mood of optimism and seemed poised for a major breakthrough on all fronts. By 1880, old Africa seemed to be dying, and a new and modern Africa was emerging" (1987: 1). Ranger offers a somewhat different overall assessment with regard to East and Central Africa, though he too emphasizes the increased military strength and political centralization of African societies. "Many scholars have argued that the nineteenth-century history of the area was a progress to disaster which left African societies on the eve of colonization greatly weakened and divided. Perhaps the century saw a decline in terms of agricultural production, of population growth or life expectancy" (Ranger 1994: 76).

Such scholarly disagreements are of course to be expected, and their final resolution here is neither possible nor necessary for our purposes because I am not claiming that the antecedents highlighted above were true of all parts of the continent. It is sufficient for the point I am trying to make that, as Boahen argues, the impetus for constitutional experimentation essentially stemmed from larger numbers of the population staking a claim to a role in governance:"the number of educated people and ulamas [Islamic scholars] steadily increased throughout the century and they began to demand a share in the administration of their countries" (Boahen 1987: 9). Conflicts between those emerging elites and traditional rulers were in some cases resolved by force, as in the Fulani Jihads or Dyula rebellions. However, "in other parts of Africa, especially on the west coast, this confrontation was resolved in a constitutional manner, with the educated seeking, not to replace the traditional rulers, but to become their partners" (9). Boahen lists three such constitutional experiments: the Fante Confederation formed in Ghana in 1868, the Egba United Board of Management (EUBM) formed in Nigeria in 1865, and the kingdom of the Grebo in Liberia (10).

For example, the constitution of the Fante Confederation in Ghana detailed the political structure of authority, from the king-president, his advisors, the Ministry, the Executive Council, and a Representative Assembly. It provided for the framing and enactment of laws and for a provincial court (Boahen 1987: 10). That constitution also outlined plans for social and economic development. Those significant and visionary proposals called for constructing roads and promoting agriculture and industry. They also emphasized education "not only of a literary but also of a technological and practical nature—as well as the pride of place given to female education and the education of the youth" (11). Moreover, those proposals were characterized by a "spirit of self-help and self-reliance underlying the proposals," and emphasized "harmonious cooperation between the educated elite and the traditional rulers for national development" (12). In Boahen's view, had the implementation of that confederation not been blocked by the British in 1873, "the course not only of the history of Ghana but indeed that of the whole of West Africa would have been different."

The need for critical assessment of such antecedents, as indicated earlier, would raise the question whether there is a negative association between traditional values and institutions, on the one hand, and constitutionalism in the present context, on the other. That is, in terms of the thesis of this book, can the persistence of precolonial or traditional antecedents hinder or obstruct the incremental success of constitutionalism in the modern African context, as opposed to supporting and sustaining it, as suggested by the preceding discussion? For example, Suberu assesses the perspectives offered by scholars who partly locate the failure of democratic institutions in traditional political cultures in Nigeria. The premise of this line of thinking is essentially the view that Western democratic practices have no correlates, and hence are fundamentally incompatible with traditional Nigerian culture and society. This argument cites as evidence the absence of limitation of power in some traditional political structures and the association of absolute authority with political power. Another problem is said to be "that the strong sense of communal obligation, which is a defining feature of virtually all traditional societies in Nigeria, fosters such destructive patterns of values and practices as social coercion and authoritarianism, ethnocentrism or intercultural distrust and corruption or nepotism" (Suberu 1995: 202). Suberu refers to this as "the ruinous patterns of public behavior which are animated by the logic that state resources and positions may be competed for and then utilized for the personal benefit of officeholders and their sectional reference groups" (202).

But Suberu himself also stresses the diversity of traditional political cultures within present day Nigeria, pointing out that it encompasses "the theocratic authoritarianism of the Hausa-Fulani emirates in Northern Nigeria, through the monarchical republicanism of the Yoruba kingdoms of southwest Nigeria, to the democratic egalitarianism of the 'stateless' or decentralized societies of the Igbo in the southeast and several minority communities in the middle-belt or lower north" (1995: 202). He indicates that, while analysis of traditional political cultures may provide valuable perspectives on modern political practices, the complexity and variation across contexts effectively prohibit any simple generalization about their overall impact. Nevertheless, he argues that it is inaccurate to conclude that traditional political practices and structures have had no influence on modern political culture in Nigeria, even though the influence might be limited.

One reservation I have about this line of thinking is that it may be dichotomizing "traditional" and "modern" notions of both community and politics in a somewhat simplistic manner. Although communal ties and notions of identity in a contemporary context may have important historical continuities that are preserved through social networks, they are also profoundly transformed by more recent and current developments. For instance, since modern political structures themselves reshape communities, as well as power relations within and among them, the meaning and implications of communal ties and identity is likely to change. Another reservation is that the argument about traditional loyalties determining contemporary politics cannot explain why any democratic change should occur at all, why individuals across communities, and different communities across a society, would share democratic aspirations and risk their lives in trying to realize them, as indeed happened in Nigeria and many other African countries, most recently during the last decade of the twentieth century.

In my view, earlier antecedents as well as more recent and contemporary developments are all elements in the same process for each society. This perspective is illustrated by the recent constitutional experiences discussed in Chapter 3 of this book. The point is also made in the possibilities and risks of incremental success in the case of Nigeria. It is probably true to a large extent that Nigeria "has been a model in adopting and utilizing federalist principles to mediate and contain centrifugal tendencies" (Suberu 1995: 206). Favorable features include "the preservation of the corporate existence of the federation, the integration of a variety of ethnic minority communities into the mainstream of national politics, the dilution of the hegemony of the north" (206). But limitations of Nigerian experience include over-centralization and continuing inequalities among social and ethnic groups (208), as well as the risks of reversal or serious setbacks, as may happen over the implementation of Shari'a by the northern states, as discussed in Chapter 5. The interaction of such contradictory factors emphasizes in my view the contingency of outcomes, and hence the role of human agency in directing developments in the direction of promoting and sustaining constitutionalism.

Constitutionalism Under Colonial Rule

Although some parts of Africa were colonized by European powers earlier, the high point of colonial occupation of most of the continent can be roughly divided into three phases. During the first phase, from around 1880 to the end of the First World War, the continent was partitioned among European powers. Following the defeat of Germany in that war, its "possessions" were repartitioned and designated as League of Nations mandates, with colonial control vested in France, Britain, Belgium, and South Africa. The second phase broadly covers the period from the early 1920s to the Second World War. The third phase, from the end of the Second World War to the 1960s, overlapped with the gradual process of decolonization and achievement of political independence which continued into the 1970s, and even the late 1980s in the case of Namibia.

Colonial rule is by definition a negation of constitutionalism at both the formal and informal levels of relations between political authority and the colonized population. However, as several scholars have pointed out, both colonialism and anticolonial resistance in Africa cannot be understood as monolithic or motivated by any single purpose (Collins 1994). Moreover, despite its inherently oppressive nature, colonialism did not mean that Africans were completely helpless subjects who lacked all political and economic initiative (Ranger 1994: 74; Boahen 1987: 41). In any case, one cannot overlook this critical phase in the constitutional development of each African country, whether it is viewed in negative or positive terms.

It may therefore be useful to envision two forms of constitutional development in Africa during the colonial period. The first form imposed an external alien political authority and transformed traditional political structures. Premised on notions of the superiority of European civilization, this discourse sought to render Africans subjects, not citizens, with minimal participation in political power. This form of "colonial constitutionalism," if it may be called that, in its complex varieties of the different territories ruled by European powers during that period, was characterized by the structural denial of access to Africans to the ultimate source or bases of political power. The second form preserved some measure of autonomy for African populations, which enabled them eventually to mobilize themselves into anticolonial resistance and develop their own nationalist movements. This is not to suggest that these two forms of constitutional development evolved separately, or were completely distinct, as they did in fact interact and overlap in various settings and over time. It is also clear that colonial policies as well as anticolonial resistance were conditioned by contextual and strategic factors that tended to generate an internal inconsistency and ambivalence on each side, and its interaction with the other.

If constitutionalism is understood as the struggle of the people to challenge and secure political power, the different reactions of African populations to colonial power was certainly a continuing constitutional negotiation. In other words, according to the thesis of this book, the precolonial, colonial, and postcolonial experiences of African societies should be seen as interactive stages in the same process by which each society was constructing its own path to constitutional governance, and continues to do so into the future. From this perspective, the earlier remarks on the precolonial antecedents should be linked to the following reflections on these processes and how they evolved during the colonial phase.

STRUCTURES AND ASSUMPTIONS OF COLONIAL ADMINISTRATION

British rule in colonial Africa was generally carried out through what is commonly known as "indirect rule," whereby colonial authority was exercised through local structures, including "recognizing" existing chiefs, appointing new, more compliant chiefs, or establishing new "native administrations" often with no African correlates for that purpose. In contrast, French colonial authorities attempted to govern through a more unified framework based on the principle of treating all colonized subjects as part of a French entity through the doctrine of "assimilation" or the fiction of French second-class citizenship. After the First World War, French administrators employed a different strategy known as "association," which allowed for more flexible patterns of administration in different regions.

The irony is that the theoretical or ideological rationale for these strategies of colonial domination was presented as consistent with European constitutional and democratic ideals. The British doctrine of indirect rule was claimed to "recognize" and even respect indigenous culture, customs and authority. The British colonial administrators "were skeptical that their own institutions could survive when transplanted to Africa, and they deeply believed that any system of government must take into account African institutions and traditions. In theory, at least, indirect rule was a happy combination of "expediency and high purpose" (Collins 1994: 102). The French policy of assimilation claimed, in contrast, to include all colonial subjects in consonance with the universalist ideals of the French Revolution and the Enlightenment ideas of the power of reason and universal equality of all men (but not necessarily women). These egalitarian principles were supposedly "applied to the French colonies that were promptly incorporated as constitutional and administratively equal parts of continental France" (Collins 1994: 103). At the same time,

The authoritarianism was justified by the belief that the *assimilation* of the African masses to French culture and civilization, though still the ultimate justification for colonialism, was hardly feasible within the practicable future. So long as Africans remained attached to their traditional or Muslim customs, ways and civil laws, they could hardly become French citizens. The best that could be hoped for was that they could be *associated* with France as her subjects, men and women possessing the obligations of citizenship but not its rights. The acquisition of citizenship became a formal process, involving education in French schools, performing military service, and agreeing to be monogamous and to forswear traditional or Islamic law and custom. (Fage 2002: 411; emphasis original)

The fact that colonial rule was itself a total and egregious violation of the constitutional ideal of the sovereignty of a people was conveniently overlooked by assuming the inherent civilizational superiority of Europe and the unquestioned value of its civilizing mission of ushering Africans into modernity. The logic of such rationalizing ideologies of colonialism nevertheless required some lip service to be paid to the values of modernity and constitutionalism, thereby indirectly contributing to the evolution of African constitutionalism out of the myth of colonial constitutionalism in Africa, though that was incidental to the colonial project itself.

TRANSFORMATION OF TRADITIONAL AFRICAN POLITICAL INSTITUTIONS

As the colonial state began to consolidate its domination after conquest, it sought political alliances "in existing African political structures. Those holding authority, or having some locally recognized claim to it, could rely on a reservoir of legitimacy and the familiarity of prescriptive usage" (Young 1994: 107). But this colonial policy of employing intermediaries had important consequences for traditional political structures and the local operations of political power because "the colonial state insisted that those chiefs it recognized were the *sole* authority holders within the reconfigured political space subject to its design" (107; emphasis added). The power of the chief came to flow under colonial control from above and not from the people. In societies with no chiefs, the equation of power between political authority and the people was radically altered.

For example, four traditional societies that had no chiefs in the precolonial context, the Kikuyu, Kamba, and Maasai of Kenya and the Ibo of Nigeria, were administered as fragmented autonomous communities. "They [British colonial administrators] gave wide political influence to men of singular authority, but the influence of these men was not hereditary or authoritarian. Their positions depended on tendering good advice and having it accepted by their peers" (Tignor 1971: 342). In contrast to centralized societies such as the Hausa-Fulani emirates in Northern Nigeria, the Yoruba of southeast Nigeria, and the Ashanti of Ghana, royal lineage was not a prerequisite for political leadership among the decentralized societies. While centralized societies had "formal bureaucracies of judges, military leaders, and tax collectors, with specially designated functions," acephalous or "headless" societies had "democratic, conciliar, and diffused government of elders" (342).

Since British colonial administrators were more familiar with societies headed by chiefs, and thought it essential to rule through a single local authority, they tended to establish local leaders in order to rule through them (Tignor 1971: 342). The creation of chiefs was accompanied by colonial restructuring of administrative political and legal structures. Regardless of the differences between the administrative systems of the Kikuyu in Kenya and the Ibo in Nigeria, in both places "chiefs had extensive powers until the later 1930s, when many of their functions began to be taken over by specialist colonial officials" (343). This was necessary for colonial administrators because the chiefs essentially were instruments of colonial government for introducing and collecting taxes, recruiting labor for projects of a public nature, and maintaining order (346). Chiefs also worked in recruiting wage labor for Europeans, and people were coerced by violence if they resisted. In these ways, chiefs' rule was a factor not only in widening the scope of political activity, but also in forcing previously autonomous communities into new political units.

This is not to say, however, that the chiefs themselves always brought about political integration, for they engendered antagonisms as well as loyalties. They did, however, sometimes undermine ancient local allegiances and direct people's vision toward the location, district, province, tribe, and even nation (Tignor 1971: 346). This new role of chiefs as the farthest extension of the colonial administration and agents of social change had three important consequences: "the creation of para-administrations and military organisations on the local level; corruption; and a zero-sum game in local politics" (348). With minimal administrative support from the colonial administration, the chiefs developed their own coercive apparatus of young men or "retainers" (349). To maintain that apparatus, the chiefs were compelled to extract what colonial administrators deemed appropriate tribute from local populations (351). The third outcome, the "zero-sum" game, was a function of the unfair distribution of obligations such as taxes and communal labor among the community (354). Those with influential connections or in a position to pay bribes could escape these obligations, while "the poor, the young, very old, and women—in short, those who lacked economic and political power—shouldered these burdens" (354). The impact of this form of administration "was largely negative and coercive for it distributed hateful obligations rather than largesse. Since in neither Ibo nor Kikuyu societies were those duties distributed equitably, local administration inevitably meant that those who held office were exempt from obligations and those outside the confines of power felt the weight of coercive administration" (355).

Some African societies like the Kamba and Maasai, however, managed to avoid this scenario according to Tignor's analysis. For example, Maasai chiefs were not able to wield the same kind of authority because they were unable to develop a similar paramilitary coercive apparatus. Maasai warriors held a special cultural position, with a strong sense of identity and "a considerable amount of political autonomy, buttressed by living in special villages separate from the rest of Maasai society" (1971: 359). They not only refused to operate as the arm of colonial power, but also sometimes rose in opposition to unpopular colonial policies that chiefs tried to forcibly implement. As a result, Maasai society did not display the three characteristics seen in Ibo and Kikuyu society, namely, coercive supporting apparatus, political corruption, and politics as a zero-sum game.

Therefore, as Mamdani points out, "Though presented ideologically as a continuation of 'traditional' precolonial authority on the continent, any examination of the division between clan and administrative authority in most precolonial African state systems reveals this claim to be hollow" (1991: 242). He argues that this mode of authority was at the heart of the colonial system because it was the basis of the economic exploitation of the peasantry which continues in the independent period. Mamdani also raises an important rhetorical question: "Is it then surprising that almost every rebellion in rural Africa, had, if not the principal then one of its chief targets, this personal embodiment of fused state authority: the chief? Was it not a demand for democracy?" (243). Although such movements were unlikely to articulate formal demands for political rights, equality, or sovereignty at that time, they were at least seeking autonomy on specific issues, if not expressions of opposition to an external, alien power as such. In any case, whether consciously or not, those movements were certainly part of the decolonization struggle, and of the continuing process of building African constitutionalism, as envisioned in this book.

Popular Resistance to Colonialism as a Legacy for Constitutionalism

As noted earlier, African populations reacted to the colonial encounter in different, sometimes internally inconsistent ways. Boahen, for example, argues that during the first phase of colonialism (from the 1880s to the end of the First World War), the "illiterate and traditional rulers of the rural areas and the educated elite and the urban intelligentsia reacted differently in terms of objectives, leadership, and strategies" (1987: 63). Rural rebellions were in the context of specific colonial policies and actions, whether "taxation, land alienation, compulsory cultivation of crops, the tyrannical behavior of colonial officials, or the introduction of Western education and with it the condemnation of African culture and traditional ways of life" (1987: 63). Boahen lists numerous such rebellions in different parts of Africa (1987: 64–65), which often cut across ethnic lines, most notably in the case of the famous Maji Maji rebellion in East Africa, which sought to remove German power from Tanganyika—"the rebellion spread over an area of more than 10,000 square miles and involved over twenty different ethnic groups" (1987: 65). Traditional religious authorities also played a key role in some of these rebellions.

In his analysis of the Ndebele-Shona (1896–97) mass anticolonial uprising in what is now Zimbabwe, and the Maji Maji (1905) in East Africa, Ranger argues that two traditions of charismatic authority in particular played a key role in giving these movements their mass character cutting across social groups. These were prophetic authority, with its revolutionary potential, and witchcraft eradication movements, which had the ability to spread rapidly across clan and tribal boundaries, sweeping people into a unity that overrode suspicions and allegations of sorcery (1967: 231).

There were also several forms of passive resistance, like refusal to comply with orders or to cultivate compulsory crops, and rejecting all the "civilized" notions introduced by or connected with the colonial system (Boahen 1987: 67). An important form of protest was "hidden or everyday struggles . . . work slowdowns, pilfering, sabotage, dissimulation, flight, and the other *weapons of the weak* were more than just a nuisance to the powerful. The sum total of these otherwise insignificant acts could and sometimes did have far-reaching consequences" (Isaacman 1990: 31, emphasis original). Such localized forms of insurgency were not classified as rebellions, revolutions, or other broad-based social movements. To their perpetrators, however, "these actions embodied at least some vague notion of collective identity and possessed an internal structure and logic even if it is not easily discernible to scholars" (32). In Isaacman's assessment, none of these recurring and localized actions "attacked the structures of class, racial, and gender oppression. In this respect they have been characterized as *weak* forms of resistance. Yet to varying degrees they did enable embattled peasantries to protect a measure of autonomy, and they reduced the level of oppression, however marginally" (40).

Translating such events into the formal vocabulary of political opposition is theoretically problematic, especially in constitutional terms of struggles for accountability and rights. If constitutionalism is understood as fundamentally concerned with the operation of law and order, then the gains procured via reform by the educated elite of colonized societies might be viewed as more properly "constitutional." However, it may be possible to envision an African legacy of mass-based "ordinary" protest as a positive political force from colonial, and even precolonial, to contemporary times. In the colonial period such resistance was itself mobilized on the basis of established ideas of justice and traditional political values as Isaacman (1990) has suggested. Regarding the post-colonial period, Cheru argues that

It would be a great mistake to attribute the growth of democracy movements in Africa strictly to the mobilization efforts of elite-led parties that have sprung up in recent years. Rather, the movements owe their success to the debilitating economic impact of the "silent revolution" on the part of ordinary peasants in protest at the incapacity of African governments to provide even the most basic services to previously protected groups (teachers, civil servants, doctors etc.). . . . The impact of such resistance to the policy decisions of government may not always be visible on the surface; its significance must be measured by long-term effects. In reality, these actions have been effective in eroding the foundations of many autocratic regimes. (Cheru 2002: 45–46)

The main point I am drawing from the preceding review is that earlier, more diffused, forms of popular political protests provide historical depth and indigenous meaning to current forms of "civil society" agitation that appears more coherent to constitutional theorists. New actors in civil society like civic and peasant associations and human rights and environmental groups have now become important agents promoting social change and demanding it from the state. "The overall consensus among these social movements is that the process of poverty alleviation must go hand-in-hand with the institution of far-reaching political change" (Cheru 2002: 46). The additional point I am making is that there is historical depth for these modern forms of organization and objectives if we are flexible and imaginative about where and how to look for that in the histories of African societies under colonial rule.

My concern so far in this chapter has been to integrate precolonial and colonial manifestations of civil society into the same narrative, and appreciate the continuity of the process of building constitutionalism by each society in its own locally relevant and coherent terms. Some of the issues and concerns about the continuation of this narrative to the present time are discussed in subsequent chapters of this book. However, while the next phases of these ongoing processes cannot be anticipated or predicted with certainty, it may be helpful at this stage to reflect on the underlying values and institutions by which "relative success or failure" may be judged. The next question for now is whether the conception of sovereignty on which present African states are founded is conducive to constitutionalism or whether there is a need for rethinking this principle, and to what ends. That discussion is followed by a focus on issues of accountability, human rights, and dignity. To my mind, these are elements of the "standards" by which the success or failure of African constitutionalism should be judged, though such evaluations should be specific to the context of each society. As I have already emphasized in Chapter 1, the need for a deeply contextual understanding and evaluation does not mean there are no identifiable standards that can be applied in judging the constitutional "performance" of present African societies. But such evaluations are to be made with a view to implementing strategies to improve performance, instead of accepting the status quo as somehow inevitable or permanent.

Sovereignty in Postcolonial Africa

As observed by Jackson and Rosberg two decades ago, although many postcolonial African states are internally deficient and externally weak, their sovereignty has been guaranteed by the world community of states and the Organization of African Unity (OAU; now the African Union). This situation, they argue, stands in sharp contrast to the "classical historical pattern [in Europe] in which external recognition is based on empirical statehood, usually achieved in alliance with other states under strenuous conditions of international rivalry" (Jackson 1984: 2). Thus, the modern states of Europe, and their successors elsewhere, were built with the use of force under strong pressures of disintegration, both domestic and international (4). The international law that emerged was created by statesmen who respected it only to the extent that it was to their countries' mutual advantage, and considered part of the balance of power but was never a substitute for it. It came to embody Eurocentric concepts of sovereignty and standards of civility as conditions for the recognition of states. Non-European parts of the world that failed to qualify as full members of the exclusive club of sovereign states (as determined by European powers) became vulnerable to European colonialism and its drastic consequences.

Except for ambiguous cases like the relationship between Ethiopia and Eritrea, all present African states are direct successors of the colonies that were constituted as united political entities by European colonial powers for the first time in the history of each territory. The constitution of these states in the belly of colonialism, as well as their legal legitimacy at independence derived from agreements among European states, rather than the consent of their own populations. Their borders were usually defined by international rules of continental partition and occupation established by European powers for that purpose, instead of local or regional political facts or geography. Previously and through the decolonization process itself, the governments of these countries were organized according to European colonial theory and practice (tempered by expediency), and were staffed almost entirely by Europeans at decision-making levels. Their economies were managed with imperial and/or local colonial considerations primarily in mind, and their laws and policies reflected the interests and values of European imperial power, which usually included strategic military uses, economic advantage, Christianization, European settlement, and so forth. While the populations of the colonies were overwhelmingly African, the vast majority had little or no constitutional standing in their own countries (Jackson 1984: 5–6).

Moreover, the African populations of those colonies had little control even in the timing and dynamics of the process of decolonization that is supposed to have "restored" their sovereignty. A combination of internal agitation for independence and shifts in the dynamics of European domestic politics and international relations after the end of the Second World War resulted in the transfer of negative sovereignty, whereby juridical statehood ensures general legitimacy and freedom from acts and threats of foreign intervention. This came about in sharp contrast to the European tradition in which the modern conception of sovereignty was based on demonstrable capacity, or positive fact of empirical sovereignty, the capacity of states for self-government and ability to enforce their territorial jurisdiction. In the formative European context of sovereignty, a state was a credible entity that existed as such, whether recognized or not, and whose reality required recognition sooner or later. Classical international law was the child, not the parent, of states in Europe, while the international law of decolonization and juridical statehood became the parent of the postcolonial African state. The basic point to emphasize out of all these remarks is that almost all present African states acquired sovereignty before they were necessarily sovereign as a matter of positive, inescapable reality (Jackson 1984: 26).

With due regard to the fact that their perspective and objectives are different from mine in this book, the following features of Jackson and Rosberg's analysis (1984, 1986) are pertinent to my own thesis:

- The minimal colonial administration by a remarkably thin layer of European decision-makers assisted by a few educated local elites and traditional rulers, employing divide and rule tactics, came to be accepted as the "natural" order of things by African populations. The exercise of sovereignty was therefore seen as necessarily requiring authoritarian power structures and relations, and elitist politics, rather than popular participation in governance and the defusion of authority and powers.
- The fact that territorial defense was a function of Pax Europa among imperial powers since the conference of Berlin, and supported by the Pax Africana of the OAU since 1963, contributes to perceptions of

state security as directing military forces inward at African populations as protection against rebellion or riot. National security came to mean the security of the regime in power, with very little transparency and political or legal accountability in the operation of security forces. It is too early to tell whether the transformation of the OAU into the African Union in 2002 will have a significant impact on this state of affairs, but it is difficult to expect the same governments to change their policies in this regard without pressure from their own populations, as suggested below.

- As independence came suddenly without preparation in most cases, the emerging African states had little capacity and competence to cope with the responsibilities of the sovereignty that was thrust on them on short notice. Zambia, for instance, had fewer than 100 university graduates and fewer than 1000 high school graduates by the time of independence (Hodder-Williams 1984:86). Lacking the strength and competence to govern effectively and humanely, postcolonial governments tended to compensate by using oppressive and authoritarian methods, a "natural" continuation of the colonial state and its administrative "traditions."

- The new African states were defined by political boundaries originally determined by European imperialists, whose territorial claims were made in relation to one another without regard to traditional African rulers or their peoples. This state of affairs was hardly conducive to the development of a strong sense of political community ("nation") among the diverse populations united by external force.

- The political parties established by African leaders in their struggle for independence were more of an expedient for retaining leadership and control over the new state than a means for providing indigenous structures or gaining the genuine loyalties of local African populations. For decades after independence, the majority of ruling parties remained auxiliary institutions of personal power rather than authentic organizations of public opinion or expressions of popular sovereignty.

In relation to constitutional principles in particular, since the real authority of the state did not necessarily cover its whole territorial jurisdiction, ruling African elites tended to focus on controlling the government apparatus and patronage system, and strove to retain the support of key ethnic leaders, instead of seeking genuine legitimacy and accountability to the population at large. Ironically, those seemingly expedient political strategies in fact facilitated the loss of power by the independence leaders of most African countries to military usurpers who succeeded in controlling the whole country by simply physically holding a few officials and key government installations in the capital. Once they were in "effective control of the government," military usurpers gained automatic recognition by "the international community" in almost every single case. In this way, both the domestic and international sources of sovereignty have tended to be exclusively concerned with sovereignty of the government, not of the people.

The reasons for the repeated failure of the first constitutions of the vast majority of African states are complex and vary from one country to another. But part of the explanation is that those constitutions were alien frameworks that had little meaning for most Africans. They were also usually established too late in the colonial period, often within a few years of independence, to become a familiar part of the political and legal institutions of the country. Many were unnecessarily complicated or clearly unfair. The Ugandan constitution, for instance, involved provinces with a "fully federal relationship, quasi-federal relationship and a non-federal relationship to the central government; in Zambia, there were a number of preferential arrangements for whites entrenched in the constitution" (Hodder-Williams 1984: 68). Despite the weakness of their own legitimacy and accountability under the constitutions of their respective countries, ruling elites everywhere managed to retain power and enjoy all the benefits of sovereignty, and so did the military usurpers who took over from them without any form or degree of accountability to the population. This reality seems to have sponsored a culture of indifference to accountability as a condition for the attainment and exercise of absolute political power.

To explore the underlying issues here, it seems to me that there are two aspects of sovereignty in relation to constitutionalism. The first one is that it is the will of the population to govern itself that finds expression through an institutional framework of democracy. The second in this context is the notion that one people is distinct as a political and territorial entity from another people. This latter conception is particularly important for the basis of the modern territorial "nation" state, which continues to be the dominant form of political organization of present societies as politically autonomous entities. Moreover, the constitution is usually taken to be a means for affirming the sovereignty of the state through a formal declaration at the beginning, in contrast to those of developed and establish countries in the West where that is assumed as the basis of constitution-making without the need to expressly declare what is taken to be obvious or self-evident. This contrast of the assertion of sovereignty, as opposed to its assumption, is partly due to the historical fact of decolonization during the last part of the twentieth century. The fact of political "restoration" or "creation" of sovereignty through political independence needed to be expressly affirmed.

However, given the continuing power dynamics of inequality that characterizes international relations at a regional or global level, the importance of this secondary aspect of sovereignty as the basis of political independence should not be underestimated. Constitutionalism is usually understood as an "internal" doctrine whose mandate and province pertains to a nation or nation-state. Yet the threat to constitutionalism may well be external through some form of intervention that repudiates even the possibility of internal sovereignty. Sometimes the threat comes from the willingness of political actors to use extra-constitutional means to protect their perceived interests, often with external assistance or encouragement, as has frequently been the case in many African countries. In such cases, the first sense of sovereignty is probably undermined or diminished, while the second sense is maintained. A military coup, for instance, seriously undermines the ability of the population to govern itself, while the sovereignty of the country as a political and territorial entity is not affected. Indeed, the coup makers have traditionally received international recognition as the government of the country, regardless of the manner in which they achieved control of the state, or the consequences of their actions for the ability of the people as a whole to govern themselves.

I am not suggesting here that one sense of constitutionalism is more important than the other. Rather, I am concerned with sustaining sovereignty in both senses of the term. To this end, I am proposing a rethinking of the concept of sovereignty in the interest of sustainable constitutionalism. The dual purpose of this proposed reconceptualization of sovereignty addresses the question of internal and external legitimacy of the state, while being rooted in institutions and processes that represent the people and secure and protect their interests.

As commonly understood today, sovereignty signifies the state's claim to exclusive control over its territory and people subject to its jurisdiction, including the monopoly of the competence and capacity to set and implement policy, enact and enforce laws, and permit or prohibit activities by any type of actors, whether internal or external (Hinsley 1986). This claim needs to be accepted and openly acknowledged by other states individually and collectively, thereby declaring their acceptance of the internal sovereignty of the new emerging state. As noted earlier, this is the juridical sovereignty that African states achieved through decolonization, regardless of their ability to be sovereign in an empirical sense, on the ground. At the domestic level, this exclusive claim is founded on the state's constitutional order, as recognized and acted upon by other states and actors at the international level. Here, the reference to a state's "constitutional order" does not require that it has a written constitution, nor does it assume a certain quality of conformity with the principles of modern constitutionalism and protection of fundamental rights. In this functional minimal sense, every state has a constitutional order at any given point in time, though judgment can be reserved about its legitimacy and efficacy.

Sovereignty is therefore established and regulated by international as well as national or domestic law. But not only are these two foundational sources of sovereignty interdependent and mutually reinforcing, but the distinction between the domestic and international is becoming increasingly blurred in ways that call for the reformulation of this conception of sovereignty. To place such renegotiation and reformulation in context, it may be useful to reflect on the current status of the European understanding of sovereignty as the dominant paradigm that is being challenged on its own terms. This European conception of sovereignty is premised on a view of the world where states are the principal actors, centers of power and object of interest (Falk 1992: 2). It is also

part of a more general discourse of power whose function is not only to describe political and economic arrangements but to explain and justify them as if they belonged to the natural order of things. . . . It is integral to the structure of Western thought with its stress on "dichotomies and polarities," and to a geopolitical discourse in which territory is sharply demarcated and exclusively controlled. (Falk 1992: 11)

Over time, however, the invention of the sovereign state in this sense, as a product of human expediency and practice, came to be reified and deified, whether in viewing a monarchy as sanctified by god or in the "secular deification" of a republic as conceived by the framers of the U.S. constitution (Anderson 1990). "Given the far-reaching transformation of the social and political landscape we have witnessed this century, and especially these past several decades," Falk suggests, "there is a pressing need to rethink the concept and practice of sovereignty" (Falk 1992 :11).

That may not be easily done, however, not only because of the vested interest of those who are in control of the apparatus of the state, but also because of the nature and assumptions of traditional international law and relations. Those who control the state prefer to keep the traditional view of sovereignty which enables them to retain exclusive control over power and resources as long as they can suppress any internal opposition. That view is also expedient for other governments because it enables them to continue the business of international trade, security, diplomatic relations, and so forth, as usual. Nevertheless, there are mounting calls for reconsideration of this traditional European conception of sovereignty, to address the push and pull of contradictory tendencies to centralization and decentralization, the tendency toward autonomy for national units and ethnic groups, and calls for greater popular control over national sovereignty (Rosenau 1992; Giddens 1990).

Traditional international law itself signifies limitations on sovereignty in that it creates obligations on the state, at least toward other states. Sovereignty is also limited by virtue of membership in international organizations which are created by states precisely because they recognize that there are issues which they cannot adequately address alone. To achieve their purpose, these international organizations have now come to operate in ways that encroach upon sovereignty, as traditionally conceived. Thus, whereas the League of Nations was only able to make decisions by the unanimous agreement of its members, the United Nations now generally operates by majority-voting system, except in the Security Council where the five permanent members have the power to veto resolutions. Traditional sovereignty is encroached upon by states being bound against their will, either by the decision of the majority or by veto power over all other members who are not permanent members of the Security Council. Yet, ironically, rapid decolonization has led to the creation of new states that are hyper-sensitive to violations of their domestic jurisdiction without being capable of maintaining their own sovereignty against internal challenge or external threat.

A number of processes and actors are now challenging state power and authority, both within and across its borders. States are "becoming enmeshed in a network of interdependencies and regulatory/collaborative arrangements from which exit is generally not a feasible option" (Zacher 1992: 60). Some of the communication, economic, and environmental issues and concerns that bring states into collaboration and compromise their sovereignty may also go beyond states' ability to respond even collectively. Governments benefit from recent technological developments in keeping a closer watch on their citizens, but the combination of computer and communications technologies have allowed citizens and corporations to evade governmental control in a number of important ways. The globalization and decentralization of production, made possible by global telecommunications and changes in transportation and production technologies, is allowing transnational corporations to supersede traditional national political jurisdiction. Governments are also losing control over their own currencies to traders whose decisions to buy and sell are based on their independent assessment of government financial decisions and economic policies and activities which are now instantaneously accessible to global market actors. Although global trade and speculation in national and foreign currencies can result in serious economic and political consequences for states and their populations, there is little that governments can do about it, especially those in Africa and other Third World countries which are most vulnerable to such pressures (Wriston 1992: 8–9).

Another area exposing the inadequacy of traditional notions of state sovereignty is the environment. Phenomena like the dramatic cross-border effects of the Chernobyl disaster, ozone depletion, and global warming clearly illustrate the permeability of state borders as well as the inability of most states, as autonomous sovereign entities, to deal with direct threats to their territories and populations (Mathews 1989: 168). Moreover, a variety of increasingly powerful national and international nongovernmental actors are challenging the sovereignty of states through their independent campaigns over environmental issues.

Social movements calling for self-determination in various senses and degrees threaten traditional notions of sovereignty from within the state's borders. These social movements "are in the process of redefining the meaning and boundaries of civil society . . . reaffirming the priority of civil society over the state, of popular sovereignty over state sovereignty" (Camilleri 1990: 35). Mounting tension in the context of tremendous ethnic diversity, diminishing ability of existing states to respond to rising demands for self-determination, and more disintegration and weakening of state sovereignty should be expected (Gellner 1983: 44–45). These trends may be seen as merely increasing the number of states, when an oppressed people seek secession and separate statehood, which may well end in the same sort of sovereignty under which they were oppressed within the previous borders, thereby signaling another triumph of the sovereign state over the sovereignty of the people. Moreover, these trends and the factors contributing to them should also be seen as a reflection of the push and pull of globalizing and localizing trends. The tension between economic and technological integration is decreasing the importance of borders, thereby rendering the state that is appropriating the sovereignty of the people increasingly weaker and less able to exercise that sovereignty. Calls for secession and independent statehood, or for limiting the exclusive control of the state within existing borders in favor of some type or degree of autonomy and devolution of power, are therefore less likely to lead to satisfactory outcomes for the people concerned.

These and related tensions can be negotiated, I propose, through a rethinking of sovereignty whereby the people's ability to govern themselves can be secured within existing borders, instead of risking separation that may result in similar oppression (An-Na'im 1997). The rethinking of sovereignty I am proposing would make the former conditional upon the latter, requiring state sovereignty to be a true reflection of the sovereignty of the people. I would also argue that constitutionalism is both a necessary means and desirable outcome of this process. But the viability of this proposed reconceptualization of sovereignty should be assessed in relation to other theoretical and practical aspects of constitutionalism in the African context. In particular, it seems to me, the basis and rationale of sovereignty should be linked to the state's willingness and ability to protect the equal human rights and dignity of all persons and groups under its jurisdiction. I will now elaborate on this dimension of the standards for assessing the constitutional performance of present African states.

Accountability, Human Rights, and Human Dignity

If we understand constitutionalism as the limitation of political power for the protection of rights and liberties of the population, then sovereignty must be rooted in notions of human rights and human dignity to help achieve this objective. However, while human dignity and human rights usually overlap and reinforce each other, dignity is not always taken to mean *equal* dignity for all human beings by virtue of their humanity as required by the concept of human rights. To the extent that this is true in a society, these two concepts would not readily provide coherent and categorical standards by which sovereignty is to be held accountable. Thus, differing understandings of these two concepts may yield contradictory standards of accountability where, for example, gender, religious, or ethnic differentiation are observed as expressions of human dignity, contrary to equality and nondiscrimination on such grounds as a human rights principle. In my view, however, such tensions and conflicts should be mediated with a view to mobilizing the moral and political force of both human dignity and human rights toward protecting the vital interests of individuals and communities. In striving to maintain, promote, and effectuate the international human rights system, a sufficiently broad and dynamic approach should be taken to address the combined concerns of these two concepts. This effort should neither confuse human dignity with human rights, if the two are perceived to be in conflict, nor undermine or weaken the existing normative and institutional strength of human rights.

By the international human rights system I mean the complex and dynamic set of norms, institutions, mechanisms, and processes concerned with the promotion and protection of human rights at the intergovernmental level through the United Nations and regional organizations. Part of this system is what is sometimes referred to as the human rights movement, which consists of a wide variety of nongovernmental organizations, groups, and individual activists and scholars concerned with the protection and promotion of internationally recognized human rights. The motivation and operation of the system and movement clearly overlap and interact, but it may be useful to maintain a distinction between the two.

The term "human dignity," in one form or another, appears in a variety of international documents and national constitutions, without authoritative definition or elaboration. While this is to be expected at this level, there is also little explanation of the term by way of jurisprudential and scholarly exposition, perhaps because its meaning is assumed to be self-evident or it has not been the subject of judicial deliberation as such. The presumably "intrinsic meaning [of human dignity] has been left to intuitive understanding, conditioned in large measure by cultural factors. When it has been invoked in concrete situations, it has been generally assumed that a violation of human dignity can be recognized even if the abstract term cannot be defined" (Schachter 1983: 849). Taking the word dignity in this general context to mean "intrinsic worth," it follows that to respect a person's human dignity is to treat her with proper regard for, or due recognition of, her intrinsic human worth, as an end, not as a means, that individuals are not to be perceived or treated merely as instruments or objects of the will of others.

This line of thinking leads to interpreting human dignity in ways that uphold the principles of a wide range of internationally recognized human rights, economic, social, and cultural as well as civil and political, while acknowledging a collective dimension to individual autonomy and choice. "The idea of human dignity involves a complex notion of the individual. It includes recognition of a distinct personal identity, reflecting individual autonomy and responsibility. It also embraces a recognition that the individual self is a part of larger collectivities and that they, too, must be considered in the meaning of the inherent dignity of the person" (Schachter 1983: 851–52). But the derivation of human rights from human dignity apparently favor a liberal view of rights as intrinsic to the person as an individual, beyond abridgment by the state or other authority, which may be problematic for other cultural or ideological traditions:

Respect for human dignity may be realized in other ways than by asserting claims of rights. In many cases, the application of a "rights approach" to affronts to dignity would raise questions involving existing basic rights such as free speech. In other cases, respect for dignity may be more appropriately and effectively attained through social processes such as education, material benefits, political leadership and the like. . . . Informal channels for dealing with alleged affronts to dignity might be more suitable and effective than litigation in many cases. (Schachter 1983: 853–54)

Accordingly, while some understandings of human dignity that may be seen as more readily in accord with international human rights norms, other conceptions might be quite different yet still being perceived as treating others with "proper" regard or "due" consideration. This contrast is to be expected because people and societies vary in their understanding of what is proper or appropriate in treating persons of different race, gender, religion, and so forth. The meaning of human dignity, in a practical concrete sense, can therefore be quite different, depending on the culture and context as well as the personal and psychological orientation of the person making the determination. According to Rhoda Howard,

> The principle of human rights represents one particular way of looking at morality, justice, and human dignity. . . . Human Rights, in fact, imply a particular form of relation of the individual to society and the state that differs from what most cultures mean by human dignity . . . They are not merely a set of values expressed in religious or secular culture but also a set of rights that the law, government, and all other social institutions are organized to defend. (Howard 1995: 79)

In contrast, the social order of many cultures stratifies individuals and groups in ways that enhance dignity for some categories of people but leave other categories dishonored, without dignity or respect; some deserve honor, others do not. In most cultures, Howard emphasizes, "Most people's claims, privileges, powers, and obligations (not human 'rights') are dependent on their social status, reflected in ascribed social roles" (Howard 1995: 63).

While I accept Howard's main point about the relative meaning of human dignity, I would also note that various understandings of human rights are also conditioned by culture and context. The present international concept of human rights evolved out of political struggles and intellectual developments within specific Western societies, though they began to be more globally accepted through a gradual process since the adoption of the Universal Declaration of Human Rights by the United Nations in 1948. This evolving "universal" conception is still contested within Western societies (regarding economic and social rights, for instance) as it is among and within other societies. The significant point in my view is that concepts of human rights as well as human dignity are dynamic and open to adaptation to changing conditions in each society. I would therefore urge that the necessarily "relativist" origins of both concepts be openly acknowledged with a view to exploring or promoting more inclusive understandings of each concept, and in relation to the other.

In other words, I am calling for mediation between two possible views regarding the relationship between human dignity and human rights in providing a normative framework for sovereign accountability. One view would subject conceptions of human dignity in all social and political life to liberal standards of individual human rights. The other would uphold traditional or communitarian conceptions of dignity, even where inconsistent with international human rights standards. The continuing challenge, it seems to me, is whether it is possible to sustain the conceptual and institutional integrity and efficacy of international human rights, which include collective as well as individual rights in my view, while striving to articulate and implement a supplementary paradigm for human dignity.

I have argued elsewhere for a deliberate process of internal discourse and cross-cultural dialogue to promote an "overlapping consensus," drawing on John Rawls's idea, over the universality of human rights, that is, to achieve greater acceptance and legitimacy for the same standards as applicable to all human beings, everywhere (An-Na'im 1992). This process should emphasize the shared need for the protection of human rights in all present state-societies, and draw on the possibilities of internal transformation within each cultural and religious tradition to uphold the same rights for all human beings. This is already happening, as culturally specific understandings of human rights are becoming increasingly accepted by diverse cultures and supported by their respective conceptions of human dignity. The same should be true for human dignity in relation to human rights. Since conceptions and implications of dignity in any culture are neither monolithic nor static, it should be possible to achieve an increasing degree of compatibility with human rights which are, in turn, also open to reconceptualization and adaptation in response to different contexts and challenges.

This does not mean, however, that adjustment and adaptation should always be by transforming communitarian notions of dignity into individual human rights in the liberal sense, though that may well be necessary in some situations. Nor should this process seek to specify in detail how universal norms of human dignity and rights must apply in each society because there will always be need for adaptation and specification of broad formulations of norms to the concrete circumstances of time and place, local priorities, and so forth. Such adaptation and specification should, in turn, be evaluated in terms of agreed universal norms of human dignity, and may also give rise to ideas for refining and expanding the norms.

The main conclusion of this last section of the chapter is that respect for and protection of both human rights and human dignity should be part of the standards by which African constitutionalism should be evaluated. As emphasized in the preceding section, sovereignty should be a means to the end of realizing and safeguarding genuine and effective self-determination for all persons and groups, as well as the totality of population at large. Notions of human rights and dignity can provide concrete standards for evaluating the constitutional experience of a country, though the precise meaning and application of these standards to any specific situation may require further clarification. As I have tried to show in the last section of this chapter, both human rights and human dignity are necessarily conditioned by cultural and contextual considerations everywhere, and for all societies, and not only in Africa or for African societies. This need for clarification and specification or adaptation is necessary and desirable from the perspective I am trying to advance through this analysis of African constitutionalism.

In the first two parts of this chapter I attempted to highlight some of the precolonial and colonial resources from which present African societies could draw in developing their own modern constitutional experiences. In the third section I briefly examined the notion of sovereignty as a foundation and rationale of constitutionalism, and as such a standard by which particular constitutional experiences can be assessed. The last section discussed human rights and dignity as substantive content of the sovereignty standard of constitutionalism. All of these elements of African constitutionalism are tentative and contested, which makes their constitutional outcome contingent on a variety of factors. But it is not possible to determine such factors and their dynamic interaction in the abstract, without reference to particular historical context and specific demographic facts, political actors. To give a general sense of how such factors might work in one setting or another, I will attempt to further clarify this approach through a brief evaluation of the recent experiences of a few African countries in the next chapter. Although I will attempt to present those experiences as part of the process of "incremental success" of constitutionalism in those countries, more definitive conclusion will require much more detail and analysis than I am able to offer here.

Chapter 3

Evaluating Experiences in Incremental Success

As already indicated, the deeply contextual and incremental approach to African constitutionalism proposed here does not mean that the experiences of each country cannot be evaluated or improved, or that one has to wait for that to happen entirely on its own. Far from taking a fatalistic or deterministic view of the process, the object is to understand the role of various actors and forces, the combination of internal and external factors and dynamics that shape the development of constitutional governance in each setting in order to explore strategies for promoting the necessary norms and institutions. These processes must be primarily undertaken by Africans for themselves, who can draw upon the experiences of other societies and benefit from the solidarity of all those who wish to support internal initiatives, not impose external models. But outside actors also have a role to play at various levels, though that is not discussed in this book.

I now highlight the recent constitutional experience of six African countries, namely, Ethiopia, Ghana, Guinea, Rwanda, Tanzania, and Uganda. Another three cases (Sudan, Nigeria, and Senegal) are discussed in more detail later in connection with the contingent role of Islam. The six experiences highlighted in this chapter are selected to represent a cross-section of countries with different colonial and post-colonial experiences, political and cultural profiles. Other reasons for this sampling will I hope emerge from the comparative analysis and tentative evaluation in the last section of the chapter. However, I readily accept that other countries could be selected, in a variety of combinations, which is part of my point: the thesis and analysis of this book can be illustrated by the constitutional experiences of any African country.

Overview of Recent Constitutional Experiences

The following review of constitutional developments in these six countries is not intended to be comprehensive or up to date, but simply to provide some basis and context for the comparative analysis. Another caveat to note here is that this review of recent experiences will not be fully uniform or symmetrical, as it is intended to illustrate the variety of experiences for the purposes of the comparative reflections and tentative evaluation offered later.

Ethiopia

The Ethiopian state, within its present boundaries, was created by a process of imperial expansion and conquests instigated and led by Emperor Menelik II during the late nineteenth and early twentieth centuries. For most of its previous history, Ethiopia consisted essentially of two closely related ethnic groups, the Tigreans/Tigrinya and the Amhara, ruled in a highly decentralized manner, with the king of kings at the top (Negash 2000: 6). Over half of present-day Ethiopia was added under Menelik's reign to include eighty ethnic groups (Selassie 1997: 101). Control over various parts of the country was achieved and maintained by force in a centralized state power under an absolute monarchy and aristocracy to perform the basic functions of government. At that time, the state was based on a feudal system of land ownership and agricultural production, which made control over land a highly political matter. For example, Menelik confiscated land from the Oromo and distributed two-thirds of it to his own family and courtiers, feudal lords, army chiefs, and the high clergy. The remaining third was then turned over to peasants and local chiefs who were subjected to tribute, high taxes and forced labor (Selassie 1997: 102). As part of his effort to restructure the feudal system, Emperor Haile Selassie enacted the country's first constitution of July 1931, which consisted of only seven articles. Citizens' rights were confined to one article that provided for equality before the law.

In 1955 the constitution was amended to include 85 articles, providing for such fundamental rights as freedom of movement, due process of law, privacy and property rights, and freedom of religion, assembly, and occupation. The revised constitution also redefined the authority of the emperor, who was to govern "in conformity with the provisions of the constitution" (Ashenafi 2003: 30). The amended constitution also established an independent judicial branch of the government to interpret the constitution, but the emperor retained unlimited emergency authorities. The laws enacted under the 1955 Constitution to enforce constitutional rights remain in force today.

In 1974, a successful military coup by a group of army officers known as the Derg (military committee) sought to transform Ethiopia into a socialist country, based on a Marxist-Leninist single-party state model (Erlich 1999: 67). The Derg claimed that one of their major concerns in taking over the state was to grant the various ethnic groups autonomy

(53). Accordingly, they developed and implemented the Program of National Democratic Revolution of Ethiopia in 1976 that granted regional autonomy to different ethnic groups, and claimed that "no nationality will dominate another since the history, culture, language, and religion of each nationality will have equal recognition in accordance with the spirit of socialism" (Wagaw 1997: 395).

In 1987 the military rulers adopted a constitution that was debated at the community level. But because the government maintained careful control and direction over the entire process some Ethiopians as well as outside observers concluded that the whole idea of regional autonomy was a sham intended to give the illusion of legitimacy (Ashenafi 2003: 31). It was intended to give legitimacy to the new ideology, leadership system of government and political culture. The constitution also provided for a wide array of civil rights, subject to the government's ability to restrict them to "protect the interest of the state and society as well as freedoms and rights of other individuals" (31, quoting Article 58).

After a long and bloody civil war, the Derg military government fell in 1991. On July 1–5, 1991, the interim government of the Peace and Democracy Conference drafted the Transitional Period Charter to be the basis of government until the new constitution was adopted. The charter "endorsed the Universal Declaration of Human Rights and specifically provided for freedom of conscience, expression, and association and the rights of ethnic groups referred to as nations and nationalities to self-determination" (Ashenafi 2003: 31). The interim government established a constitutional commission that was highly representative of diverse groups within society to draft a constitution. The commission organized meetings of specialized panels and plenary sessions. It consulted legal researchers and experts in Ethiopia and abroad. The commission also examined the constitutions of other countries and conducted local and international meetings to discuss conceptual and practical constitutional law matters. Furthermore, the commission disseminated a concept paper for public discussion, outlining alternative positions on important constitutional issues, including the structure and form of government. The public then voted on alternative proposals and the commission followed the outcomes of the vote (32).

The constitutional commission deliberated for two and a half years before forwarding a draft constitution to the House of Representatives for debate. This initial draft included alternative minority views on several points. The House of Representatives then forwarded the draft to the Constituent Assembly, a body composed of more than five hundred individuals elected directly by the population for the sole purpose of ratifying the constitution (Ashenafi 2003: 32). The Constituent Assembly ratified the Constitution of the Federal Democratic Republic of Ethiopia on December 8, 1994. This constitution limited the power of government and guaranteed human rights protection according to international standards. It also affirmed a renewed commitment to the right of ethnic groups (nationalities) to self-determination. The preamble to the constitution stipulates that the objectives of the political forces require respect for individual and group freedoms and for the right to live as equals without any religious or cultural discrimination.

The central point in the new, restructured state is the provision for an ethnic-based federalism (Selassie 1997: 125). Under the current constitution the country is divided into fourteen regions based on presumed ethnic demarcations, and there are nine member states of the Federal Democratic Republic of Ethiopia. Within those states the nations, nationalities, and peoples have the right to establish their own states, while each region and subregion has the right to secede. But some critics of this approach charge that the drafters of the Ethiopian Constitution ingrained and glorified ethnicity by establishing a federal government based on tribal affiliation (Haile 1996: 4). They argue that the geographical boundaries of the nine states, defined by ethnicity, separate the Ethiopian people and create tensions among groups that had once learned to live together. This, it is said, gives ethnic groups too much autonomy and undermines national unity (Selassie 1997: 126). Ethnic divisions and artificial regions have weakened the central government and created a fragmented political system (Erlich 1999: 53).

Critics also charge that, while the Ethiopian Constitution attempts to project an aura of constitutionalism and provides for an impressive set of human rights, there are no effective limitations on the power of government. The constitution is seen as a tool for the ethnic groups who overthrew the Marxist regime, namely the Tigrayans, to keep complete control over the state (Erlich 1999: 57). In theory, the powers of the Ethiopian government may be scrutinized by the Federal Council, a group composed of representatives of the ethnic regions which have the final authority to interpret the constitution. In this way, the representatives of the regions in the Federal Council have the hypothetical power to establish the extent of their own authority (62), leaving the federal government with virtually no power. In reality, critics argue, the state and federal government have unlimited powers under the constitution because of the absence of separation of powers, lack of genuine federalism that divides power between the central government and the subunits, and absence of judicial review as a means for limiting the powers of government (Haile 1996: 51–52). Although there are more than 70 languages and 200 dialects spoken in the country, the constitution does not establish a national language for conducting business and official government transactions.

Other commentators argue that the use of ethnicity in this way has served a useful purpose for the nation as a whole by promoting the empowerment and effective participation of all ethnic groups (Twibell 1999: 453). This approach allowed for the release of tensions that would have built up if Ethiopia became too centralized or nationalistic after hundreds of years of monarchal rule, and a decade of dictatorial military rule during which one ethnic culture was dominant (435). However, due to extensive public involvement in the drafting process, the Ethiopian Constitution contains an exhaustive list of every objective the government should implement and an extensive array of democratic and human rights. This lack of clear criteria for setting priorities in effect allows for the treatment of important policies as urgent needs, thereby justifying extraordinary measures (440). Many of the rights listed are vague on what exactly the right is and how it should be implemented by the state, making them more in the nature of resolutions than constitutional rights as such (441). Thus, the text of the constitution presents a problem for its implementation because it enables the government to claim that any action, however remote, is sufficient.

Despite such criticisms, the country is apparently stable and successfully operating its complex regional and federal system. There is a good mix of political parties represented in the House of People's Representatives (lower elected House of Parliament). Meles Zenawi, the leader of the Ethiopian People's Revolutionary Democratic Front (EPRDF) that defeated the Derg regime seems to be firmly in control of the country, was Prime Minister (executive head of government) in 1995, and was reelected in 2000 through a coalition of several parties in the House of Representatives. The threat to political stability in Ethiopia appears to be linked to the all too familiar problem of one party or ruler seeking to hold on to power at any cost, more than to presumed or anticipated risks of ethnic federalism. Charges that the May 15, 2005, elections were rigged by the ruling party provoked a series of strikes, processions, and civil disobedience by opposition parties. In the crackdown that ensued, dozens of people lost their lives, and opposition leaders and journalists were charged with treason.

GHANA

Ghana has been ruled since independence in 1957 by alternating cycles of military regimes and democratically elected civilian governments in near equal measure. The former, four military governments, have held power for 22 years and the latter for 25 years. However, accordingly to Nana Busia, "in spite of the frequent overthrow of democratically elected civilian governments by the military, the Ghanaian political system and constitutional development has always been liberal democratic in character" (Busia 2003: 53).

The 1957 Constitution (The Independence Constitution) was patterned after the British parliamentary system of government. The Convention Peoples' Party (CPP) came to power upon independence and remained the ruling party until 1966. The Independence Constitution included certain principles and rights, such as prohibition of racial discrimination, protection of freedom of conscience or religion (with exceptions for considerations of public order, morality, or health), and prohibition of taking private property without adequate compensation. It did not, however, provide a comprehensive bill of rights as such, and the CPP determined that: "In order for Ghana to develop rapidly and catch up with the rest of the developed world, human rights should not impede the objective of rapid development" (Busia 2003: 54). Although the Supreme Court of Ghana had original jurisdiction over "matters concerning the validity of any law in the country (Article 31(5))" (54), it was unable to prevent clear violations of constitutional rights. For example, the Deportation Act of 1957 allowed the executive branch of government to deport political opponents of the socialist regime, who were perceived as representatives of Western imperialism. Similarly, the Preventive Detention Act of 1958 allowed the government "to detain without charge persons suspected of endangering national security" (55). In July 1960, a Republican Constitution was enacted, thereby ending the role of the Queen of England as the Head of the State, as she is for former British colonies which become members of the British Commonwealth. This Republican constitution made no reference to the protection of human rights except in the president's oath of office, which guaranteed equality and certain freedoms. However, the Supreme Court of Ghana ruled that this oath had no legal significance (56).

The CPP government was toppled by military and police forces that formed the National Liberation Council (NLC) government, which ruled the country from 1966 to 1969. The CPP had grossly abused the Preventive Detention Act, and approximately 2000 people, mostly political or personal opponents of the CPP leaders, were in detention at the time of the coup. Although it promised to redress such injustices, the NLC retained the Preventive Detention Act, changing the name to the Protective Custody Decree of 1967, and used it to oppress its political opponents, just as the CPP did earlier. On the positive side, the NLC transferred power back to an elected civilian government in 1969, thereby initiating what is known as the Second Republic.

The Second Republican Constitution, drafted the same year, was strongly influenced by the failures of the first Republic, which were seen as due to the constitutional principle of parliamentary sovereignty, the

British notion that parliament is not limited by the constitution. As the CPP government had a huge majority in parliament, it was able to do whatever it pleased, including massive human rights violations. To safeguard against the recurrence of excesses and abuses of power, the 1969 Constitution provided for pluralistic politics, regular elections, entrenched human rights provisions, separation of powers, and an independent judiciary (Busia 2003: 57). That constitution also apparently set the mode for all subsequent Ghanaian constitutions, which tended to incorporate the following principles (57):

1. The concept of parliamentary sovereignty was discarded in favor of that of supremacy of the constitution as the fundamental supreme law of the land from which Parliament derives its authority to make laws. Any act or conduct inconsistent with the constitution was null and void to the degree of its inconsistency.
2. Inclusion of clear and explicit provisions on human rights, with elaborate statements defining the content of the rights.
3. Affirmation of the role of the courts as the guardians of the constitution. The Supreme Court has always had original and exclusive jurisdiction to interpret the constitution, but came to share concurrent jurisdiction with the High Court on the enforcement of the human rights provisions provided for in the various constitutions.
4. The notion of "standing" (*locus standi*) to initiate litigation about the constitutionality of law or official action has been broadened to grant "any person" access to the Supreme Court for that purpose.

The Progress Party (PP) won the 1969 elections, and its government was, on the whole, respectful of human rights and the constitution. But this government, commonly known as the Second Republic, was overthrown in 1972 by another military coup, and various military governments ruled Ghana from 1972 to1979, during which time serious human rights violations occurred. Each regime suspended the 1969 Constitution and declared that the coup leadership was invested with all legislative and executive powers. The most brutal of the military regimes was that of the Armed Forces Revolutionary Council (AFRC), led by Jerry John Rawlings, which lasted only three months in 1979. The AFRC committed numerous atrocities but granted itself amnesty before relinquishing power.

In 1979 the Third Republican Constitution was enacted and the democratically elected People's National Party (PNP) took power, but was overthrown two years later in 1981 by another military coup. This coup was also led by Rawlings, this time under the name of the Provisional National Defense Council (PNDC). Ghana was in a severe economic crisis at the time, and Rawlings claimed that "liberal democracy could not address the social needs of the people with respect to education, health, transportation, and other basic needs" (60). The PNDC established in 1982 "organs and institutions for the expression and exercise of popular power" that "enabled the peasants, the illiterate, the economically deprived and marginalized youth and women to exercise power and take part in decision making" (60). However, by 1984 the PNDC abandoned that claim, and accepted the plans of the International Monetary Fund/World Bank for combating the economic crisis. The PNDC implemented various austerity policies and restricted civil rights in an attempt to control the economic situation. As opposition to the economic austerity policies grew over the next few years, the PNDC responded with increasing brutality, torturing and sometimes killing opponents in the name of state security (61). During that period, "arbitrary detention, torture, harsh prison conditions, and death sentences meted to political opponents were common occurrences in Ghana" (62). The Ghanaian economy improved and political stability persisted. These successes have been attributed to what has been called the "Rawlings factor," a combination of charismatic leadership, economic pragmatism, and high-handed personal rule (Ibrahim 2003: 8–23).

Despite its serious violations of civil and political rights, the PNDC did promote certain economic and social rights, such as the "right to housing, access to justice, inheritance rights, and the establishment of the Ghana National Commission on Children to protect the rights of children" (Busia 2003: 62). Nevertheless, the PNDC faced tremendous public pressure to return the country to democratic governance, which they were obliged to do in 1992, after the failure of their attempt to retain power through the appointment of a new government. The Consultative Assembly was formed in May 1992 to establish a new constitution, and implemented the following changes desired by Ghanaians as expressed in the report of the National Commission on Democracy (NCD):

1. repeal repressive PNDC laws, most of which were still operative;
2. affirm freedom of the press by abolishing the newspaper licensing law and removing any ban on newspapers and magazines;
3. release all political detainees;
4. dissolve the paramilitary organizations created by the PNDC to intimidate political opponents; and
5. dissolve the election committees, which were created during and after 1988.

In April 1992, 92 percent of Ghanaians voted in favor of the draft constitution, which became known as the Fourth Republican Constitution. Presidential and parliamentary elections took place in November and

December 1992 respectively. The PNDC turned itself into the National Democratic Congress (NDC), and Rawlings was its presidential candidate. Rawlings won 58.3 percent of the vote and became president of the Fourth Republic, but his opponents claimed that the 1992 elections were not free and fair.

The Fourth Republican Constitution is highly respectful of human rights, civil and political as well as economic and social rights. It guarantees equality regardless of "race, place of origin, political opinion, color, religion, creed or gender" (2003: 65). A healthy competitive multiparty system seems to be thriving under this Constitution.

In the parliamentary elections of December 2000, the New Patriotic Party (NPP) captured 100 seats, with the NDC a close second with 92 seats, and John Kufuor was elected executive president in January 2001 with 56.4 percent of the popular vote, with John Mills making a credible opposition candidate receiving 43.6 percent. In the elections held in December 2004, Kufor was reelected for a second term with 52.4 percent of the vote. Recalling the caveat at the beginning of this chapter, these election results are noted here as reflecting the stability of the constitutional democratic process in the country, without claiming to be comprehensive or up to date.

GUINEA

When Guinea gained independence by referendum on September 28, 1958, France severed all contact with its former colony immediately. The country was led by the Democratic Party of Guinea (PDG), which quickly formed governmental institutions and established a fifteen-member constitutional commission. The PDG essentially dictated the contents of the constitution, which became known as the First Republican Constitution. The 1958 Constitution did provide for the protection of a range of rights, but "the rights protecting life and physical integrity are conspicuous by their absence from the text, which is also silent on the right to a fair trial and to free movement within Guinea" (Kane 2003: 101).

The First Republic lasted from 1958 to 1984 under President Ahmed Sékou Touré, who quickly transformed it into a single-party "constitutional dictatorship . . . with numerous coup attempts, either real or invented, which led to arrests and arbitrary detentions, 'people's' trials organized against the 'enemies of the Guinean Revolution,' [and which] forced millions of Guineans into exile in neighboring countries (mainly Senegal and Côte d'Ivoire) and Europe" (Kane 2003: 99). Guinea became among the first African countries to establish a single-party state, a trend that later came to be copied widely in Africa. The ruling party became a "hollow shell whose functions were unclear and whose utility was uncertain"

(Chazan 1992: 62). The party was turned into an omnipresent tool of control, with patronage often replacing ideology. Coercion was used as a "substitute for acquiescence" (144). Whatever level of democracy may have been promised at independence receded farther and farther as a consequence. As a result of mounting international and domestic pressure, the PDG regime was forced to liberalize somewhat in 1982 by adopting a new constitution with greater human rights protection. The new constitution included the right to integrity of the person (Article 23(1)) and the right to develop freely (Article 23(2)), although this must occur while respecting the democratic and social order as determined by the PDG. It also permitted each citizen to institute legal proceedings with the Party-State authorities against any authority or person who has caused him prejudice (Article 25) (Kane 2003: 101). The constitution also significantly expanded the scope of protected rights to include rights to education, health and social security, assistance for the elderly, handicapped and disabled.

At the same time, however, the constitution removed the right to association, because the PDG was to be the "meeting place and debating hall for all currents of national life and the supreme means of the people to exercise power and the principal guiding force of its actions" (the preamble to the 1982 Constitution). The legislature was given authority over most civil and political rights, other than freedom of conscience and the prohibition on arbitrary arrest. The 1982 Constitution also included a number of duties that the citizens of Guinea were required to fulfill in exchange for the rights afforded them. The extensive list of duties included the obligation to carry out their civic duties (Article 15), to show solidarity with all other citizens (Article 17), to work according to their abilities (Article 18) and with the strictest respect for discipline and working hours (Article 19), to care for collective property, to fight against the misuse and squandering of public property, and to be "constantly striving to safeguard and develop the best interests of the people" (Article 27). Even more problematic were the vague obligations not to betray the people or the country (Article 16(2)) and to maintain "revolutionary vigilance toward all elements hostile" to the regime (Article 31). It was also not clear how this exchange of rights for duties was supposed to work in practice: who is to determine if duties were properly discharged, and how are the consequences of failure to do so be determined? As was to be expected, the extensive and vague nature of these duties was used by the regime against its opponents and critics (Kane 2003: 102).

When Sékou Touré died suddenly in April 1984, the military took power and established the Military Committee for National Recovery (CMRN), which designated a six-year transitional period during which the repressive laws of the previous era were repealed and replaced by laws which took greater account of civil liberties. But the economic, social and political situation in the country deteriorated during the military transition of 1984–1990 (131–32). In 1990 discussions of a new constitution started, and democratic institutions began to be established for the first time since independence. According to Kane, however, those "discussions represented more of a token gesture to donors and international opinion than the laying of the foundations of a real democracy in Guinea" (2003: 132).

On December 23, 1990 Guinea adopted the Basic Law, which "integrated certain principles and rules of the liberal democratic model with the rule of law, without really breaking with the country's constitutional heritage" (100). The 1990 Constitution incorporated the Charter of the United Nations, the Universal Declaration of Human Rights, the Charter of the Organization of African Unity and the African Charter on Human and Peoples' Rights. The Constitution proclaimed a dedication to democracy and the democratic establishment of the rule of law, and affirmed "the sacrosanct nature of the person and the inviolability, inalienability, and irreversibility of the rights and freedoms described in the constitution which 'are the foundation of all societies and guarantee peace and justice the world over'" (Article 5) (102). In addition, the 1990 Constitution provides for a wide range of fundamental rights, some in unusual formulations, like the right to free personal development (Article 6(1)), and the right to resist oppression (Article 19(4)). Freedom of association is also provided for (Article 10(2)), subject to two conditions on political parties: they must have representation throughout the country and they must not be identified with a particular race, ethnic group, religion, or territory. Expanded social and economic rights include the entitlement of workers, the elderly, and the handicapped to assistance and protection by the state (Articles 17(2) and 18(5)). Guineans were also given a right to the preservation of their heritage, culture, and environment (Article 19(3)), and young people were given the right to be protected against exploitation and moral neglect (Article 17(1)).

On the other hand, the 1990 Constitution also maintained and expanded the requirement of duties owed by Guineans, requiring them to abide by the constitution, laws, and rulings (Article 20(1)), be loyal to the nation, promote tolerance and the values of democracy (Article 20(2)), respect the dignity and opinions of others (Article 20(3)), pay taxes "according to one's means," and fulfill social duties (Article 20(4)). While the constitution mixes liberal democratic provisions with the maintenance of links to the country's constitutional heritage by retaining the hegemony of the president of the republic, "these measures resulted, for the first time in Guinea, in a real opening up of the political space with the emergence of a whole range of political movements, trade unions, and media" (133).

The past continued to cast its shadow during the presidential elections of December 1993, in which incumbent president General Lansana Conté was elected after "an exceptionally violent campaign during which ethnic tensions increased to such an extent that the results from nearly all the electoral constituencies of highland Guinea were quite simply canceled by the Supreme Court. These first elections confirmed the administration's lack of impartiality (at the central, territorial, and judicial levels) and showed it to be totally subservient to the elected president's party" (134). The 1993 elections were followed by legislative and local elections in 1995, and the Second Republic was thereby established. Conté was reelected in December 2003 with 95.3 percent of the popular vote, after the constitution was changed to allow him to run, and he appointed the prime minister and cabinet. There are several political parties represented in the unicameral People's National Assembly, with the Party for Unity and Progress (PUP) of President and Conté dominating the last election of June 2002, receiving 61.6 percent of the popular vote, with the Union for Progress and Renewal (UPR) a distant second at 26.6 percent

The political culture inherited from the PDG combined with the social and political circumstances made it almost impossible for constitutional rights and guarantees to be protected. Curbs on freedom of speech and association, harassment of media, detentions, and torture continued. At the same time, "it is also true that there was increased recourse to legal institutions with the aim of putting an end to these practices and this was showing significant results. For instance, the Supreme Court has been trying, through its use of precedents which are increasingly available, to reinforce its role as guardian of the constitution and public freedoms" (135).

RWANDA

Rwanda is populated by three ethnic groups; the Hutu are the largest group, followed by the Tutsis and the Twa, who are a small minority. Mentioning Rwanda tends to evoke images of extreme violence among these ethnic groups since the eve of independence, especially the horrific genocide of 1994. Although the following brief overview of the recent constitutional experiences of the country is not an attempt to explain those cycles of violence, they are clearly part of the specific context within which constitutionalism has to evolve in this part of Africa.

Rwanda was a Belgian colony until it gained independence in July 1962, with Grégoire Kayibanda, the chairman of Party for the Emancipation of the Hutu People (PARMEHUTU) as its first president. Tutsi refugees, who had fled the country as a result of earlier ethnic violence, especially in 1959, began to conduct guerrilla attacks in 1963–64, and the government retaliated against Tutsis who remained in Rwanda. Periodic massacres of Tutsis continued through 1973, when a military coup established a single party government led by Major Juvénal Habyarimana and the Movement for National Revolution and Development (MRND), which supposedly extended membership to all Rwandans. But the unrest continued and a full-scale civil war broke out on the first of October 1990 between the MRND government and the Rwandan Patriotic Front (RPF). "In response, the government adopted a new constitution in 1990 that recognized the multiple-party system, and the Arusha Peace Agreement was signed between the government of the Rwandan Republic and the RPF in 1992–1993" (Gahamanyi 2003: 253). However, opposition to that Agreement continued, including among elements within the MRND, culminating in the assassination of President Habyarimana on April 6, 1994, which marked the beginning of the genocide of Tutsis as well as Hutus deemed to be traitors for supporting the "enemies" of the Hutu majority. The genocide claimed the lives of some 700,000 Rwandans by the time it ended when the RPF took Kigali on July 4, 1994, but that also prompted the massive exodus of Hutus to neighboring Zaire and Tanzania (Gurevitch 1998). On the other hand, a National Union Government was established in Rwanda under the auspices of the RPF in November 1994, which managed to gradually bring peace and resume the constitutional development of the country.

That Transitional Government had to deal with the huge and delicate problems of recovery and reconstruction of the whole country, at a time when more than half the population had fled. A particularly delicate task was how to deal with the hundreds of thousands of Rwandans accused of participation in the genocide in a balanced and constructive way when the country lacked any level of human or institutional capacity in the administration of justice and related fields. Another major political issue was how to reintegrate Hutus in the government and army in the aftermath of the genocide. This process seems to have been reasonably successful, but perhaps a brief overview of the post-independence constitutional development of the country would be useful in evaluating the post-genocide phase in broader context.

The Constitution of November 1962 abolished the monarchy and established the republic on a parliamentary system in which the National Assembly could have a vote of no confidence in the president at any time. The constitution incorporated the rights provided for in the Universal Declaration of Human Rights, but expressly made them subject to Rwandan law. The 1962 Constitution was amended in June 1963 to provide for universal suffrage in presidential elections and again in May 1973 to designate "democratic socialism" as the economic system; it extended the length of the presidential term in office from four to five years and to a maximum of three successive terms, and abolished the age limit (sixty years) for candidates in presidential elections. Those amendments were obviously designed to enable the first president of the Rwandan Republic, Grégoire Kayibanda, to remain in power beyond his initial eleven years. Moreover, the multiparty system was effectively replaced by a de facto one-party system because PARMEHUTU, a party representing only Hutus, was the single party allowed to operate. "Other parties, including UNAR (Rwandan National Unity), RADER (Democratic Assembly for the Republic), and APROSOMA (Association for the Social Progress of the Masses), were dissolved and their leaders were exiled, imprisoned, or killed. Politics became increasingly intertwined with ethnicity between 1962 and 1973. There were no Tutsis in the government, the territorial administration, or the army" (Gahamanyi 2003: 255).

The Constitution of December 1978 was enacted to incorporate changes that came as a result of the coup of July 5, 1973 which suspended the 1962 Constitution. The MRND (the Movement) was founded in 1976, and every Rwandan was deemed to be a member of it from birth. The 1978 Constitution also expressly established a one-party system under a presidential regime headed by a single person, required that only an MRND candidate could run for president, and permitted an unlimited number of consecutive presidential terms of office. The constitution abolished the Supreme Court and replaced it with the Supreme Judicial Council, which had to approve the president's appointment and removal of judges. The president was the chairman of the Council and had complete control over its actions. The keynote speeches of the president and the by-laws of the Movement became more important than the constitution and the laws of the country (256).

In response to the civil war with the RPF, as noted earlier, and international pressure to democratize, the 1991 Constitution "was meant to guarantee democracy, eliminate the one-party system, and show a commitment to human rights. It established a virtually unlimited multiparty system; the only constraint on this new system was that monarchists remained banned (Article 7)" (257). That constitution also created a prime minister's office and delegated some of the power previously held by the president to the prime minister. The new constitution limited the ability of one person to hold the office of president to only two five-year terms. In addition, judges were given the power to elect the Supreme Council of Judges, but the Supreme Court was not reestablished, and there was no provision for security of judicial tenure, thereby leaving judges vulnerable to arbitrary removal from office.

The 1995 Basic Act, which is the current constitution of Rwanda, incorporated the 1991 Constitution, the Arusha Peace Agreement of 1992–93, the RPF Declaration Relating to the Establishment of Institutions of July 1994, and the November 1994 Protocol Agreement concluded by all the political forces except the MRND on the establishment of national institutions. The Arusha Agreement was in fact a collection of texts, like the Nsele Cease-Fire Agreement, which provided for the establishment of the rule of law, based on national unity, democracy, pluralism, and the respect for human rights; the formation of a national army integrating government and RPF forces; and broad-based power sharing in the transitional government (259). To implement these principles, the Agreement superseded many sections of the 1991 Constitution but left unchanged the provisions on civil liberties, which were already reasonably good, if enforced. The Protocol Agreement on the Rule of Law sought to secure equality of all citizens before the law, and guarantee equal opportunity and nondiscrimination. It provides for the inalienable right of refugees to return home, and that the Universal Declaration of Human Rights and the African Charter on Human and Peoples' Rights are the basic principles of democracy. There is also the Protocol Agreement on Broad-Based Power Sharing, which defined the institutions required for the transition, instituted specialized committees, organized the various branches of government, and developed a political code of ethics binding on all political groups involved in the transition (260). The president's powers were significantly reduced, while those of the prime minister and Parliament were increased. This Protocol reestablished the Supreme Court and established the Transitional National Assembly (261). Other elements of the Peace Agreements also incorporated into the 1995 Basic Law include the Protocol Agreement on the Repatriation of Refugees and the Resettlement of Displaced Persons; the Protocol Agreement on the Integration of the Armed Forces makes the military representative of entire country, not just one ethnicity.

The RPF Declaration of July 17, 1994, also incorporated into the 1995 Basic Act, "reaffirmed the RPF's commitment to the principles of establishing the rule of law, forming a national army open to all Rwandans, and power sharing in the transition government" (263). Another element of the Basic Act is the Protocol Agreement between the Political Powers which "confirms the partnership between the RPF and the other Rwandan political forces. It adopted the RPF's July 17 declaration and distributed assembly seats evenly among the participating parties (thirteen seats each)" (264). Moreover, subsequent amendments to the Basic Act include the Basic Act Revision of January 1996, which allowed people without legal training to serve as judges on the lower courts because the genocide depleted the available lawyers and judges. The amendment was also intended to facilitate the operation of military tribunals to try those who participated in the genocide, both military and civilian. Retroactivity of law was also established to cover "acts and omissions which were not punishable at the time they were committed . . . if they were considered criminal in the light of the general legal principles recognized as such by the law of nations" (265).

Despite the tragedy of the genocide, difficulty of the transitional process, and the complexity of the present constitutional structure, Rwandan constitutionalism seems to be developing well. The president Paul Kagame and prime minister Charles Muligande, appointed in April 2000, were both democratically elected to their respective offices in August 2003, the first presidential elections since the 1994 genocide. Paul Kagame was reelected in the first round with 95.05 percent of the popular vote, and the other two candidates received 3.6 percent and 1.3 percent. Elections of the National Assembly were also held in September 2003. As indicated with other countries, the point of this review to provide a sense of the development of the constitutional democratic process, without attempting to offer an accurate political assessment of the situation.

Tanzania

Present-day Tanzania came to being in 1964 as a result of the union of the People's Republic of Zanzibar and the Republic of Tanganyika. For the limited purposes of this chapter and due to space limitations, the following brief review of the recent constitutional experience of the country will begin with developments in Tanganyika, by far the larger and dominant part, and include Zanzibar as part of the union without attempting to outline its very special history.

The 1961 Independence Constitution of Tanganyika followed the British parliamentary model, with a prime minister drawn from the majority party, a government subject to the supremacy of parliament, rather than the constitution as such, and an independent judiciary. The constitution also provided for a "governor-general" who represented the Queen of England as the head of state (Shivji 1998: 24). But that constitution did not provide for a bill of rights. This was the standard model for former British colonies worldwide, and tended to prompt similar responses from African leaders soon after independence, as discussed later in this chapter. As elsewhere in Africa also, the 1961 Independence Constitution was shaped by the broader economy of external political relations and pressures, reflecting the negotiation between colonial powers and nationalist leaders, rather than the relationship between people and the state. Moreover, the "eleventh hour conversion of colonial rulers to constitutionalism was not without ulterior motives," which included seeking to promote a liberal ideology as a barrier to the threat of communism (1998: 24).

Another source of tension from the beginning was that the imposition of liberal ideology, with the weak government it implied, cleared the ground for privileged classes to disproportionately control power, while the elite who came to power preferred a strong state. The ideologies of development and nation-building promoted by this class made the state itself the "primary site of accumulation" (24). Shivji cites Julius Nyerere defending the extensive powers granted to him as president by the 1962 Republican Constitution (enacted the second year after independence and terminating all constitutional links with the British Crown) on the grounds that institutional checks on the presidency would hinder the urgently needed social and economic development of the nation. The powers held by the prime minister and governor-general under the 1961 Constitution came to be collectively vested in the president under the 1962 Constitution. The assumption of the powers of the governor-general by the president extended to acts liable to misuse, such as "the Deportation Ordinance, 1921 (cap. 38), the Collective Punishment Ordinance, 1921 (cap. 74), and the Emergency Powers Order-in-Council, 1939" (25). In addition, the government enacted the Preventive Detention Act, 1962, which authorized indefinite detention without trial. The responsibility of the government to parliament was, for all practical purposes, negated. In fact, the manner in which the Republican Constitution was brought into being was itself patently unconstitutional, by first passing a law that allowed for converting a national assembly into a constituent assembly, and thereby completely leaving the people out of the process. This political practice, "first applied in Ghana. . . . has bedeviled the political process to this day" (1998: 26).

Two years later, the Articles of Union between the People's Republic of Zanzibar and the Republic of Tanganyika were signed. Shivji suggests that external compulsions and pressures played a critical role in the establishment of the union, more than its being a "logical outcome of long standing relations between the peoples of Zanzibar and the mainland" (1998: 26). The Acts of Union of 1964 amended the 1962 Republican Constitution, which was renamed the Interim Constitution of the United Republic of Tanganyika and Zanzibar, 1964 and was soon merged into the Interim Constitution of Tanzania 1965. According to Shivji, the Republican Constitution, Acts of Union, and the Interim Constitution of 1965, each contributed "one of the three foundations of the Tanzanian constitutional order" (28). The 1962 Constitution introduced the executive presidency, the 1964 Acts of Union established the two-government union (one for Zanzibar and the other for the Union as a whole), and the Interim Constitution established the "party-state" which, in Shivji's view, is often, mistakenly called the one-party state (28).

The 1965 Interim Constitution was passed not by a constituent assembly but as an ordinary act of parliament, once again bypassing "the people and the public debate in the process of adopting a new constitution" (29). The 1965 Constitution formally recognized the constitutional status of the party state in Tanzania, while still failing to include a bill of rights. A presidential commission appointed by Nyerere in 1964 to inquire into certain aspects of the party state gave the following reasons for that omission: (a) A bill of rights would constrain the efforts of the new nation to establish order and security. (b) It could become a source of conflict between the judiciary and the executive. Since the judiciary consisted of expatriate judges (as explained later in this chapter), and was not really an "indigenous institution," giving the judiciary political power over the executive might run inimical to the objectives of law and order. (c) It could stand in the way of the government's agenda for economic development and the social restructuring that such development might well entail.

The Interim Constitution underwent several amendments between 1965 and 1977 that brought a greater number of matters under union control, hence, limiting the autonomy of Zanzibar. The 1975 amendment affirmed party supremacy, which "was only a constitutional formalisation of what had already occurred *de facto*. . . . It is not so much that the Party became supreme and the national assembly was reduced to rubber stamping. Rather the state and the party merged to form a one-party state . . . concentrating executive power under one and the same chief" (30). The process of making the 1977 Constitution itself "sheds further light on the relation between the constitution and constitutionalism, between the constitution as a reflection/mapping of power and constitutionalism as the legitimation of its exercise" (30). Through this process, the political parties of Tanganyika and Zanzibar merged to form the Chama cha Mapinduzi (CCM), the national assembly was designated a constitutional assembly, and the constitution itself came into existence, without any public consultation or debate. The 1977 Constitution did include a Special Constitutional Court, but that seems to have been a nominal gesture to address the apprehensions of Zanzibaris. Supposed to be comprised of equal representation from Zanzibar and the Union Government, the mandate of the court was to adjudicate disputes between the two regarding constitutional matters. In any event, the court has never been convened.

In 1982, proposals for constitutional amendments were brought to the public for a year-long countrywide debate. The moment was significant, although the proposals were not radical in themselves—"they proposed to modify somewhat the powers of the president, enhance the stature of the Parliament and consolidate the Union" (32). But the debate, which was not confined to those proposals, also produced two major themes, namely, the democratization of the state including a bill of rights, and a federal structure of the union (32). Zanzibar was the main site of the demand for autonomy, as President Aboud Jumbe called for the Special Constitutional Court to be convened, where he intended to challenge the 1977 Constitution in the light of the 1964 Articles of Union" (32). Nyerere confronted Jumbe at a National Executive Committee meeting, and as a result Jumbe had to resign. In that way, the national debate was cut short after eight months.

The bill (for the Fifth Constitutional Amendment, 1984) based on the preceding debate did include a bill of rights, but that was more a compromise with the leadership of Zanzibar than in response to public demand. Since the leaders of Zanzibar were determined to have a bill of rights in their new constitution, "it would have been politically foolhardy to have a bill in one part of the union and not another" (32). The bill, which drew on international human rights documents, makes civil and political rights provisions enforceable by the courts, though "circumscribed by claw-back and derogation clauses" (32). Social and economic rights, on the other hand, were presented as directive principles that are not supposed to be enforced by the courts. In Shivji's view, "just as the liberal 1961 Constitution was a superimposition on the authoritarian colonial legal order, the 1984 bill of rights was a super-imposition on an otherwise authoritarian polity described by the 1977 Constitution" (1998: 33).

The next significant stage in the constitutional experience of Tanzania is the multi-party debate of 1990. Once again, it seems, the impetus for the multi-party debate and its implementation came from "the global context of the crumbling of the socialist block and the onslaught of western imperialism to re-establish its world hegemony" (35). It is interesting to note here that, as shown by the case of several African countries, including all cases considered in this chapter, the impact of international power relations can be ambivalent. While the unstated agenda of the major powers may be neocolonial hegemony, international forces can result in pressure for domestic consensus as much as they can inhibit consensus-oriented debate, as happened during the cold war period.

Inside Tanzania, the National Executive Committee of the ruling CCM under Nyerere provided the initiative for the multi-party debate to be taken to the public arena, the ruling party organized some seminars, and the press joined in. A Commission to coordinate the debate on multi-partyism was appointed under Mr. Francis Nyalali, the Chief Justice (36).

The Commission's recommendation that the multiparty system be implemented (despite 80 percent of the sample choosing the single-party option) "sailed through the National Conference of the party unanimously and eventually the government presented the Eighth Constitutional Amendment, 1992 to the National Assembly, to make provision for a multi-party system" (36). The Commission's report included a strong analysis of the rise of the party-state and recommendation that the union with Zanzibar be placed on equal federal footing with three governments (one for the territory constituting the former Tanganyika, along with Zanzibar and Union governments). The report also listed some forty pieces of legislation which it considered oppressive and which ought to be repealed or amended (36). But the government accepted only the recommendation to establish the multi-party system and disregarded all the others.

Shivji also assesses various perspectives on constitution-making in the experience of Tanzania and other African countries, namely, constitution-making as consensus-building, constitution-making as a technical exercise, constitution-making as change (*mageuzi*) from the party-state to state parties, and constitution-making as tinkering with the status quo (36–39). His own preference, with which I fully agree, is that

the *process* of arriving at a multi-party political and constitutional order was as important as the establishment of the system itself. That should be a protracted process in which the people are fully involved. In the light of the fact that the previous experience of constitution-making in Tanzania had always been one from the top, it was necessary to reverse the order and establish a new national consensus embodied in a new constitution so as to give it legitimacy on a new basis. Only such a constitution could possibly lay the foundation for a new political order as well as address the problem of transforming the party-state on the one hand and lending acceptability and legitimacy to the union on the other. (37, emphasis added)

In 2005, CCM chose Jakaya Mrisho Kikwete, a former military officer and foreign affairs minister, as its presidential candidate in the general elections. In December 2005 Kikwete was elected president and Ali Mohammed vice president on the same ballot by popular vote for five-year terms. Kikwete achieved 80.3 percent of the popular vote, while his two rivals got 11.7 and 5.9 percept. It is therefore clear that CCM continues to be the dominant political party in Tanzania, but the recent elections also indicate that the country enjoys a dynamic and stable constitutional democratic process. One question I will discuss in the comparative analysis section is whether Tanzania and other African countries which went through similarly agonizing stages had to go through those various "experiments" to arrive at the "right" formula. The following review of the experience of Uganda may help frame that question and related issues for the discussion later in this chapter.

UGANDA

Like almost all other African countries, present-day Uganda was brought together as a single entity through European colonialism. The country was made up of many ethnic groups or states, in most cases, independent of one another, and possessing different social and political organizations ranging from centralized kingdoms to segmented societies. The concept of Uganda as a territorial state was therefore "a direct result of Uganda's colonial experience after the British arbitrarily carved out the boundaries of today's Uganda, including within its borders a diversity of tribes who must evolve a common destiny in an indivisible sovereign state" (Ibiranga 1973: 4).

For our purposes here in particular, the precolonial constitutional arrangements of these groups were as diverse as the groups themselves. Some groups like the Acholi, Alur, Iteso, and Bakiga organized themselves along decentralized clan-based political and social organizations. Those who were organized into centralized kingdoms included the Baganda (the Kingdom of Buganda), the Banyankole (the Kingdom of Ankole), the Banyoro (the Kingdom of Bunyoro), and the Batoro (the Kingdom of Toro). The Baganda are the largest ethnic group in Uganda, and their monarchy was the strongest and the most pronounced during colonial rule. The preexisting constitutional structure of Buganda played a vital role in the British colonial expansion and rule in Uganda, and the monarchy was so powerful as to create a major constitutional crisis for Uganda on the eve of independence and beyond. More generally, like some other countries, including Sudan and Nigeria discussed later, the strong ethnic diversity, variety of political and social institutions, and consequent multiplicity of interests and how to meet them presented the greatest challenge to nation-building and constitutional development throughout the colonial era and since independence.

Between 1884 and 1912 Britain used several strategies including treaties and agreements with traditional leaders, military conquests, and coercion to patch together the diverse ethnic and linguistic groups of Uganda into a single entity. The Buganda kingdom and its strong kingship institution, and similar structures in Ankole, Bunyoro, and Toro, provided an expedient vehicle for British colonial administration through traditional leaders and institutions, commonly known as "indirect rule." To that end, Britain signed agreements with the local rulers, with Buganda in 1900, Ankole and Toro in 1902, and Bunyoro in 1933. Those agreements could be regarded as the first constitutional documents in the modern history of Uganda (Mukholi 1995: 3).

In areas that did not have centralized monarchies, the colonial administration issued a series of ordinances to create chiefs in those areas and gave them powers, rights, and privileges to maintain order on behalf of the colonial government in their territories; to collect taxes; and to recruit labor for public works. In time, the interests of the chiefs and the government became more closely interwoven, as the former collected taxes, received fixed salaries, and promoted centrally initiated policies. The more the chiefs became associated in the public's mind with the colonial administration, the more they also associate their own interest with those of the ruling power (Low 1960: 173). In Ibiranga's view, that system of indirect rule was to a large extent responsible for the strains and stresses that Uganda went through, including encouraging Buganda's demand to secede from the rest of the country, demands by the western kingdoms of Busoga for federal status and extravagant powers (Ibiranga 1973: 28).

As demands for independence began to rise by the 1950s, Ugandans began to focus their attention on constitutional arrangements that would define power sharing when the British colonial rule ended. In response, the colonial government set up the Wild Constitutional Committee in 1958 to work out plans for a general election on a common roll for the members of the Legislative Council, which would be introduced in 1961. This was the first step in the field of nationwide constitutional developments dealing with a central legislature. The committee deliberated extensively on a system of government for Uganda, but two major questions presented very serious problems in that regard: the problem of minorities, especially the immigrant Asian minority, and the demands of the Kingdom of Buganda for political independence from the rest of country (Ibiranga 1973: 115).

The Wild Committee published its report in February 1960, detailing steps toward independence and recommending that direct elections to the Legislative Council be held in 1961. The Kingdom of Buganda however, rejected the report on the grounds that it did not take adequate account of its demand for full federal status in the independent Uganda, and threatened to secede completely (Karugire 1980: 177). Though the secession threat did not materialize, Buganda refused to participate in the political process, boycotted the 1961 elections, and generally continued to present a huge stumbling block toward the realization of Uganda's independence.

In 1961, the colonial government appointed a commission headed by the Earl of Munster to work out a constitutional framework as part of the transition toward full independence for Uganda. The Munster Commission carried out extensive consultations and deliberations with various categories of people and interest groups in Uganda. Meanwhile Buganda and some other kingdoms and monarchies like the Ankole, Toro, and Bunyoro kept campaigning intensively for some form of constitutional recognition in postcolonial Uganda. The Munster Commission published its report in June 1961, recommending acceptance of the demands of Buganda for federal status, and recognition of its king (the Kabaka) as a constitutional monarch. For the kingdoms of Ankole, Bunyoro, and Toro, however, the Commission recommended a semifederal position because the agreements those kingdoms signed earlier with the British colonial government, noted above, had not given them administrative autonomy equal to that of Buganda (Mukholi 1995: 10). For the rest of the country, the Commission recommended a unitary relationship between the districts and the central government. At the Constitutional Conference that convened in London in September 1961, the status of Buganda dominated the discussions. Other matters were postponed for another conference in 1962, which discussed the final details of the Independence Constitution.

Consequently, the Independence Constitution of 1962 established a British parliamentary model of government, gave Buganda federal status, semifederal status for the kingdoms of Toro, Bunyoro, and Ankole, and a unitary system for the rest of the country. By that hybrid federal and unitary system, members of the federal legislature were to be elected directly, except those from Buganda, who served as an electoral college for the kingdom's representatives. That complicated compromise survived for a very brief period of peace and unity, as the country was engulfed in political and constitutional crises soon after independence due to the conflict between Buganda and the central government on how to implement the constitutional formula. In an effort to defuse the crisis, the constitutional amendment of 1963 provided for the position of a ceremonial head of state (president), and the national assembly (parliament) elected the Kabaka of Buganda to that position. But that solution created even more constitutional problems as conflicts of interest emerged from the Kabaka's dual role as both king of Buganda and president of Uganda. While he was constitutionally required to act in accordance with the advice of the national assembly and the cabinet, he was often more loyal to the kingdom than to the country. As the interests of the kingdom were often at variance with those of the country as a whole, there was a constant power struggle between the Kabaka/president and prime minister.

In 1966, Prime Minister Milton Obote deposed the resident and declared himself executive president. He abrogated the Independence Constitution and singlehandedly introduced a new constitution that he called the interim constitution. Obote summoned the national assembly, which was intimidated by a heavy deployment of troops outside the parliament building, to approve the interim constitution. At that session, Obote told the members that "this [new constitution] is now a provisional Uganda constitution till another enactment . . . If you go down to your pigeon holes [mail box in the building] you will find your copies of the new constitution" (Mukholi 1995: 16). The "Pigeon Hole Constitution" of 1966, as it came to be known, abolished the federal arrangements that were enshrined in the Independence Constitution and provided for a highly powerful executive president. It also provided that rent from the Kabaka's land should no longer go to the Kabaka but be paid to the central government. When the Buganda kingdom rejected the new constitution and its assembly voted to expel the central government from Buganda territory, Obote sent in troops that engaged in a bloody massacre. The Kabaka managed to escape to Britain, and died in exile three years later.

In 1967 Obote introduced another constitution that was basically an amended version of the 1966 Pigeon Hole Constitution, except that it abolished all the kingdoms and declared Uganda a republic. It also provided for extensive concentration of power at the center, away from local governments. Obote then began a systematic process of arrogating absolute power unto himself; all opposition parties were banned and political opponents killed, thrown into jail, or forced into exile. This was the situation until 1971, when General Idi Amin Dada ousted Obote and elevated his dictatorial reign of terror to a completely new level.

During the following nine years, the 1967 Constitution was completely disregarded as Amin ruled by decree and all representative institutions were abolished or subordinated to his will. Suspected political opponents were detained, tortured, and sometimes publicly executed, and terror and gross human rights abuses were commonplace. Also during this time almost 90,000 Asians were expelled from Uganda.

Eventually, Amin brought about his own downfall when he threatened to invade Tanzania in 1979 and take over a part of its territory he claimed belonged to Uganda. In response, Tanzania launched an anticipatory attack by a combination of Tanzania's military and forces of Ugandan exiles. The invasion succeeded in overthrowing Amin, who fled the country.

Between 1980 and 1986, Uganda had a succession of different leaders. First, Amin was replaced for a short time by a government of the Uganda National Liberation Front (UNLF), an amalgam of several political and military groups. However, when a national election was conducted in 1980, it brought Obote back to power again. As disagreements and squabbles by the politicians and different interest groups continued, Yoweri Museveni, the leader of one of the parties in the UNLF, launched a campaign of guerrilla warfare against the government. In 1986, Museveni's forces overran Kampala, and he was sworn in as the president of Uganda.

By 1988, the country had started a long and exhaustive constitution-making process involving extensive consultation with the Ugandan people, until a new constitution was adopted in 1995. The Constitutional Commission conducted an extensive series of public debates, seminars, workshops, and meetings throughout the country and provided various forums for discussion and constitutional education of the people. It also looked to newspapers, interest groups, and educational institutions for input on the new, more legitimate constitution, and conducted comparative studies. The Commission received over 25,000 submissions from the general population on what they wanted to see in the constitution. From these submissions, the commission drafted a constitution that retained the principle of the country as a republic under a presidential type of government, and yet restored the kingdoms that were abolished by Obote in the 1967 Constitution. The draft constitution provided for a comprehensive bill of human rights and freedoms with special focus on women, children, and disadvantaged groups. The draft constitution was debated by a Constituent Assembly during 1994 and 1995 and, on September 22, 1995, the new constitution was enacted.

At the time of writing, Museveni remains the executive president and head of state since 1986. He was reelected in 2001 for the second time under the 1995 Constitution, and again officially declared the winner of the February 2006 elections, the first multi-party elections in 25 years. Museveni was declared to have received 59 percent of the votes, the opposition leader Kizza Besigye got 37 percent and the three other candidates just over 3 percent. The opposition candidate and foreign observers objected to the fairness of the election process and validity of the official result.

The unicameral National Assembly consists of 214 members directly elected by popular vote, 81 nominated by legally established special interest groups (women 56, army 10, disabled 5, youth 5, labor 5), 8 ex officio members. The last elections were held in 2001, and the next is due to be held in 2006. The only political organization allowed to operate freely is the Movement (formerly the NRM) of President Museveni, who maintains that it is a mass organization which claims the loyalty of all Ugandans, rather than a political party as such. There are, however, several political parties which are not allowed to sponsor candidates for election, including the Ugandan People's Congress of Milton Obote, the former prime minister/president.

Uganda's experiment in non-party politics was not totally new, as can be seen from the experiences of other countries, reviewed earlier. While the legitimacy of the 1995 Constitution may have been generally acknowledged, many groups hold that their views and needs were not accommodated in the drafting process (Mukholi 1995: 82). The advocates of a multi-party system in particular argued that the restrictions on their political activities constitute a violation of freedom of association in order to consolidate the Museveni's Movement control over the country (83). That argument eventually prevailed and multi-party politics has been restored, but it remains to be seen what the people of Uganda will make of these developments in securing constitutionalism in their country.

Comparative Reflections and Tentative Evaluation

I turn now to an attempt to compare and tentatively evaluate these experiences, within the framework of the proposed deeply contextual and incremental approach to African constitutionalism. The main question for this section, as indicated earlier, is how to understand the role of various actors and forces, the combination of internal and external factors and dynamics that shape the development of constitutional governance in each setting for the purpose of facilitating successful and sustainable constitutionalism in each African country. Some of the points I am drawing from the six experiences, reviewed above, can also be made in relation to other countries not covered in the review. I am also drawing in this section on various sources cited elsewhere in this book (such as An-Na'im 2003; Collins 1994; Fage 2002; Jackson 1984), without citing them specifically, as that might be distracting from the reflective nature of what I am saying here. The evaluation I am offering in relation to various aspects of this comparative analysis will have to be tentative because the subject is open to genuine difference of opinion. For instance, an underlying theme of this whole process is whether various aspects of the constitutional experiences of each country were avoidable or really necessary as experiments in the process of arriving at the "right" formula for that country. In my view, this is a matter of judgment and personal opinion, rather than a product of a purportedly objective calculation.

To begin with some general framework, Ghana, Guinea, Rwanda, Tanzania, and Uganda came into being as unified states as result of colonial consolidation of control over territories that were previously governed in a wide variety of centralized and decentralized regimes. In fact, these countries were governed during their colonial periods as parts of a wider colonial region, rather than as discrete or separate political entities. Ghana, which is the slightly oldest among these five countries, has less than 50 years of existence as a separate or self-contained state in any sense of the term, that is, since independence in 1957. To put things in perspective, one may wonder about the constitutional status of Britain, France, the United States, and other developed countries at corresponding stages of their histories, whatever their starting date may be taken to have been. In the case of the United States, for instance, within the first fifty years after independence, the country had drafted a constitution (with some lamenting an "excess of democracy") (Woody 2005), fought a war in 1812, expanded its territory through what is known as the Louisiana Purchase, and amended its constitution 12 times. The twelfth amendment, in particular, set the election of presidents through an electoral college, thereby settling an issue that has dogged many African countries since independence.

The main difference between those Western countries and postcolonial African states is probably that the former were dealing with their own homegrown solutions to constitutional problems, rather than attempting to implement a "formula" that was imposed from outside. Even in the case of the United States, the constitutional framework being implemented was a continuation of the Western intellectual tradition which early Americans brought with them to North America. In contrast, African countries have to deal with a peculiar accumulation of complex problems, some arising from their particular traditional political situations, others inherited from the colonial era, as briefly highlighted below. While most African countries were experiencing centrifugal forces dictated by a need for national cohesion, they were also being pulled apart by the lure of Pan-Africanism, or regional and continental unity. For example, between 1960 and 1963 Guinea and Ghana united with Mali, then under Modibo Keita, a like-minded ruler, to form what was called the Union of African States (UAS). In 1963, African countries formed the Organization of African Unity (OAU), with the aim of creating some form of political federation. Although the OAU has failed in that regard, it has had significant influence on constitutionalism in Africa by sponsoring constitutional documents such as the OAU Charter, the Cairo Declaration of Border Disputes, the Banjul Charter, the Lagos Plan of Action, and the OAU Decisions on Good Governance. It is also relevant that African countries are dealing with issues of constitutionalism in a drastically different global context, particularly the impact of economic globalization on domestic African economies and politics.

Ethiopia came into existence more than half a century earlier through what might be called "African colonialism" of Emperor Menelik II, but the modern constitutional history of the country is much more recent, if one excludes the 1931 document, which consisted of seven articles whose implementation was seriously interrupted by the Italian occupation in 1935 and the exile of Emperor Haile Selassie until the early 1950s. However, the constitutional experience of the country is still dominated by the legacy of that imperial past, including the underlying cause of civil war, persistent conflict with Eritrea, and intense ethnic rivalries and conflict, in addition to problems of weak basis of constitutional governance and general underdevelopment shared with the rest of the continent. Some of the tensions in Ethiopia's relations with Eritrea, which was for a long time a province of Ethiopia, can be traced to Italian incursions into Ethiopia, from 1882 to 1930s, often using Eritrean forces (Negash 2000: 7). In other words, although it was not colonized like other African countries, Ethiopia is as much a postcolonial state as any of them.

Some of the common difficulties facing constitutional development in all six countries include weak state formation and lack of human and institutional resources for constitutional governance under the rule of law; mutually exclusive and antagonistic ethnic identities constructed or cultivated by colonial administrations that continue to undermine the basis of national unity and political stability; and the ambivalent role of international actors and forces, due to competing ideologies and power politics of the cold war era, global capitalism, and the more recent democratization trends. In attempting briefly to explain some of these problems and related issues in the following remarks, I am simply trying to place the constitutional experiences of African countries in context, without offering an apology for the failures and setbacks suffered by these countries since independence. As these difficulties have frequently been cited, and continue to be used, by various types of African elites to escape responsibility for their own conduct, it is better to note them in this tentative evaluation.

To begin with, the way these countries were rapidly rushed into single states and propelled into juridical sovereignty without being empirically sovereign on the ground, as explained in chapter 2, meant that none of them were ready for independent statehood. On the contrary, the only experience their independence leaders and general population had with modern state management under colonial administrations was that of oppressive authoritarianism and unaccountable government that manipulated ethnic and religious divisions among the population for its own narrow political interests. The only knowledge early African nationalists and founders of African states had of the rule of law was as a tool for the suppression of political dissent through indefinite detention without charge and forced exile, and exploitation and pilferage of state resources which would then be repatriated to the metropolis. The counter-insurgency measures employed by the colonial authorities in putting down civil unrest involved "political arrests, farcical public court trials, resulting in manipulated guilty verdicts calling for jail terms for convicted nationalist leaders" (Assensoh 2001: 67). It is true that, a chosen few like Kwame Nkrumah and Jomo Kenyatta had lived and studied abroad, mainly in Western countries. But the negative experience those African leaders had there, like Nkrumah's with pre-civil rights racism in the United States and Kenyatta's in Britain, may have been counterproductive for their perception of constitutionalism and made them susceptible to totalitarian socialist ideologies fashionable at the time. After independence, African leaders responded to political opposition with treason laws and detention without trial in the name of preservation of public security. In Sékou Toure's Guinea, for instance, the first Organization of African Unity secretary general, Diallo Telli, died in political detention under unexplained circumstances. In Nkrumah's Ghana, Dr. Joseph Boakye Danquah, who had helped Nkrumah with finances when he was a student, was detained and subsequently died in prison after he spoke openly against Nkrumah's dictatorship.

None of the countries discussed here, or any African state for that matter, inherited a functioning and credible domestic judiciary or security apparatus that was accountable to political leaders at independence. Most countries have therefore continued to rely on foreign judges for decades, some up to the present time. Such judges mostly come from former colonial countries, or the weak clubs of formerly colonized countries such as the British Commonwealth and what is loosely referred to as la Francophonie. Accused persons have no access to legal assistance, whether government provided or free legal aid. Police forces and prison services are poorly trained, do not usually understand the law they are supposed to uphold, and are generally incompetent and corrupt. The aggregate of these shortcomings results in a pervasive culture of arbitrary authoritarianism. A sense of 'business as usual' enabled generations of ruling elites and government officials to continue to enforce the same oppressive security laws, through the same authoritarian institutions, in order to perpetuate their own power and avoid responsibility for corruption and incompetence. This was as true of Kwame Nkrumah of Ghana, Ahmed Sékou Touré of Guinea, Sanni Abacha of Nigeria, Milton Obote of Uganda, among many others, as it is still true now (at the time of writing in 2005) of Robert Mugabe of Zimbabwe and Omar El-Bashir of Sudan. Mostly illiterate, politically uninformed, disempowered at the national level, and inhibited by parochial traditionalism, African populations apparently tended to accept arbitrary and authoritarian government, violations of human rights, and general economic and social hardship as simply the way things are supposed to be.

African dictators also coopted individuals from their own ethnic groups, probably to ensure personal political loyalty, reinforcing the notion that the emerging "national" state "belonged" to a particular ethnic community, to be defended as such by that group and resisted by other communities for the same reason. The 1994 genocide in Rwanda is a tragic and extreme manifestation of the common problem of mutually exclusive and antagonistic ethnic identity that was constructed or cultivated by colonial administrations to facilitate their own rule. Whether under the British doctrine of indirect rule or the French principle of assimilation, colonial administrators tended to cultivate and manipulate local ethnic and/or religious affiliations into rigid and closed categories. As noted in Chapter 2, these features of colonial expediency that often distorted traditional, relatively more democratic institutions and consolidated rigid social and political stratification in the past continue to seriously undermine political stability and constitutional government after independence. Moreover, such underlying tensions are sometimes manipulated by various elite groups to instigate and sustain civil strife and war, as happened in Nigeria, Kenya, Rwanda, Ethiopia, Sudan, and Uganda and, more recently in Sierra Leone and Zaire, to mention but a few examples.

The ambivalent influence of international actors and forces was reflected in the ideological and geopolitical competition of the cold war, the drastic "experimentation" with Pan-Africanism and Non-Alignment (resisting alliance with either side in the cold war) of Gamal Abdul Nasser of Egypt, Nkrumah of Ghana, Kenneth Kaunda of Zambia and Julius Nyerere of Tanzania. Those same leaders and others, like Sékou Touré of Guinea and Jaafar Numeiri of Sudan, also engaged in experimentation with ideological notions of state socialism and/or one-party state. Such one-party regimes claimed that the challenges posed by ethnicity, poverty, ignorance and disease were analogous to the kind of emergencies that prompted developed countries to declare emergency powers—that these mutually reinforcing crises were a threat to national security. In Ghana, Nkrumah's regime eliminated political parties by using the law to proscribe opposition parties like the Muslim Association Party, the Northern People's Party, and the Asante-dominated National Liberation Movement in the late 1950s. In Guinea, the PDG claimed that the single-party state was in fact the actual realization of independence, because, as a mass party truly representative of the nation, PDG was Guinea (Winchester 1995: 349).

Similar ambivalence also resulted from global geopolitical competition between the Western and Soviet blocs during the cold war, and sometimes among Western powers like France and the United States in the Great Lakes region. Ironically, Western powers condoned and sometimes even encouraged military coups and oppressive regimes in the name of combating the spread of Marxist-Leninist ideology in the region. Examples include al-Numeiri in Sudan, Amin in Uganda and Mobutu Sese Seko in Zaire. Although not strictly speaking a military regime for its total disregard of democracy, the apartheid regime in South Africa falls in this category. The ambivalence continued in the post-cold war period through the conflicting agenda of the global capitalism and superficial political liberalization as experienced by Ghana during the latter part of the Rawlings years, Kenya under Daniel arap Moi and Uganda under

Yoweri Museveni, among many countries over the last decade of the twentieth century.

In general, the usual difficulties facing all emerging states that were artificially created by colonial administrations were frequently manipulated by some of the first generation of independence leaders to justify suppression of political opposition, usually followed by a bid to extend their hold on power indefinitely, all in the name of national unity, stability and development. This was done by Ahmadou Ahidjo in Cameroon, Nkurumah in Ghana, Sékou Touré in Guinea, Moussa Traoré in Mali, Ngwazi Kamuzu Banda in Malawi, Obote in Uganda, and Kaunda in Zambia, among others. These leaders manipulated the African cultural identities of their populations by adopting fancy titles for themselves, including African traditional veneration monikers like Osagyefo, Ngwazi, Mzee, or Oga. The military dictators also often promoted themselves; Amin called himself Al-Haji Field Marshal Dr. President Idi Amin Dada, Conqueror of the British Empire, while Mobutu's full title was Mobutu, Sese Seko Kuku Ngbeandu Wa Za Banga, meaning the "allpowerful warrior who, because of his endurance and inflexible will to win, will go from conquest to conquest leaving fire in his wake."Although a direct connection cannot be empirically established, the model of Emperor Haile Selassie's monarchy in Ethiopia may have been influential as the only "authentic" African imperial leader, particularly in this early stage of African independence. That African dictators often took a leaf from each other's book is not far-fetched; Malawi Banda lived in Nkrumah's Ghana before returning to his country, and appears to have brought with him Nkrumah's draconian detention laws (Assensoh 2005: 64–65), while Uganda's Amin learned his brutality uninhibited as a colonial soldier fighting Mau Mau in Kenya.

The high-handedness of African leaders became so pervasive that military intervention through coup d'etat became the only option for getting rid of them. In many countries, armed forces seized power under some pretext of combating corruption, restoring "genuine" democratic government, or saving the country from total economic collapse. This happened with Jerry Rawlings in Ghana, the Military Committee for National Recovery (CMRN) in Guinea, and Amin in Uganda. Military intervention by self-appointed savers or ideologues has occurred repeatedly in some countries, like Nigeria where the first protracted and complex military coup of 1965 brought Yakubu Gowon to power, setting off a series of coups by military commanders over the next two decades, and in the case of Ghana three times by the same commander, Rawlings. Military coups were also used to initiate ideological regimes, like that of Mathieu Kérékou's Marxist-Leninist People's Revolutionary Party of Benin from 1977 to 1990, and the Marxist-Leninist Program of National

Democratic Revolution of Ethiopia of the Derg in Ethiopia from 1976 to 1991.

Comparative reflection and evaluation of African constitutional experiences can be approached from a variety of perspectives. But I will limit myself here to a few comments on some pertinent questions to clarify some aspects of the thesis and analysis of this book. A broader or more comprehensive discussion which requires a high degree of detail and focus on individual cases and specific periods (like Ghana or Uganda during the 1960s–1980s) would be appropriate for a different kind of analysis from the one I am attempting here. The first set of questions relate to whether any type of government (military or civilian, single or multiparty state) experienced by each country can be evaluated from a constitutional point of view, and by which standards such an evaluation can be made? That is, whether a regime was good or bad as a matter of *constitutional* government, and not by some other measure like maintaining law and order or reducing the foreign debt of a country. This is not to suggest, of course, that such other criteria are invalid or unimportant, but only that they are not the subject of this study. Second, if some regimes were better than others, as one would expect, how were the relatively bad regimes allowed to govern or tolerated by the population at large? Third, whatever answers one may find regarding the first two questions, is it true that all these experiences, good and bad, were necessary, or could the bad ones have been avoided by the countries that experienced them?

On the first question, the constitutional measure of any type of government must be its fidelity to the principles of constitutionalism as outlined earlier in this book, basically to what extent it is accountable to the general population, attentive to their well-being, and respectful of their human rights. In other words, the measure must be the extent to which the government has realized and safeguarded the right of the people to self-determination in terms of promoting general development, public security, democratic self-government and respect for human rights. The application of such indicators, however, should take into account the processes of securing institutionalized and sustainable development of these features, not simply their presence or practice at a specific point in time. Thus, some military governments or single party states may express a willingness to be accountable, and do in fact take steps to improve the protection of human rights, quality of life and public safety for the general population. For instance, General Olesegun Obasanjo of Nigeria became the first military man in Africa to relinquish power to civilian rulers in 1979, but the civilian regime of his successor Shehu Shagari became so corrupt and inept that it literally invited the military to take over.

The fact that Museveni's faction of the Uganda National Liberation

Front (UNLF) and the Ethiopian People's Revolutionary Democratic Front (EPRDF) seized power through armed rebellion and protracted civil war does not necessarily deem these regimes to be inherently and permanently incompatible with constitutionalism. The question should be how these governments behaved after coming to power, rather than simply the manner in which they seized power. But this perspective should not be assumed to automatically yield categorical evaluations, because the whole premise of the incremental success approach adopted in this study is to consider each stage as part of the constitutionalism process for the country in question. For nearly two decades, Museveni curtailed democratic freedom by proscribing political parties and favoring his non-party movement system. However, it can also be argued that Uganda has in the interim recovered from years of devastation, and established a minimum foundation for competitive politics. Conversely, one can also note the failure of the regime to fully transform into constitutional democratic government. Similarly, the EPRDF has made important strides in constitutionalism, including the promulgation of one of the most progressive constitutions on the continent. Yet, serious concerns can be raised about the successful transition to constitutionalism in view of the 2005 elections and their aftermath. While there is no final judgment when constitutionalism is seen as a constant work in progress, interim or tentative evaluation is still important for corrective strategies and informing current practice.

Since some military or revolutionary regimes may do relatively better than some civilian governments elected through fair and open elections in a multi-party state, the question must therefore be whether the implementation of constitutional principles is likely to be as institutionalized and sustainable under a military regimes or single party state as under civilian democratic government. A negative answer is clearly indicated by the essential nature of military regimes which rely on the force of arms to seize and keep power, or single party states which rely on oppressive measures to suppress dissent and exclude electoral competition. This is not to say that either type of regime does not need some degree of popular acceptance and political support. Rather, it is that the primary means of political control by such regimes are more coercive than voluntary, and that dictators are more likely to resort to violent suppression of political opposition than to give up their control of the state. In contrast, a civilian elected government is by definition more dependent on acceptance and support by the public, though it may use force to keep the peace or combat an armed rebellion. In other words, peaceful pressure by public opinion is more likely to influence an elected government than a military regime, especially in the long term. If that is the case with military regimes and single-party states, as compared to elected governments, then why or how do the former succeed in seizing or holding power in so many African counties? Why do people accept or tolerate military rule or single party states despite their inherent incompatibility with constitutional government?

A comprehensive or exhaustive response to these questions will require a detailed discussion of a wide range of issues against the background of a lot of factual information for each country and specific period of time. In any case, whatever conclusions I might draw from that type of analysis may not be widely accepted because such assessments cannot be isolated from the ideological orientation, value judgment, or personal bias of the researcher. For example, much of the debate about the utility or rationale of military regimes and single party states in the 1970s and 1980s involved the notion of "trade-off" of constitutional governance for national security or development—the idea that a country has to postpone the implementation of the former in order to achieve the latter. In my view, the notion of trade-off in this context is false and counterproductive: national security and development must be founded on constitutional governance if they are to be worthwhile and sustainable at all. It is also clear to me, however, that while I can argue for this response on the basis of my assessment and evaluation of the available evidence, such an argument is ultimately grounded in my own ideological orientation and value judgment. Others may take a different view of the same evidence, or blame some internal or external factors for the failure of one regime or another to deliver on its promises. Instead of engaging in such a protracted debate which will probably lead to conclusions others will probably reject as too subjective or biased, I wish to make a very limited, and hopefully readily acceptable, twofold proposition.

The first part of my limited proposition is that, whatever general explanation one may be inclined to accept, it seems that part of the reason for the willingness of Africans to accept or tolerate military regimes or single-party states was a combination of four elements, namely, frustration, hope, fear, and justice. That is, as they became increasingly frustrated by the decline in their material well-being and safety, and/or deterioration of the country as a whole, Africans were willing to give a military regime or one-party state a chance to govern, in the hope that it might do better than the previous regime, in addition to the fear of the harsh consequences of opposition. People may not be consciously aware of these factors as such, and their role and relative impact would probably vary greatly from one person or group to another, one setting to the next, as well as over time in the same setting. The frustration with the incompetence and corruption of an elected government may have been the primary or at least initial motivation for welcoming a military regime which is hoped to do better, as happened repeatedly in Ghana,

Nigeria, and Sudan. Aware that thieves, torturers, and murderers go scot-free during dictatorship, Africans have tended to welcome the military in the hope that the executions of national leaders that invariably follow offer some kind of justice, and Africans have often expressed this idea of justice in biblical terms; he who lives by the sword dies by the sword. As the hope fades away, and the military or single-party state turns out to be as incompetent and corrupt as the civilian elected government it replaced, fear of harsh repression of political opposition may become the main factor in the acquiescence to being ruled in that way.

The second part of my limited proposition relates to the question of how to break the inertia in order to achieve the replacement or transformation of the military regime or single-party state into a multi-party, democratically elected, and constitutionally accountable government. Since this repeatedly happened in many African countries by the early 1990s, the question can also be framed in terms of explaining the rise of resistance that ultimately results in this replacement or transformation. Again, seeking a comprehensive or definitive answer to either formulation of this question will probably require engaging in a protracted and value-loaded debate drawing on the specific details of each case. On the one hand, for instance, one can emphasize the personal charisma and political skills of military commanders turned civilian rulers like Kérékou of Benin and Rawlings of Ghana, or leaders of single-party states like Obote of Uganda, who managed to get democratically elected after their regimes ended. On the other hand, it can be argue that such "survivors" benefited from the restrictions they had imposed on political activities during the dictatorships that inhibited the emergence of even more charismatic and skillful leaders and supported by sufficiently experienced organizations to defeat the former dictators.

In all cases, it seems to me, the "frustration, hope, fear, and justice" combination of factors that permitted or sustained military rule and single party states reflect an underlying lack of confidence in constitutionalism, impatience for it to bear worthwhile fruits in due course, and unwillingness to risk personal safety or other hardship in its defense. Since local developments in the late 1980s and early 1990s leading to the replacement or transformation of unconstitutional regimes clearly indicate that people were willing to take those risks, the question becomes how this happened and why. What made people willing to demand constitutional governance, despite earlier experiences indicating it to be likely to produce incompetent or corrupt governments? Why did they come to accept the costs of political opposition, as the ruling regime probably grew more brutal in its desperate effort to keep power? Such questions, with their obvious policy implications for the prospects of constitutionalism in African countries, directly raise the question of the cultural or religious legitimacy of constitutional principles. The claim here is that popular perceptions of the legitimacy of constitutionalism will influence how people relate to these principles, whether they will be willing to wait for good outcomes and risk hardship in their defense of constitutional governance. It is from this perspective that I think it is critical to examine the role of Islam in the constitutional development of African Islamic societies, which will be attempted in the next two chapters.

In conclusion here, it seems clear to me that, while each situation should be viewed as a distinctive experience in the incremental success of constitutionalism in that particular setting, comparative reflection and tentative evaluation are possible and necessary for guiding strategies to support and sustain the relevant principles and institutions in each country. While no experience should be subjected to an arbitrary dichotomy of "success or failure" according to some preconceived notions of where it is supposed to be along the way to perfect or total constitutionalism, it is indeed necessary to draw lessons in order to improve "performance" in the future. Otherwise the process-based incremental approach I am proposing can be used to justify deterministic complacency which enables the elite in power to claim that nothing needs to change or can be done to improve the situation. The fallacy of that logic is that one will not be able to tell in advance whether all that can be done has in fact been done. In other words, making a country's constitutional experience its own model and standard of evaluation does not provide any justification for failure to develop and implement appropriate policies to improve the situation. Every effort must be made to understand the process and develop and implement reforms because that is the only way to know what we need, which direction to take, and how to get where we need to be.

Chapter 4

The Contingent Role of Islam

In this chapter I introduce and try to clarify the notion of contingency as a possible framework for mediating tensions between traditional understandings of Islam, on the one hand, and modern principles of constitutionalism, on the other. This framework can contribute to facilitating the development of constitutionalism by enhancing its cultural and religious legitimacy in African Islamic societies. Here I am seeking to apply to African Islamic societies the same basic premise discussed earlier, namely, that the sustainable development of constitutionalism needs to come to terms with the indigenous values and institutions of those societies. This is not to say that is only and exclusively in terms of Islam, but merely that there is an Islamic dimension to relevant values and institutions of predominantly Islamic societies in Africa. Moreover, such reconciliation cannot be assumed to exist or be readily available in any specific setting, nor should it be presumed to be impossible to promote through internal debate. These two chapters are therefore intended as a study in a proactive approach to the incremental success of constitutionalism in African societies whose cultural and institutional resources have a strong or clear Islamic dimension.

Given the ambivalence and contingency of the relationship between Islam and constitutionalism, as explained in chapter 1 and further elaborated below, the basic question is whether it would be possible to develop deliberate strategies for promoting a positive relationship between the two. The rest of this chapter will be devoted to clarifying this notion of contingency in the role of Islam in politics, broadly defined. For our purposes here this means that the outcome of the interaction of Islam and constitutionalism can vary according to a variety of factors, rather than being permanently settled one way or the other. If this is true, it should be possible to influence this relationship by addressing the various factors that shape its outcome in any given context. To elaborate this thesis, I will begin with recalling some earlier theoretical reflections, and then outline the processes of the spread and adaptation of Islam in Africa in relation to the colonial and postcolonial stages, as the context in which the proposed contingency analysis is supposed to be applied. The chapter ends with a discussion of a proposed approach to reconciliation, to be further explored in the next chapter.

Islam and Constitutionalism: Tensions and Possibilities of Mediation

To recall the caveat in Chapter 1, the premise here is not that Islam is the sole or even primary determinant of the status of constitutionalism in Islamic countries (that is, those where Muslims constitute the majority of the population). Indeed, it is integral to my argument that the present status and future prospects of constitutionalism in those countries should be assessed in terms of the historical experience and present context of each country, like any other country in the world. The role of Islam in that experience and context would necessarily vary from one country to another, but always as only one among many factors and forces that may influence the course of developments in each setting. However, even where it is not so obvious or dominant at some point in time, the role of Islam in this field should not be underestimated because of its implications for the legitimacy and efficacy of the notion of constitutionalism itself in those societies. In other words, the role of Islam in this connection should be taken seriously, without unduly exaggerating or underestimating it.

This relationship is problematic since Islam is commonly taken to be synonymous with historical understandings of what is commonly known as Shariʿa. Whereas the term Shariʿa refers to the normative system of Islam in general, the specific content Muslims have given to this system is necessarily a product of the history of their own societies. This point is extremely important for our purposes here, namely, that the term Shariʿa always refers to human interpretation of the Qurʾan and Sunna (traditions of the Prophet), and as such is neither divine nor immutable. The particular understanding of the content of Shariʿa prevalent among Muslims today contains some principles that are incompatible with fundamental principles of constitutionalism, as briefly explained earlier and further elaborated below. This does not mean that Shariʿa as such is incapable of being understood by Muslims in ways that are fully consistent with constitutionalism for their own society, but the contradictions must first be acknowledged before the reinterpretation can begin. In this first section, I will briefly explain this basic tension, and outline a theoretical approach to its mediation. The notion of contingency elaborated in the rest of this chapter indicates that there is "space" for this mediation to happen within the local context of each Islamic society. But let me first recall aspects of the understanding of constitutionalism on which my argument is founded.

Constitutionalism, Universal and Specific

Essentially, constitutionalism is a particular response to a basic paradox in the political, economic, and social life of every human society. On the one hand, it is not practically possible for all citizens to participate equally in the conduct of the daily affairs of their country at large. It is also clear, on the other hand, that people tend to have different views and conflicting interests regarding matters of sharing political power, development, and allocation of economic resources, social policy, and service. The state is the agency charged with the mediation of these differences of opinion and conflicts of interests. But since this function is supposed to be performed by those who control the apparatus of the state, who are human beings with their own biases, opinions, and interests, the question is how to ensure that they will not exceed or abuse their powers. Constitutionalism signifies a system of government that seeks to enable those who have no direct control over the apparatus of the state to ensure that their views and interests are well served by those who are in control of the state. All aspects of constitutionalism, whether regarding the structures and organs of the state or their operation in the making and implementation of public policy, administration of justice, and so forth, follow from this basic reality of all human societies today. This relationship between the population at large and those who are in control of the apparatus of the state can be understood and evaluated in terms of how representative and accountable is the government of a country to all segments of its population. In other words, a society enjoys constitutional governance to the extent that processes of representation and accountability are working properly.

This conception of constitutionalism is sometimes expressed in terms the right to self-determination, namely, the right of people to freely determine their political status and pursue economic, social, and cultural development. But the realization of this right should be seen as a continuous process, rather than being exhausted or extinguished by the achievement of political independence from external colonial rule. Political independence is a necessary but insufficient condition because a people can be as oppressed by the internal hegemony of a ruling class or group, or an exclusive ideology, as they can be by external colonial rule. While internal hegemony is generally harder to resist than external colonial rule, it is even harder to resist when it is justified in the name of religion.

To conceive constitutionalism in terms of the ability of people to influence the course of events that shape their lives at the personal, familial, and communal level would emphasize the need to safeguard the necessary "public space" for people to safely and freely seek and exchange information regarding public policy issues, and to organize with others for action in furtherance of their own objectives. This basic conception of constitutionalism would also indicate that equal access to and ability to use such public space must be secured for all citizens of a country. It would therefore follow that the essential nature and basic function of constitutionalism preclude the exclusion of any citizen from the full benefits of citizenship because of gender or religious beliefs. This point is of particular concern in this chapter, as I explain later.

It may also be helpful at this stage to note the relationship between structures, institutions, and processes of specific constitutional traditions, on the one hand, and the values and objectives that can be extrapolated as universal features of constitutionalism in general, on the other. Commonly accepted features of constitutionalism, such as the principles of popular sovereignty, separation of legislative, executive, and judicial powers, and independence of the judiciary, are normally realized through different structures, institutions, and processes in various countries. As discussed in the final chapter, for example, separation of powers and independence of the judiciary can be secured either through structural and institutional arrangements, as in the United States, or by means of deeply entrenched political "conventions" and traditions of practice in the political culture of a country like the United Kingdom. A sharp distinction between conventions and traditions in this sense, on the one hand, and structures and institutions, on the other, can be misleading because each model requires or presupposes some degree or form of the other for its proper functioning. That is, structures and institutions require conventions of practice for their proper functioning, and constitutional "conventions," in the British sense of the term, also rely on some structures and institutions. Differences in emphasis on one or the other model are the product of the historical experience and context of the country, rather than the result of a deliberate single choice that was made at a specific point in time. In the final analysis, what is important is the ability of the system to achieve the desired constitutional objectives, rather than the precise manner in which it seeks to do that.

But this does not mean that all conceivable systems are equally conducive to the sustained realization of the separation of powers or independence of the judiciary as principles of constitutionalism. While this is usually a matter of degree, there is a point where some mechanisms are too inadequate to be acceptable if the principle in question is to be upheld at all. For instance, while some executive discretion in the appointment and tenure of judges is unavoidable, total reliance on the "good faith" of those responsible for such determinations without external checks or safeguards will defeat the principle of the independence of the judiciary. For example, allowing such executive discretion to discriminate on grounds of sex or religion in making judicial appointments amounts to the total repudiation of the principle of constitutionalism itself. As explained below, this is the sort of constitutional objection to traditional formulations of Shari‘a that cannot be overlooked as merely minor variation in practice.

Nevertheless, it does not follow that unacceptable models can easily and quickly be replaced by more appropriate ones. As clearly illustrated by the post-independence experiences of many African countries high- lighted in chapter 3, the transplantation of structures, institutions, and processes that are found to be successful in one setting or another is a profoundly difficult task that requires extensive adaptation and careful development. This requires time and patience for such institutions to work, which is why I am arguing for withholding categorical judgment, while working for the incremental success of constitutional governance in each case. The point to emphasize here is that both the emergence of consensus on certain features of constitutionalism, and their detailed formulation and implementation in each country, are the product of particular experiences in specific global and local contexts. In other words, the meaning and implications of constitutionalism for a given country is the product of the interaction between broad universal principles and specific local factors and processes. The universal principles themselves are distilled from the specific experiences of a wide variety of countries, which were in turn produced by a similar interaction between the uni- versal and the local in their respective context.

Islam, Shari‘a, and Constitutionalism

To begin with, I recall a point emphasized earlier, as human interpreta- tions of the foundational religious sources of Islam (Qur’an and Sunna), conceptions and principles of Shari‘a that are accepted by Muslims at any given time and place can be neither divine nor immutable. Any formu- lation of Shari‘a is simply a human effort to interpret and implement Islamic principles, and not Islam itself as a religion. I would also recall here other relevant points made in chapter 1 earlier, in order to intro- duce the following discussion of the "contingency" thesis presented in this chapter. In particular, the premise here is that the relationship between Islam and constitutionalism is important for all Islamic societies in gen- eral, and not only where Shari‘a is supposedly enforced by the state as pos- itive law, whether by conservative governments as in Saudi Arabia and the Gulf States, or by radical regimes like those of Iran and Sudan. Debates and strategies regarding the enforcement of Shari‘a by the state are often connected to the rise of so-called Islamic fundamentalist movements and their calls to establishment of an "Islamic state." It may therefore help to begin with some clarification of these and related issues.

Except when used simply as a shorthand way of referring to a state where Muslims constitute a clear majority of the population, the adjective "Islamic" logically applies to people, rather than to a state as a political institution. More importantly the notion of an Islamic state as a political institution is conceptually incoherent, historically inaccurate, and practically not viable today (An-Na'im 2000). It is conceptually incoherent because for a political authority to claim to implement the totality of Shari'a in the everyday life of a society is a contradiction in terms. Enforcement through the official institutions of the state is fundamentally inconsistent with the nature of Shari'a, as a religious normative system that is the product of human interpretation of the Qur'an and Sunna by early Muslim scholars (An-Na'im 1990). This last point can be briefly explained as follows.

It is misleading to think of Shari'a as "Islamic Law" because it is different from positive law that is supposed to be enforced by the state in the usual sense of the term. To begin with, Shari'a is believed to be the divinely ordained total way of life for all Muslims; its norms cover the full range of human activity, from purely religious articles of faith and worship practices to social relations and personal hygiene and fairness in personal relations and vocational activities. It is also supposed to provide broad political principles of participation in the public affairs of the community and organization of its economic and social concerns. As such, Shari'a is different from positive law because its binding force is supposed to be derived from the convictions of believers rather than the coercive power of the state. It is only this type of voluntary compliance that is consistent with the nature of Shari'a as the product of scholarly interpretation of religious texts. Moreover, the manner in which this system has actually evolved in practice has resulted in extensive diversity and disagreement among the founding scholars of the various schools of thought (*madhahib*). In contrast, the enforcement by the state today would require formal enactment as the law of the land or adoption of clear policies specifying certain action by organs of the state. To meet such requirements of the way a state must operate today, the legislature and government will have to choose among equally authoritative but different interpretations of the various madhahib, as well as of individual scholars within each one. Yet the leading individual scholars who founded those madhahib are unanimous in insisting that such choices are to be made by the believers according to their own conscience. Thus, what is represented as Shari'a is no longer the religious normative system of Islam once it is formally enacted for enforcement by the state.

Moreover, as a matter of historical fact, there has never been an Islamic state that consistently and systematically enforced Shari'a in the sense advocated today by some Muslims. The Prophet's state of Medina

(622–632) was of course of foundational normative importance, but it can neither be replicated, since the Prophet is no longer among us, nor compared to any of the subsequent Muslim imperial states, let alone with present-day increasingly complex states in their global context. The Medina state ruled over a very small area and population who lived in direct interpersonal contact under the immediate guidance of the Prophet, with no institutionalized organs, system of public administration, or security forces to enforce the will of the state within its own territory. It is clear that that form of political organization, if it can be called a state at all, is nowhere to found in the rest of Islamic history to the present day.

Even if one assumes, for the sake of argument, a degree of conceptual coherence or historical experience with states that can be called "Islamic" in the past, it would still be clear that such a state is not practically viable at the present time. A state that seeks to enforce some general principles of Shari'a regarding public affairs and governance would find it extremely difficult to fulfill its essential domestic and international functions in the present increasingly global context. A number of problems will arise from this perspective. First, the basic structure and political order of the state would be impossible to operate even for a small population of a few million people, as highlighted in chapter 1. Second, the denial of basic citizenship rights for women and non-Muslims will face serious challenge by these groups internally, and by the international community at large. Third, enforcement of corporal punishments for *hudud* offenses faces serious unresolved procedural and evidentiary objections, let alone human rights concerns about cruel, inhuman, or degrading treatment or punishment (An-Na'im 1990). Fourth, economic activities would be crippled by the prohibition of a fixed rate of interest on loans (*riba*), and of insurance as based on speculative contracts (*qharar*). Regarding this last point, however, the point is that it is not possible to operate a modern economy on these principles, and not that individual Muslim believers cannot or should not observe such prohibitions in their personal dealings. In other words, the state should neither impose religious prohibitions by law, nor prevent or interfere with voluntary compliance by believers as a matter of freedom of religion.

To note such limitations or problems with the modern application of Shari'a is not in the least to criticize that system in its own historical context, but only to object to its enforcement by the state today. The Shari'a principles that I find objectionable from a constitutional or practical point of view today were in fact consistent with the political and social values of the historical context in which they evolved and practically applied in building a major world civilization that flourished for many centuries across vast regions of the world. Being consistent with the values and institutions of their time (seventh to ninth centuries), the founding jurists of Shari'a did not address the need to limit the powers of the Caliph through notions of separation of powers or independence of the judiciary. Moreover, while those founding jurists were careful to explain a certain set of rights for women and those non-Muslims accepted as People of the Book (mainly Christians and Jews), they did not envision the possibility of equal rights of citizenship for these groups. Besides refusing to grant equal access for members of these groups to the highest ranks of public office, traditional Shari'a principles deny them equality before the law even in the daily administration of criminal justice, all on the grounds of gender and religion. For example, women and non-Muslims are denied the competence to testify in trials for capital offenses (*hudud*), and the monetary compensation that is to be paid for their homicide is less than that paid for Muslim men. While such aspects of Shari'a represented significant improvements on political and legal systems that prevailed throughout the premodern world, they are totally unacceptable from a constitutional point of view today.

Theoretically speaking, as I have argued elsewhere (An-Na'im 1990), these constitutional problems can be overcome through a particular degree of reinterpretation of the Qur'an and Sunna, but that process can only begin when the incompatibility of Shari'a with the principles of constitutionalism is acknowledged as a serious problem. Instead of taking this essential first step, the proponents of an Islamic state today tend to undermine the legitimacy of constitutionalism itself in the name of upholding the Islamic authenticity of the state and its institutions. What is more serious, however, is that the Muslim public at large finds it extremely difficult to resist these claims, which are presented in the name of Islam as a religion. That is, when ordinary Muslims are faced with claims that the absolute powers of the ruler (though not as a Caliph in the traditional sense) and the limitations on the rights of women and non-Muslims are decreed by Islam itself, in contrast to the demands of constitutionalism, which is presented as a secular Western notion, it becomes extremely difficult for Muslims to choose the latter over the former. This is the core of the unavoidable yet problematic relationship between Islam and constitutionalism I am concerned with in this and the next chapter.

It is not relevant for our purposes here to discuss the validity or viability of any specific Islamic reform methodology as such, whether the one I have argued for or another approach, because that is a matter of detailed, and probably highly technical, debate among Muslims. The more pertinent issue here is the practical difficulties facing the mediation of the tensions between Shari'a and constitutionalism, regardless of the precise reform methodology one is proposing to resolve those tensions.

Part of the problem, it seems to me, is the attitude of scholars and policy makers, both within Islamic societies and elsewhere, who take claims of the unity of Islam and the state at face value. Realistic mediation of the tensions can begin only when the issue is taken seriously, and framed in terms of historically conditioned forms of the relationship between Islam and the state, rather than a sharp dichotomy between total unity or categorical separation of religion and the state.

Given a clear understanding of the particularity of the relationship between Islam and constitutionalism in each Islamic society, the issue becomes one of understanding the basis and dynamics of this relationship as a historical process that is capable of change and transformation, rather than a permanent or inescapable fact. What is really at issue is the organic relationship between normative systems like constitutionalism, on the one hand, and the religious/cultural worldview, values, and institutions of any people who are expected to accept and implement such a system, on the other. The question is how can people of different religious/cultural traditions, even though they all live in the same country, agree to accept the same normative system? In other words, tensions in the relationship between Islam and constitutionalism in Islamic societies are simply specific manifestations of the broader problem of the cultural legitimacy and contextual sustainability of constitutionalism in those countries. To explore possibilities of mediating this tension I will now introduce the notion of contingency of the role of Islam in the African context.

Islam in Africa and African Islam: An Overview

Islam spread in different parts of Africa through a number of means, routes, and agents, from the initial conquest of North Africa in the seventh century, to gradual diffusion through trade and economic networks, the work of charismatic preachers and sufi (mystic) masters, conversion of political elites, and so forth. Gradually over four centuries beginning with the Muslim Arabs conquest of North Africa that began with the invasion of Egypt in 639, the whole North African region not only became predominantly Muslim but also increasingly culturally Arab. Islam began to spread significantly in West Africa in the tenth century through a peaceful process, as the Berbers propagated the religion across the Sahara desert, and the Sonike took it further south. This "relaying" of Islam, through local ethnic groups, helps explain why it was able to spread peacefully in West Africa, where its adaptability allowed it to become Africanized and accepted in the region. This mixing of African and Islamic religious elements "was typical of Islam in West Africa before the eighteenth century" (Levtzion 1994: 208). As traders represented Islam in this area many chiefs began adopting aspects of Islam to "maintain a middle position between Islam and paganism" in order to serve both communities (211).

In tropical Africa generally, Islam spread along trade routes. North African caravans moved south along the west coast, inland and down the Nile. The Red Sea coast provided direct access to Eastern Sudan, Ethiopia, and Somalia, while trade routes along the Indian Ocean led inland into tropical Africa. Muslim traders and artisans "seem often to have been the first bearers of Islam and to have at least prepared the ground for a later expansion of their faith, even where they made no efforts at direct proselytization" (Lewis 1980: 26). Teachers and holy men came with the traders to teach their children, and often married into the local communities. Leaders also brought teachers from West Asia. Eventually some self-perpetuating centers were established in key cities. Muslim clerics began to undertake secular roles. *Malams* and *sheikhs* (Islamic teachers and religious leaders) were "acting as negotiators and mediators, both internally—particularly in uncentralized societies—and externally, where in kingdoms and chiefdoms their knowledge of Arabic and participation in the para-ethnic culture of Islam made them especially valuable as agents and emissaries in external affairs" (Lewis 1980: 30).

The process is sometimes described in terms of three stages of conversion to Islam by nomads who settle in a particular place. The first stage is the quarantine stage in which these newly settled nomads live separately from the local population. The second stage is mixing in which the "local people begin to adopt Islamic ideas and Muslim clothes; the court begins to celebrate Islamic festivals as well as traditional ones and so on" (Hiskett 1984: 305). The third stage, which seems to come in cycles, is reform, in which puritan reformers seek to end the mixing stage, forcing everyone to observe "true" Islamic practices. The scope and manner of the spread of Islam in sub-Saharan Africa included local political, social, historical, and geographical factors, as well as the strength of traditional beliefs in an area before the introduction of Islam. In coastal East Africa, however, with long traditions of welcoming immigrants from great distances, cultural change was an inescapable fact of life (Pouwel 1987: 2). Although conversion to Islam may have been a conscious decision to distinguish oneself from other native Africans, the local understanding and practice of the religion not only was influenced by African culture, but also exhibited elements of Asian influence that created a culture distinct from coastal East African culture.

Trimingham proposed a model for the spread and integration of Islam in Africa that consists in juxtaposing African traditional religions which are assumed to precede the advent of Islam and historically independent from it, on the one hand, and Islam as a more or less alien, coherent body of beliefs and practices, on the other (Trimingham 1970, 1980).

His conception of Islam assumed it to be initially alien to the African continent and to have progressively invaded it, striking all sorts of locally specific compromises with pre-Islamic traditions. Van Binsbergen is critical of this model and proposes an intercultural philosophical perspective to demonstrate that African societies "are much more intricately a part of the wider world, and have always been, than would be suggested by the entrenched reified and utterly othering images of African religion and culture" (Binsbergen 1999: 2–3).

I find this view more helpful in evaluating the contingent role of Islam in Africa because the kinds of social, and political, and cultural changes and transformations associated with Islam cannot be reduced *solely* to either an "African" or "Islamic" agency or motivation. Moreover, to view the spread of Islam in a given context primarily in terms of its appeal as a religious ideology may draw on certain assumptions regarding the role of "religion" for the society in question. In contrast, I am using the phrase "contingent role of Islam" in this chapter in order to suggest that there are multiple possible directions and a complex set intersections leading to different outcomes of the relationship in different times and places. Within each context, the roles and meanings of Islam can be apparently contradictory and ambiguous, which is exactly my point. The notion of contingency means that a particular outcome can be simultaneously viewed as, on the one hand, local, African, and Islamic, and on the other hand, religious, ideological, social, cultural, and/or political. Indeed, the diversity of patterns of the spread of Islam indicates the different roles and purposes it served for different social segments, such as specific local communities, groups defined by vocation as traders or artisans, and so forth. In this long process of diffusion and growth, Islam played various pragmatic, ideological, political, cultural roles and functions, or a combination of some of them, in different contexts. In other words, after initial contact, Islam already becomes an integral part of the local networks and structures:

In Africa, diversity has produced rich traditions of widely varied religious meanings, beliefs, and practices. Islam energized, enlivened and animated life in African communities, and at the same time Islam has been molded by its African settings. As a result of the interaction between Muslim and African civilizations, the advance of Islam has profoundly influenced religious beliefs and practices of African societies, while local traditions have "Africanized" Islam. The ways Islam has thrived in the rich panoply of continent-wide historical circumstances have fostered discord at least as often as these ways of Islam have helped realize unity and disagreement. (Levtzion 1994: ix)

One domain of the mutual transformation that might be called the dynamic of Islamization in Africa and Africanization of Islam can be seen is relation to political authority, where different elements of Islam appear to have had varying degrees of importance in different locations. In West Africa, for instance, which had political traditions of centralized states, the legal traditions of Islam took root, whereas in North East Africa, with comparatively less centralized political organization, sufi (mystic) traditions were established. There is also evidence of the adoption of Shariʿa by nomadic people because it offered them some "political cohesion" despite their "geographical mobility" (Lewis 1980: 36). Leaders in centralized societies used various aspects of Islam to reinforce their power before they actually adopted Islam, which also gave them a legitimate reason to expand their territory in the name of conversion. Unlike indigenous African systems that lacked a cohesive unit to hold the polity together, "Islam provided a more cohesive pull and a stronger basis for empire building. It was no accident that the Islamic empires, such as Ghana and Kanauri, lasted the longest in Africa's history. Egalitarian elements of Islam, on the other hand, encouraged subject peoples to rise against their rulers" (37).

Hiskett argues that Islamic states in West Africa have been established by influencing existing states or by creating states where none had existed before (Hiskett 1984: 311). Pilgrimage to Mecca also helped increase the status of rulers and allowed them to create links with other Islamic states. Although in many cases states had existed before the introduction of Islam, Shariʿa played a role in creating empires out of these states in places like Mali, Songhay and Kano. However,

Islam was, of itself, never the sole agent in forming these states and empires. Many other factors such as conquest, trade, incoming strangers, slave-raiding and slave-trading, were also involved; what mattered was whether the persons engaged in these activities were Muslims or non-Muslims. If they were Muslims, the political organisations they created, whether simple states or more complex empires, naturally bore the marks of Islam to a greater or lesser extent. Otherwise, these organisations remained non-Islamic. (Hiskett 1984: 314)

Hiskett also points out that literacy played a most important part in the process of conversion to Islam and the establishment of an Islamic state (314–15).

Military conquest was also part of the processes of Islamization in Africa. For instance, the Almoravid Islamic sect, which flourished in the eleventh century in what is now Mauritania, "overwhelmed much of the western Sahel" (Griffiths 1995: 14). Their conquest "set the pattern for the ebb and flow of Islamization, of adaptive and reforming Islam, which remains a characteristic of Muslim communities ever since" (Quinn 2003: 19). The Maliki school, which was introduced into the region by the Almoravid movements as a fundamental framework of West African Islam, gave the region "a shared intellectual-legal frame of reference with the Maghrib (in a wide sense), Spain and (later) the Sudan" (Sanneh 1997: 30). But Islamic theocracies, like the Fulani Empire, did not appear in West Africa until the eighteenth and nineteenth centuries (Lewis 1980: 40–41), as a result of reformist movements which sought to purify West African Islam through *jihad* (religiously motivated war). Usman dan Fodio's "early nineteenth century jihad against the Hausa rulers of what is now northern Nigeria represents something of a revolution in Islamic thought in as much as it was a call for jihad against other Muslims" (Hunwick 1997: 31).

However, jihad was also a basis for anticolonial struggles in northwest Africa and the Sahel region across sub-Saharan Africa during the first quarter of the twentieth century, where it "continued to provide powerful motivation for diverse Muslim communities, although its focus was not so much internal reform as a defense of Muslim lands against the encroachments of European infidels. Most of these militant Islamic movements sought to maintain or re-establish an Islamic state that was either under attack or had been recently occupied by the European powers" (Stewart 1990: 194–95). Yet, by the mid-1920s, "jihad had been rejected as an anachronism in Muslim Africa. Islamic leaders and communities who sought to distance themselves from their Christian rulers joined others who, from the advent of colonial rule, had simply withdrawn from the political realities of colonial occupation" (200). Strategies of withdrawal included migration from colonially occupied territories, and calls by some reclusive religious leaders for non-involvement in temporal affairs as a way of ignoring the European presence (201, 202).

An important characteristic of African Islamic political authority is prophetic and charismatic leadership among sufi brotherhoods (*tariqas*). Although *tariqa* literally means "method" and is used to indicate a mystical path to Islam, the English translation "brotherhood" depicts another connotation of the word in Sufism as an identifiable, corporate group, though this quality varied and did not necessarily follow a specific formula. "The nature of this corporateness, and the extent to which it is employed for social and political ends, varies considerably among Sufis. And these variations depend less on the particular doctrine or religious rule of the *tariqa* than upon the intentions of a given leadership in the context of a given set of social, political, and religious conditions" (Brenner 1988: 34). Thus, it was the leader of a *tariqa* who would engage the brotherhood in social and political arenas, though in different ways, as illustrated by the following two cases.

Sidi al-Mukhtar al-Kunti (1729–1811) "clearly perceived the social and political, as well as religious, potential of the *tariqa* as a corporate entity" (Brenner 1988: 36). He saw himself as the religious leader who would renew Islam, but he did not believe in doing so by force. Instead, he believed that he could achieve renewal "by establishing a religious community which could serve as a refuge for those Muslims who wished to renew their own faith" (38). Al-Mukhtar's *tariqa* remained an independent religious brotherhood, unaffiliated with the secular state. This fact was probably facilitated by the fact that he lived among scattered desert communities. In contrast, Sheikh'Uthman b. Fudi (1754–1817), who lived in a more centralized state, did not establish an exclusive religious community, and required less absolute loyalty to his religious system while resisting the existing state at the same time. Brenner attributes the differences in these examples to the leaders' different "ideas about *tariqa* as a corporate organization, and differences in the socio-economic milieux in which they operated" (50).

The *tariqas* are described by Hunwick as a kind of pan-Islamic network, which "stress spiritual rather than intellectual knowledge, a feature that has enabled them to become mass movements—in a sense the 'churches' of Islam." In sub-Saharan Africa, the most extensive networks have been "(a) in the west, the Qadirriya and the Tijaniyya, and (b) in the Nile valley and the east, the various *tariqas* deriving from the teaching legacy of the early-nineteenth-century Moroccan mystic Ahmad b. Idris— notably the Sanusiyya in Chad, the Kahtmiyya in the Sudan/Eritrea and the Salihiyya in Somalia" (Hunwick 1997: 31–32).

Cruise O'Brien (1986) argues that Islam has benefited from its participation in democracy and locates democratic elements in West African Islam in three forms, namely, traditional or sufi, reformist, and revolutionary. Regarding traditional or sufi Islam, although critiques of Sufism have often focused on the complete subservience of the disciple to the master, teachers usually have "conditional authority" in which they provide services to their disciples in return for their devotion. Many *tariqas* are pan-Islamic but have had difficulty retaining a centralized authority over a wide area, especially as the colonial powers "remained distrustful of the interterritorial links of Sufism with a particular vigilance reserved for any 'pan-islamic' associations" (75). Sufis have participated in West African politics, but have also opposed existing authority. Reformers who want to "return to the original principles of Islam" are often directly opposed to traditional Islam in West Africa, while using instruments of modernity and the European-created territorial state to disseminate their message. One of the primary models of this type is the Wahabiyya, which was brought to French Sudan (now Mali) in the 1920s and 1930s by merchants returning from the pilgrimage (*hajj*) to Mecca, where the Wahaby Saudis were taking control of Arabia. The revolutionary Islam of the jihad movements prior to the consolidation of colonial powers in West Africa had a "charismatic democracy . . . in the fervent devotion of the charismatic following to the leader of holy war" (80).

For our purposes here, it is interesting to note that the constitutional model of the Medina state of the Prophet continued to influence the political thinking of African Islamic leaders, especially during the jihad periods in West Africa. As noted in the preceding review, they often tried to resurrect that model as the ideology of the states they established, or for the reform movements they initiated. At the same time, however, a different model of Islamic political organization was often attempted by Sufi leaders who sought to reconcile their followers with living under a secular state that did not attempt to enforce Shariʿa as the positive law of the land. In this sense, the Sufi tradition, which is the more popular approach among African Muslims, appears to be more consistent with modern principles of constitutionalism. It is also clear, it seems to me, that the contingency of the ideological and political role of Islam throughout the region has reflected a dialectic relationship among internal and external actors and factors, ranging from the possibilities of transregional pan-Islamic networks earlier, whether traditional, sufi, or militant Wahaby doctrine of Saudi Arabia, to the impact of confrontation with European colonialism. Some elaboration on the impact of the colonial encounter may be particularly relevant for its impact on the contingent role of Islam in the postcolonial context.

Islam and the Colonial Encounter in Africa

The role of Islam in African societies has partly been shaped by its encounter with colonialism, as the two had complex and often contradictory relationships, varying according to the shifts in colonial policy. At the same time, Islam also provided a zone of autonomy and resistance to colonialism. For instance, although the "anti-Islamic" dimension and fear of Islam was an integral aspect of French colonial policies, this period witnessed the fastest expansion of Islam in the region (Triaud 2000: 169). The hostility was rooted in various sources, religious as well as the tenets of the Enlightenment which called for a separation of religion and the state, thereby conditioning French perceptions of Islam by the struggle of republicans and radical secularists against Roman Catholicism in France itself. "French colonialism always experienced the Muslim presence in the guise of a counter-revolutionary conspiracy" (170). Thus, when the French first encountered the Muslim Sufi brotherhoods in Algeria, they "were immediately likened to their presumed European counterparts, in particular to the Jesuits, who were a "secret society" par excellence, being conspiratorial and subversive in the eyes of republicans of the epoch" (170).

The classification of all Muslims according to brotherhood affiliation that was initially adopted in Algeria, sometimes contrary to the available evidence, was applied across the Sahara, and "remained one of the found-ations of colonial administrative taxonomy up to independence" (Triaud 2000: 171). Theories of French specialists and ethnographers devalued Islam in the evolutionary chain. "The intensive use of polemical anti-Islamic literature, which was sometimes obsessive, created a common 'culture of Muslim affairs' with which a large number of civil and military functionaries became permanently infused" (172). However, there were also competing perspectives among colonial administrators, some favorable and others hostile to Islam and Islamic groups. For instance, in Senegal and Mauritania, the Qadariyya were marked and treated as the "good" brotherhoods and the Tijaniyya were the "bad." In Algeria, it was exactly the opposite.

After World War I, it seems that "the fear of Islam and of a conspiracy that would take its orders abroad, in Germany and in Turkey, finally over-rode all other considerations" (Triaud 2000: 172). French colonial policies accordingly reflected assessments of Islam and Muslims in terms of loy-alty to France over other European powers during the war. Different groups of Muslims won favor and cooperated with the colonial administration:

In Senegal, the talents of the Mourid brotherhood, which corresponded to the needs and the demands of the administration, won quasi-immunity for the broth-erhood in the French colonial system. Elsewhere, networks of Muslim merchants, particularly the Julula, thanks to their role as intermediaries along the railway routes and the trails, benefited from the protection of an administration with vested interests. Muslim elites and the French administration found the terms for a lasting compromise, albeit one that was at times disturbed by fits of mistrust. Under the Popular Front, de Copper, the socialist governor general of French West Africa, renewed links with "Islamophile" practices close to the British style, in-cluding attending the major Muslim feasts, subsidizing Islamic institutions, and giving instructions in this vein to the administrators. (Triaud 2000: 176)

In contrast to a general policy of compromise and cooperation, the French colonial administration of West Africa sometimes ruthlessly repressed the followers of Shaykh Hamahallah, a branch of the Tijaniyya. The Shaykh was deported to Mauritania, Côte d'Ivoire, followed by Algeria, until he eventually died in Montlucon, France, in 1940, while his followers were sent to internment camps. The crushing of the Hamallah was used as an example to intimidate those who sought to take Islamic authority beyond the control of the French administration of West Africa (Triaud 2000: 176).

After World War II, there was a focus on economic development and political liberalization, but the Arab/Palestinian conflict in the Middle East and the Algerian war of independence kept the French colonial ad-ministration deeply worried about Islam. The administration continued to utilize the theory of "Black Islam" as a means to cut the Muslims off from their Arab fellow believers, while continuing to follow the brotherhood model, most prominently in Senegal. The target of the colonial administration in this phase was Wahaby doctrine imported by young preachers with its emphasis on purity and reform. Those young preachers were regarded by French colonial administrations in the 1950s as part of a Middle Eastern/North African conspiracy. But with the imminence of decolonization and its change in the dynamics of power, and the institution of local autonomy in 1956, the colonial bureaucratic systems were no longer able to stem these changes (Triaud 2000: 177).

The relationship of Islamic movements and groups with French colonial administration in West Africa was a mixture of resistance and cooperation. The officially recognized Islamic movement benefited from cooperation with the French administrators, who always accorded a certain status to religion, even when they were generally hostile or negative to its role in West African colonies. At independence, however, French-educated elites replaced religious elites who also had to deal with the impact of the colonial French policy that sought to undermine Islamic culture. As a result, according to Triaud, there was a contradiction in the colonial period, a huge increase in numbers of Muslims, on the one hand, and "a substantial defensive conservatism, or stagnation, of thought and intellectual reflection," on the other (2000: 182).

During the next phase of decolonization, the symbols of Islam were mobilized for an essentially modern political form of the state and nation. For instance, "the key feature of Islam in Tunisia during the preindependence period was not that there was a modernist interpretation that emerged but, rather, that Islam provided the symbols and the vocabulary for a mobilization of the people in opposition to foreign rule" (Voll 1982: 209). Algerian nationalism was formed in a more complex manner, where the crux of the nationalist imperative was to define a distinctive Algerian identity in the wake of a colonial effort to destroy the basic social order through a political and cultural offensive, as well as the establishment of a large European settler population. In that context, "the struggle was to define the meaning of being an Algerian, a process in which Islam played a significant role" (209). Islam in Algeria provided the symbolism and emotion of the Algerian revolution, thereby complementing, instead of competing with, nationalism. It was also a major aspect of the resistance to European rule and emergence of nationalism in Morocco as well (212–13).

Once again, however, the dynamics of the role of Islam shifted with a change in context, from a struggle for independence to post-independence governance in the Maghrib (Tunisia, Algeria, and Morocco), despite the violence of the liberation struggle.

In this transition, the key issues relating to the Islamic experience involved the problems of modernization and nation-building. In particular, once the common enemy was removed, debate arose over the appropriate ideological and programmatic foundations for modernization. During the 1960s, the major development in the area was the evolution of a more secularist socialism. This ideological approach became a powerful force by the middle of the decade but then declined in importance. Parallel to that process was a decline and then a revival of a more visibly Islamic orientation. (Voll 1982: 215)

Another feature of the paradoxical relationship of Islam and colonial administrations relates to ways in which Islamic leaders were able to retain a degree of autonomy that was, to a significant extent, ordained by colonial policies. This paradox is illustrated by the codification of Shariʿa principles in specific fields of family law and inheritance, while at the same time separating Islam from the sphere of official political authority. That codification fixed the nature of Islamic authority, contributing to notions of "authentic" Islamic authority as being that which is officially recognized by the state. Colonial administrators also privileged certain Islamic groups over others through "indirect rule," and sponsored certain "Islamic" officials, like the Grand Mufti, who was in charge of issuing officially sanctioned religious rulings on a specific matters placed under his jurisdiction by the colonial administration. The approval of Islamic titles, sanction of the Arabic language, and acknowledgment of Shariʿa in general by colonial administrators served to confirm and reinforce the importance of Islamic institutions. The codification of Shariʿa principles in the limited field of so-called law of personal status also resulted in the establishment of a "Shariʿa judiciary" distinguished, if not institutionally separate from, the regular "civil judiciary" which had jurisdiction in all other legal matters. That colonial codification and specialization in the administration of justice also introduced a new degree of uniformity and consistency in the applications of Shariʿa throughout individual colonies or protectorates, and formalized a division between state authority and religious institutions. This process had the dual effect of undermining the adaptability of Shariʿa to local customary law, despite the long history of mutual accommodation of the two systems, while extending the application of Shariʿa in legal matters to some communities where it previously had little impact (Stewart 1990: 205–6). In that way, changes introduced by various colonial administrations set the scene for the formal and institutional relationship between Islam and the emerging independent states of Africa with majority Muslim populations. A brief discussion of this latest phase may help clarify the contingency of the role of Islam in the constitutional development of present African states.

Islam and the State in the Postcolonial Era

In this section, I first highlight aspects of the relationship between Islam and the postcolonial territorial state in the transition to independence, and then offer some reflections on the implications of this recent history for the future development of constitutionalism in Islamic African societies. To begin with the overview, Shahin (1997) locates the contemporary role of Islam in Tunisia, Algeria, and Morocco in terms of its historical role. Islam not only had a dynamic part in shaping the popular culture of the people and the structure of these societies up to independence, but also continued to affect political values and responses in these countries, despite the changes in conditions and circumstances after colonialism The state controls the institutional practice and formal public teaching of Islam, in order to silence religious-based opposition and draw mass cohesion to affirm the legitimacy of "a Westernized political elite with little in common with the masses" (Shahin 1997: 19). More generally, Islam has been both unifying and divisive in the African political context. On the one hand, African countries with majority or significant Muslim populations have developed ties with Islamic Arab and Asian countries, thereby generating solidarity regarding the Middle East conflict and decolonization in Africa. On the other hand, Islam has caused tensions between African and Arab states in relation to certain armed conflicts, such as those during the 1980s in Chad and Eritrea.

Since identities in general are constructed within sociopolitical processes, and in response to shifting needs and concerns, Islamic identities tend also to include claims of more "authentic" representation of Islam as a means of appropriating influence among Muslims and to exclude or marginalize their "competitors." This happened between the Qadiriyya and Tijaniyya in Mali. Despite the fear of Islamic institutions by the government of Mali and international development agencies, the Wahabis have actually become quite adept at creating social programs to help local communities. A tension grew into the politics of Mali as Moussa Traoré increasingly identified himself and the country as both Muslim and secular during his period of leadership in 1968–1991. This became institutionalized in the government sponsored national Muslim organization, the Association Malienne pour l'Unité et le Progrès de l'Islam (AMUPI) which paralleled the single political party of Mali, the Union Démocratique du Peuple Malien (UDPM). Thus, constructions of Muslim identity occur within multiple "social formations" as the public expression of economic and political conflict.

The use of violence as a strategy of opposition by Islamist movements in the Middle East and North Africa during the last quarter of the twentieth century can better be understood through contextual analysis instead of as a question of doctrine. Islam neither forbids violence for religious causes, nor encourages it. The doctrinal view does not tell us when or why believers actually resort to violence in some situations and not in others, or whether or why such resort to violence is understood to be Islamic. Instead, Lisa Anderson emphasizes "political circumstances or institutional environment, that breeds political radicalism, extremism, or violence independent of the content of the doctrine . . . there are circumstances that foster radical political strategies and, conceivably, resort to violence, independent of the content of political beliefs, just as there may be conditions that encourage political movements to work within the system, however radical their ideologies" (Anderson 1997: 17, 18).

In the debate over whether Islamic parties should be included in the political process in Algeria and Tunisia, supporters of their inclusion cited the positive example of Marxist parties in France and Italy who are legitimate participants in the electoral democratic process, despite their ideological advocacy of class revolution and moral and financial ties to foreign Marxist powers. Opponents of the inclusion of Islamic parties, in contrast, pointed to counter European experiences, like that of the Nazi party in Germany, which came to power through the electoral process only to turn around and change the rules to maintain exclusive totalitarian power. A particularly helpful point made by Anderson is to note the relationship between opposition and what it opposes:

Opposition, however, has the unusual characteristic of being defined partly by what it opposes; it develops within and in opposition to an ideological and institutional framework and, as such, reveals a great deal not only about its own adherents but also about the individuals, policies, regimes, and states in authority. This is particularly true of illegal political opposition, since the decision to prohibit the expression of dissident voices is one that can be taken only by those in a position to determine legality; the authorities themselves. Any examination of the nature of illegal political opposition also illuminates the nature of regimes in power. (Anderson 1997: 18–19)

The preceding remarks regarding North Africa can usefully be extended to a wider view of these issues in the Middle East in general, especially in view of the strong influence of that region on Islamic developments in sub-Saharan Africa. Throughout the Middle East and North Africa, with some possible partial exceptions like Lebanon before the civil war, nondemocratic rule was the order of the day till the mid-1970s. A variety of internal and external factors from the beginning of the 1980s onward compelled political authorities to reconsider their relations with the generality of their citizens. As public acquiescence declined, regimes had to find new incentives for political stability and cooperation. "Starting in the mid-1970s in Egypt and continuing in the next decade and a half in Tunisia, Algeria, Jordan, Yemen, and, to a lesser extent, Morocco and Kuwait, press censorship was lifted, political prisoners released, political parties authorized, and contested elections held" (Anderson 1997: 20). However, the aim of these measures was to consolidate the power of the elite, rather than promoting genuine democracy and allowing legitimate political competition. This was the political context within which Islamist movements emerged as an alternate space possessing a legitimacy that the governments themselves lacked. Since nationalism as an ideology could not, in and of itself, justify the actions of regimes nor provide a participatory space of any kind, the alternate ideological vision of the umma proved more compelling.

The early conception of Hasan al-Banna and the Egyptian Muslim Brotherhood of the "comprehensiveness of Islam" lent itself both to a broad social project and a challenge of the social welfare ambitions of the secular postindependence states.... In providing free medicine, distributing school equipment, organizing garbage collection, offering legal and administrative advice, organizing scouting groups, the Islamists also played roles in social life that governments had once claimed but then abdicated. (Anderson 1997: 24)

This dialectical relationship between government and opposition is clearly illustrated by the rise of the Front Islamique du Salut (FIS) out of popular opposition to the policies of the singleparty Front de Libération Nationale (FLN). The FIS provided social services in emergency situations such as earthquakes, and ensured law and order, which the government was unwilling or unable to do. While both sides framed the debate in ideological terms, FIS not only effectively discredited the FLN regime by becoming an alternative provider of public services, it also did better than all the secular political opposition. In contrast, the secular opposition to the FLN developed little or no grassroots following because it defined its mandate in narrowly political terms, such as contesting elections or publishing newspapers, and avoided social or economic activities (Anderson 1997: 24).

However, the ambiguity in the programs and agendas of Islamist groups was apparently a cause as well as a consequence of their support across social sectors. Their vague and often emotional appeals to popular sentiment made it difficult to ascertain their real ideological positions. At the same time, this enabled them to attract popular support for broad unspecific claims that were unverifiable for the purposes of proper political accountability. Moreover, as a general rule, Islamist movements became more pragmatic when the prospects of sharing power became stronger, although it is impossible to categorically determine whether this is tactical or genuine political compromise. It may well be true that governmental repression begets such ambivalence in the opposition, failure to recognize genuine political opposition, the tendency to treating it as disloyalty to be suppressed, leads both the regime and its opponents to resort to violence (Anderson 1997: 25–29).

Recalling earlier discussion of the postcolonial state in Africa, colonialism has radically transformed African politics by imposing the European model of the nation-state, with all its normative and institutional assumptions, extensive centralized powers to regulate economic and social activities. Colonialism also transformed international relations and trade by globalizing European models of nation state as the primary focus of political and economic relations among peoples of Africa and Asia. At the same time, however, colonial administrations had very little to do with local African communities who were politically controlled by local elites on behalf of the colonial administration, the so-called "indirect rule" or "native administration," but otherwise left entirely on their own. Other colonial administrations superimposed European "nation" state models not only in the absence or inadequacy of the presumed preconditions, but also without bothering to promote or supplement those conditions over time. Far from encouraging national unity and cohesion that might have helped adapt those models, colonial administrations vigorously pursued divide and rule strategies to keep local populations politically divided through manipulations of ethnic and religious affiliations. That is why I prefer to use the term "territorial" instead of "nation" state in relation to postcolonial African states, as explained in chapter 1 earlier.

Also recalling earlier discussions in Chapter 2, colonialism also coopted a variety of elite leaders to implement its policies, and educated some of them for middle and lower level administrative positions. By the end of colonial regimes, those who were educated in European style schools took over the state and continued its operation along colonial models that sought to perpetuate the assumptions of constitutionalism and the rule of law as they operated in European countries. With minimal preparation for the educated elites, and far less for the general local population at large, African societies were supposed to adapt and operate the complex constitutional and legal orders applied by their respective former colonial powers. Thus, most African societies were suddenly supposed to replicate British or French constitutional and legal systems, compete in global markets, and engage in international relations as sovereign states, with little preparation for these functions of sovereignty.

Moreover, those elites who came to control of the state were not in touch with the realities of their own populations, and had little understanding of how to relate constitutional principles such as protection of human rights, independence of judiciaries, and separation of powers, to the popular culture of local populations. In the case of Islamic African societies in particular, ruling elites had very little understanding of how to negotiate the relationship between Islam and the post-colonial "secular" state, with its expansive powers and ability to control the daily lives of its population. This tension was minimal in the precolonial and colonial contexts precisely because the state was a distant authority that left local Islamic communities to administer their own affairs according to their respective customary practices, including elements of Shari'a. It is only to be expected, then, that secular nationalist project failed to deliver on their promises of political liberation, economic development and social justice, especially in North African countries like Algeria, Egypt, and Tunisia. The consequent widespread disillusionment, especially among the newly educated young generations, created a most receptive environment for Islamist groups and parties in opposition to the regimes in power (Shahin 1997).

In their desperate search for a viable alternative, postcolonial Islamic societies turned to traditional understandings of Islam, which offered archaic notions of the state, law, and society that are totally unsuited for the realities of a pluralistic territorial state in its modern global context. In particular, using readily available models based on traditional principles outlined in chapter 1, Islamists appeal to legalistic, austere, puritanical perceptions of Islam, in the Wahaby doctrine sponsored by Saudi Arabia, or the discourse of the Muslim Brothers movement spreading south from North Africa. The proponents of this view deploy the discourse of a long tradition of scholarly and theological development of a more textual and legalistic understanding of Islam, presented as the vehicle of self-determination for Islamic African societies. They tend to see this view as the only viable alternative to what they perceive to be discredited colonial Western models of constitutionalism and their underlying ideology of the state. The proponents of this re-Islamization of African societies insisted on keeping the colonial notion of the territorial state and its expansive powers, but sought to transform the orientation of its policy and legal system to fit their ideas of Islam. In fact, what the Islamists of the 1980s and 1990s sponsored was a totalitarian project that seeks to transform people's lives, attitudes, and manners of behavior through controlling the state and transforming its institutions in the service of Middle Eastern understandings of Islam.

This postcolonial cycle of contestation of the meaning and relevance of Islam in relation to constitutionalism is different from previous episodes of Islam in Africa and African Islam, discussed earlier, because of the dynamic nature of Islamism in the age of globalization. Recent technological developments have facilitated previously unthinkable degrees of economic and political interdependence and cross-cultural influence.

As a result, ideas about Islam, its relationship to the state and politics, and the impact of political and social movements can have far-reaching consequences throughout Africa and beyond, over remarkably short periods of time. But these recent features do not necessarily dictate a particular outcome of the interaction of Islam and constitutionalism. In terms of the thesis of this book, these developments emphasize not only the contingency of that relationship, but also a larger scale and faster speed of one outcome or another, than was the case in the past. In other words, the present intensity of global and regional interaction of ideas about Islam and constitutionalism can facilitate either a positive or negative relationship between the two in ways that can affect more people, throughout the world, and in less time, than ever before.

However, as I hope to demonstrate by contrasting the cases of Sudan, Nigeria, and Senegal in the next chapter, the outcome of this discourse still depends on a variety of factors. In particular, the intensified contingency of this relationship is compounded by what might be described as a double crisis. On the one hand, the colonial and postcolonial territorial state has not really managed to strike roots and become legitimate among its own African Muslim population. On the other hand, relatively more inclusive, pluralistic, and adaptive local understandings of Islam are being challenged by militant legalistic and puritan notions of Islam that seek to transform local societies. That is, the principles and institutions of constitutionalism are undermined by the inability of the postcolonial state to apply them effectively, while being challenged by a re-Islamization campaign that seeks to introduce principles and institutions that are fundamentally inconsistent with constitutional governance.

To suggest mediating this complex contingency in favor of the incremental success of constitutionalism in the Islamic context of some African countries, I would invoke what might be called "the principle of cultural transformation," as spontaneous, gradual, incremental internal process of cultural adaptation and change (An-Na'im 2002b). To say that it is internal is not to suggest that it is not influenced by external forces and factors, because cultures adapt in response to both internal and external stimuli. As no human society lives in isolation from other societies, interaction with other societies is an integral part of how each culture adapts to its changing context. Indeed, as just noted, the present accelerated and intensified rate and scale of globalization generate a strong dynamic interaction between internal and external factors and forces in the processes of cultural transformation more than ever before. Moreover, to emphasize the internal transformation process is not to suggest that it is totally arbitrary or unpredictable, although the underlying notion of contingency implies that outcomes can vary depending on the role of various actors, factors, and context.

Determined and well-informed actors can make a difference to the outcome of the relationship between Islam and constitutionalism by deploying deliberate strategies to promote their own vision of the social good. In relation to the thesis of this book, the question is whether African Muslim policy makers, social scientists, and lawyers can promote an Islamic rationale of the principles and institutions of constitutionalism in ways that are persuasive to their Muslim constituencies. More specifically, I am suggesting that this process of promoting constitutionalism through the current dynamics of cultural transformation of Islamic African societies should be seen as a function of competing visions of African Islam and re-Islamization according to Middle Eastern perspectives. The appeal of the latter, which has antecedents in the West African jihad movements of the eighteenth and nineteenth centuries, is supported by the desire among local communities to be part of a powerful international entity, the Islamic umma at large. This desire is probably motivated by the promise of the benefits of modernity while maintaining a strong sense of Islamic identity. Sustainable mediation must therefore address this underlying psychological and sociological need, and work out its constitutional implications—to balance appropriate recognition of and respect for the former with the requirements of the latter. After all, constitutionalism is about realizing the people's right to self-determination, not repudiating it.

In conclusion of this section, I would emphasize that the outcome of internal debates about the political and legal role of Islam is far from settled by claims of either complete fusion or total separation. This ambivalence also runs deep. The North African Islamic historian Ibn Khaldun (d. 1406/7) maintained that if worldly affairs and religion were mixed both would suffer, yet he suggested that religion can be important only as basis of a political umma rather than as personal faith based on persuasion and choice (Sanneh 1997: 199). So far in this chapter I have sought to clarify the terms and context of this internal Islamic debate, while emphasizing that outcomes are contingent on identifiable conditions rather than predetermined by some doctrinal imperative. Part of this clarification is the need to distinguish between the necessity to secure the institutional separation of Islam and the state, while recognizing and regulating the interconnectedness of Islam and politics. In the next section, I elaborate on another perspective that might facilitate the regulation of the unavoidable political role of Islam in favor of constitutionalism in Islamic African societies.

Culture, Religion, and the State

In light of the preceding review and analysis, I am suggesting that the relationship between Islam and constitutionalism in Africa should be understood within the framework of the dialectic of what might be called "Islamization in Africa and Africanization of Islam," as aspects of the broader context of culture, religion, and politics. This constant dialectic, it seems to me, emphasizes the basic tension between certain objectives of politicization of Islam and the constitutional and legal imperatives of the postcolonial territorial states all Africans have to live in. In particular, traditional forms of Africanized Islam might provide better prospects for reconciliation between the Islamic cultural identity of African Muslims, on the one hand, and the requirements of their daily lives in multicultural, multireligious states, on the other. Though a more precise and nuanced analysis of specific situations may dispute some aspects of this generalization, I believe that it is sufficiently true of enough situations to be useful for understanding the role of Islam in the development of African constitutionalism in its various settings.

As outlined earlier, Islam came to North Africa within a few decades of its beginning in seventh-century Arabia, and spread into sub-Saharan African very gradually, primarily through migration, cultural integration, and assimilation. But that gradual Islamization of Africa also meant the Africanization of Islam, by adapting it to the social and economic realities of African communities. However, a counter re-Islamization occurred during the last three decades of the twentieth century, efforts to transform and mobilize the Islamic identities of Africans in pursuit of certain political objectives. This re-Islamization has taken a variety of forms and directions, some of which are clearly inconsistent with the need for political stability, economic development, and social justice. The question is whether it is possible to direct or orient these processes of re-Islamization to promote consensus and collaboration among Muslims and non-Muslims on principles of constitutionalism?

Essentially, the Africanization of Islam is simply a regional manifestation of a historical phenomenon of adaptation and indigenization of Islam wherever it managed to spread in the past, from southeast, southern and central Asia, to north and sub-Saharan Africa. This adaptability, whereby people can become Muslims by a confession of the faith and the practice of devotional rituals like prayer and fasting, while retaining many of their own norms and institutions, has in fact facilitated the remarkable spread of Islam over the centuries. That is, instead of seeking to displace preexisting local cultures, propagators of Islam have traditionally endorsed and incorporated local traditions into the core ethical precepts of social justice and practical expediency they sought to promote. This is not to suggest that there was no conflict and tension between Islamic precepts and the pre-Islamic norms and institutions of Islamized communities. Rather, whenever conflicts or tensions arose or were perceived, the mediation of local customary practices was so gradual and minimal that it was hardly offensive or overtly intrusive. In time, I suggest, Islam was itself localized in the process.

Africanized Islam, with its strong sufi (mystical) roots, was inclusive and tolerant of diversity among Muslims and in their relationships with non-Muslim communities. But that approach remained at the spontaneous grass-roots level, and did not manage to develop a superstructure of ideas or "theology," probably because people accepted and lived by it without much theorizing about its theological foundations or formal legal implications. But the lack of corresponding theological developments meant vulnerability to challenge as "un-Islamic" from a Middle Eastern, purportedly orthodox point of view. However, when such challenge was mounted during various jihad movements of the eighteenth and nineteenth centuries, the impact was limited in scope and/or duration because of the highly decentralized nature of precolonial African societies, with their minimal political structures that did not seek to regulate people's daily lives. One can see the contingency of the role of Islam at that time in the different ways in which the jihad movements evolved and adapted to their local contexts in sub-Saharan Africa.

The nature and possible outcomes of the current challenge to Africanized Islam is still unfolding, but one can already observe certain elements of the notion of contingency. It is possible, on the one hand, that this cycle of re-Islamization may turn out to be more effective in transforming the lives of the Muslims and non-Muslims of sub-Saharan Africa because of its ability to control and manipulate the postcolonial territorial state, with its more effective institutions and expansive powers. That is, the scope, speed, and dynamics of transformation may be on a larger scale and faster than in the previous cycle in its ability to use the educational administrative and judicial institutions of the state. But it is also reasonable to expect, that the ability of various actors to reach and compete for influence on these institutions makes it difficult to predict the precise outcomes of these processes. Moreover, the regional and global nature of the cross-cultural and political interaction adds to the contingency of the role of Islam in relation to constitutionalism. In other words, the same factors that indicate greater risks to constitutionalism also open new possibilities of its sustainable development throughout the region and beyond.

Thus, there seem to be two main competing currents of Islamic thinking and practice, or visions of Islamic identities and their political, constitutional, and legal consequences. These competing currents of thought and visions of identity correspond, broadly speaking, to the above-mentioned notion of an indigenized Africanized reality of Islam, on the one hand, and a Middle Eastern, militant, literalist theocratic vision of Islam. Each of these opposing visions seeks to transform Islamic

African societies into its own image through processes of cultural transformation that combine internal change and external influence. Culture, as the totality of institutional values that regulate social, economic, and political relations of the community, is the object of this contestation, as well being the medium through which contestation is happening. But both aspects are difficult to observe and analyze, at least within a brief timeframe, because of the pervasiveness, spontaneity, and subtlety of cultural processes.

Still, as emphasized earlier, the processes of cultural transformation are not totally arbitrary or unpredictable. Culture enables human beings to adapt to their social and physical environment, the ways each culture depends on the nature and dynamics of change in that environment. Understanding those changes can help in identifying or predicting the ways in which local cultures will adapt to them. The ability to identify or predict outcomes of processes of cultural transformation is also related to people's understanding of the parameters and dynamics of the flexibility and adaptability of culture. At the same time, I would emphasize, these parameters and dynamics are themselves the subject of constant renegotiation and transformation. In other words, dynamism and change are inherent to every aspect of culture and its operation, including perceptions of what can or cannot change about culture. However, in hoping and planning for cultural transformation in favor of enhancing the prospects of constitutional governance, I am counting on the fact that the continuous contingency of the role of Islam is not beyond the realm of human agency, and the choice and action people can take in that regard.

As an integral part of culture, the understanding and practice of religion are factors in the processes of adaptation and transformation, as well as being influenced or shaped by them to varying degrees. This is not to say that religion is exclusively defined by culture, or vice versa, because of the transcendental dimensions of religion, at least in the case of Islam. Nor is it to suggest that the identity of a community is totally determined by its religious affiliation, or that the daily behavior of its members can ever be fully consistent with their religious beliefs. Muslims are not only Muslims, nor do they behave all of the time as such, though Islam is fundamental to their cultural identity, social institutions, and daily behavior. The point here is simply that the impact of Islam on social and political institutions is itself the subject of negotiation in the processes of cultural transformation. What Islam means for a particular community at any given time is the product of Muslims' understanding of the historical scriptural tradition in their own context, which is influenced by the processes of current adaptation and transformation. Islam can only be understood and practiced by people acting through their specific social and political relations, and never as an abstract concept.

While I personally believe in the transcendental dimension of Islam, it is clear to me that that cannot be relevant and meaningful to the social and political relations of Muslims, among themselves and in relation to others, except through the role of human agency: the ability of people to construct meaning and negotiate their relationships to each other, their ability to act or their failure to act accordingly to their perceptions of their best interest.

The same analysis would suggest that the relationship between religion and the state is both the site of contestation and its outcome. Religious symbols and discourse, as cultural resources, are deployed by various actors in their effort to control the state, while state institutions are used to shape popular understandings of religion. It is therefore not surprising that competing constituencies and perspectives seek to control the state, or at least those parts they find most useful for advancing their particular religious/ideological objectives. Such instruments of what might be called the politics of culture include the educational system, the judiciary, and the legal profession, as well as popular institutions like the media, the arts and literature.

One issue arising from this view of the state as the product and object of cultural contestation in the present African context is that cultural boundaries, to the extent identifiable, are far from concurrent with the political borders of the state. On the one hand, the boundaries of culture tend to go beyond the political borders of the state, while a given territorial state normally includes a variety of cultures. The present state of Sudan, for example, encompasses many cultures, while some of them extend beyond the political borders of the country into Chad, Congo,, Uganda, Kenya, and Ethiopia. Both phenomena reflect the arbitrariness of European colonialism that often forced divergent groups into the same political entity, while keeping apart others who could have belonged well with each other. Which European power, Britain, France, Belgium, or Portugal, happened to conquer or otherwise gain control over which territories first, or trade them for another territory, as happened through the so-called mandate system of the League of Nations after the First World War, was a historical accident. In the process, European colonial powers often forced populations together or apart, and transformed their social and political institutions beyond recognition.

This state of affairs raises risks of political instability, civil war, and threats of secession to establish a separate state, due to perceptions of cultural, including religious, hegemony of some groups over others within the same territorial state. Whether Somalis in Ethiopia, or Christians in southern Sudan, the plight of cultural or religious minorities can attract external sympathy and support from neighboring countries or the international community at large. Regardless of one's view of the justice of the grievances of a particular minority, or realistic prospects of the success of their protest/secessionist movement, such situations have clear implications for the development of constitutionalism in Africa. These problems are compounded by the weakness of the postcolonial state, as outlined in Chapter 2 earlier, and its vulnerability to external pressures of geopolitical competition, economic globalization, or of structural adjustment programs imposed by the International Monetary Fund (IMF), that tend to diminish its sovereignty over its own territory, economy, and domestic policies.

The weakness and artificiality of the postcolonial state in African does not prevent it from controlling the lives and livelihood of its population. In fact, I argue, perceptions of the helplessness and indifference to the state, especially among rural populations who see little evidence of its power or resources, are both misconceived and dangerous. However weak and artificial it may be, the state is still a fundamental reality for their own populations through its almost exclusive and overwhelming power, to monopolize the use of force and mobilize economic resources and legal institutions to enforce its will on the population. The state has the exclusive authority to levy taxes and to disperse the income as it deems fit, to develop and enforce national policies on social and economic relations, regulate international trade, and so forth. In fact, the weakness and vulnerability of the state, especially in relation to external actors, may make it more determined to exercise whatever degree of control it can over its own population, regardless of the consequences for that population. Underestimating the power of such states is dangerous because it can encourage indifference to the critical need for their political and legal accountability to their own populations. For our purposes here, this situation has the paradoxical result of making constitutionalism and its safeguards more important for local populations, yet harder to achieve in a sustainable manner.

Concluding Remarks: Contingency and Legitimacy

As indicated earlier, I am arguing for using the notion of contingency to promote possibilities of alternative initiatives and outcomes of the politics of cultural/Islamic identity, including ones that are conducive or antagonistic to the incremental success of constitutionalism. The premise of this argument is that it is grossly misleading to see Islam as a given, objectified, self-contained, static body of doctrine and rituals, as if it has an abstract existence, independent of the consciousness and daily experiences of Muslims everywhere. Similarly, it is dangerously simplistic to take Islam as a totalizing ideology and theology that demands blind and unquestioning obedience from its adherents, regardless of the requirements of their lives in complex local and global conditions of interdependence and cooperation. Instead, I am calling for Muslims' understanding and practice of Islam, how it relates to various aspects of their lives as Muslim individuals and communities, as well as in their relationships to non-Muslims close and far around them, all to be seen as the subject and outcomes of constant negotiation and mediation. Assuming that the contingency thesis is accepted, how can it be applied in favor of constitutional governance in Islamic African societies?

It is critical to my thesis and argument in this regard that one should not be fatalistic or deterministic about the dynamics and outcome of the contestations of cultural/religious identify and politics, or their implications for constitutionalism. The politics of cultural/religious identity can be positive in affirming individual and collective human dignity and self-determination, which are the foundation of sustainable constitutionalism. Cultural identity is equally important for adapting universal features of constitutionalism to the immediate environment and context of the person and community, instead of attempting to implement clearly unworkable or irrelevant principles. To affirm this possible line of thinking and action is not to deny the counter-possibility that the politics of cultural/religious identity can be negative to the extent that it negates or diminishes the human dignity and self-determination of other persons and communities. Rather, it is an assertion of a personal deliberate choice as a first step in the direction of developing and implementing strategies for its implementation in practice.

Whether one type or the other of politics of identity prevails to promote or undermine constitutional governance is a result of an interaction of a complex web of factors over time, and not only a matter of personal choice. For the purposes of the incremental success of constitutionalism, which is my primary concern here, the question is what individual persons can do about this process in relation to the contingent role of Islam in their own situation. It is from this perspective that I would emphasize the role of conscious choice and ability to be self-critical. A favorable choice is more likely to be made to the extent that one appreciates that respect for one's identity is contingent on respecting the identity of others, while an unfavorable choice reflects a failure to appreciate that moral and pragmatic imperative. For example, as a Sudanese Muslim from the northern part of the country, I can either assert my cultural/religious identity with due regard to the identity of non-Muslim Sudanese from other parts of the country, or do so regardless of or even in violation of their identity. The first choice signifies confidence in one's cultural/religious identity as consistent with, if not requiring, one's obligation to concede the same right to other citizens of the same country. In contrast, the second choice indicates an unwillingness or inability to appreciate the need for reciprocity in this regard, probably in the belief that conceding the right of others to their cultural/religious identity undermines or diminishes one's own right.

The fact that outcomes of the politics of identity are totally arbitrary and unpredictable is clearly demonstrated by the manner in which Islamists have deliberately and systematically promoted their understanding of Islam, with its anticonstitutional consequences in Sudan, as explained in the next chapter. In light of this recent empirical reality, I conclude that an acknowledgment of the moral and pragmatic value of reciprocity in conceding the right of others to their own cultural/religious identity in order to secure one's own identity is a quality that can be deliberately cultivated and developed in a given population. The next step from this perspective is to investigate and attempt to change the processes by which perceptions of identity in exclusive terms that negate or diminish the right of others happen to prevail in Sudan. Such a "corrective" strategy, I argue, should first seek to understand the rationality of viewing cultural/religious identity in exclusive terms, and address the underlying reasons for it, in attempting to influence people in favor of a more inclusive understanding of the human need for belonging and solidarity that underlies this powerful urge. In speaking of the "rationality" of this sort of negative exclusivity of identity, I am emphasizing that human beings take such positions for reasons that appear to be reasonable and coherent to them at the time. But it is perhaps helpful to briefly clarify an underlying tension in this proposition.

For instance, assertions of identity are by definition exclusive; indeed, that is the common rationale of all identity politics. Whatever basis of identity one is asserting in a given context, the object is precisely to include some people in that identification, which necessarily implies excluding others. When I say I am a Sudanese, for instance, I am at the same time saying that I am not an Egyptian or Kenyan, by affirming that I am a Muslim I am confirming that I am not Christian or atheist, and so forth. Moreover, there is an implication of self-satisfaction, if not superiority, in at least some forms of identity, especially when they are believed to be a matter of choice or merit. For example, in affirming that I am a Muslim by choice, I am claiming that I believe that to be better than being Christian or atheist. Stressing one's professional training as a lawyer, for instance, implies pride in that affiliation, often in contrast to being an accountant or engineer or some other professional position. In general, identity is important to people because it affirms their own dignity and worth as human beings, satisfies their need to belong to a desirable group, and attracts the solidarity of other members of that group.

If that is the nature and function of identity, how can it be effectively affirmed while at the same time accepting other identities as of equal value? How can the unavoidable exclusivity of identity be meaningful when it does not imply some advantage that is denied to those who identify with something different, especially when it is a competing religion or a culture that is believed to be inferior to one's own? While acknowledging this inherent tension in the politics of identity, I believe that the principle of reciprocity can provide a moral and pragmatic framework for mediation. Moreover, since such mediation is unlikely to eliminate this tension even in the long term, constitutionalism can in fact provide a useful political and legal framework for the continuous mitigation of its negative consequences for social and economic relations.

By reciprocity I mean appreciating that one's claim to affirm his or her identity, in whatever terms one deems to be important and relevant, is in fact contingent upon accepting the right of others to do the same. Such reciprocity is both required as a moral justification for one's own claim, and politically necessary if others are to accept that claim. In other words, if I am unwilling to accept the right of others to assert their own identity, I cannot realistically expect them to accept my claim. If I should then attempt to impose my right against their voluntary acceptance of it, they will probably resist by any means available to them. When the realm of this contestation is a territorial state, for our purposes here, the effort of one group to impose its own cultural/religious identity to the exclusion of the right of others to do the same will probably result in severe political instability, if not civil war, as illustrated by the case of Sudan in the next chapter.

In any case, the whole basis of national sovereignty, economic development, and political participation would be repudiated by an assertion of identity by one segment of the population that denies the right of other segments of the population their right to do the same. This moral and political imperative of reciprocity is both required for, and facilitated by, sustainable constitutionalism as a framework for sustaining overlapping identities, whereby one can be Muslim or Christian, of one ethnic group or another, while at the same time sharing with people who identify in different terms the common quality of being citizens of the same territorial state. Constitutionalism also provides the legal and political mechanisms for negotiating and adjudicating competing claims to resources and services that may arise from the various identities asserted by different segments of the population of the country.

Chapter 5

Islam and Constitutionalism in Sudan, Nigeria, and Senegal

In this chapter, I attempt to illustrate the contingency of the role of Islam with reference to certain aspects of the recent constitutional experiences of Sudan, Nigeria, and Senegal. While I have argued that evaluation of constitutional experiences should always be context specific, it is also part of my thesis that African countries can learn from the experiences of others, within the continent and beyond. Comparative analysis would be particularly useful in relation to a common factor or variable, like Islam, to see how it operates in different settings. To reiterate once more, I am not claiming that Islam is the sole, or even always the primary, factor in the constitutional development of these or any other countries. Rather, I am examining its association with constitutionalism to see whether it is possible to draw some guidance for a more positive relationship where and to the extent Islam is a relevant factor.

Recall also the premise that this relationship should neither be taken for granted nor assumed to be permanent or inevitable because if it is positive at any given time, it can decline, and if it is negative it can still deteriorate further or improve. Using some of the recent constitutional history and context of three countries, this chapter explores whether understanding the role and interaction of the various actors, factors, and processes that shape and influence this relationship can assist in the development of policy interventions and strategies to enhance the incremental success of constitutionalism in African societies where Muslims constitute the majority or a significant minority of the population.

Since I am introducing new information on the three countries discussed in this chapter, as well as an analysis of the specific role of Islam in each setting, I first present a brief overview of constitutional developments in each country and highlight an apparently dominant theme or set of issues in that context. I will begin with the case of Sudan as the oldest and most drastic example of the serious implications of the role of Islam among all three countries. The case of Nigeria will be presented next as a variation on the theme of the Sudan case, and Senegal will follow as a different model of the contingent role of Islam. All three cases will be taken together in a comparative discussion in the last section of the chapter.

Sudan: Persistent Constitutional Stalemate

The territories now constituting the Republic of Sudan were first unified under a somewhat centralized colonial administration by Ottoman-Egyptian armies through a gradual process starting in the 1820s. That colonial period ended when Muhammad Ahmed, a Sudanese sufi who claimed to be al-Mahdi (divinely ordained savior), led a nationalist/religious revolt that took control of most of the country by 1884. It is pertinent to note here that the Mahdi movement along the Nile valley was in the tradition of the Islamic jihad reform movements along the Sahil region of West Africa, as outlined in the previous chapter. But that brief phase of independence was plagued by constant civil wars, military campaigns, and famine, until the Mahdist state was destroyed thirteen years later by a British-Egyptian consequent of the country that was rationalized as "recovering Egypt's possessions in Sudan." Since Britain was occupying Egypt itself at the time, as a "protectorate," and had led the conquest of Khartoum, the capital of Sudan, in 1898, it also dominated the joint colonial administration (called Condominium in the 1898 Agreement of the two colonial powers). Sudan gained independence from Anglo-Egyptian colonial rule on January 1, 1956.

Less than two years after independence, General Ibrahim Aboud lead a military coup on November 17, 1958, suspended the 1956 Transitional Constitution, dismantled the English-model parliamentary system, and ruled by decree for the next six years. That constitution was restored, however, as the Transitional Amended Constitution of 1964, when a determined civilian uprising, supported by some army officers, forced the military junta out of government, and reestablished civilian government under an elected parliament. But that second attempt at establishing constitutional government was once again abruptly terminated by the second military coup of May 25, 1969 led by Colonel Jaafar Numeiri, which forced out the elected government of Prime Minister Saddiq al-Mahdi, the grandson of the founder of the Mahdist state of 1884–98. The second military junta transformed their military regime into a single party state under what they called "The Permanent Constitution" of 1973, but was overthrown on April 6, 1985, again by a popular civilian uprising that was supported by some military officers, in a similar process to the end of the first military regime of Aboud in October 1964.

A second cycle of those events was repeated in the 1980s and 1990s, starting with the overthrow of the elected government of the same Prime Minister Saddiq al-Madhi by the country's third military coup on June

30, 1989 led this time by General Omar El-Bashir, who made himself the president of the country in 1993. A significant difference between this third military regime and the previous two is that the 1989 coup was carried out by the military wing of the National Islamic Front (NIF), a political organization that emerged from the Muslim Brotherhood, which had used various names since Hassan al-Turabi assumed its leadership in 1964. After concealing the true ideological nature of the 1989 military coup for a few months to consolidate its hold on the country through the systematic purge of all military and civilian personnel who opposed the NIF, the regime revealed its true colors and al-Turabi assumed the political leadership of the whole country, though mainly indirectly. Thus, El-Bashir was elected president in 1996, when all opposition parties and groups boycotted the elections.

In 1999, the multi-party system was formally restored under the Constitution of 1998, which allowed some of the traditional political parties to operate lawfully inside the country. But the main political struggle, as it turned out, was within the NIF itself, when some of al-Turabi's lieutenants, in alliance with the military wing that carried out the 1989 coup, challenged his leadership. In response, al-Turabi used his position as the speaker of parliament to reduce the power of El-Bashir as president, while increasing his own. In December 1999, El-Bashir responded by dissolving parliament and appointing a new cabinet and improving his position within the National Congress Party (NCP), a new name for the old NIF. As the power struggle within the NIF intensified, al-Turabi's position as secretary general of the NCP was suspended in May 2000, and he established his own opposition party, the Popular National Congress Party (PNC). In December 2000, El-Bashir was reelected president under the 1998 Constitution, and placed al-Turabi first in preventive detention, and then under house arrest until he was released in October 2003, only to be placed in preventive detention again in March 2004, as the power struggle between the two factions of the original NIF continued.

But the post-independence constitutional and political history of Sudan cannot be understood without close consideration of the civil war and its underlying causes and developments. The first phase of the civil war started as a local rebellion in southern Sudan in August 1955, four months before the country achieved independence, but developed into a full scale civil war that has continued ever since, except for about ten years of peace (1972–1983). That decade of peace came about through what is known as the Addis Ababa Agreement of 1972, negotiated by the military regime of Numeiri in an attempt to achieve a delicate balance between competing claims to self-determination, as explained below. For the purposes of this overview, it is sufficient to note that the critical terms of the Peace Agreement were enacted in the 1973 Constitution, thereby granting the south regional autonomy within the framework of a unitary state. Numeiri began to repudiate the 1972 Agreement and 1973 Constitution through a series of unilateral acts in the early 1980s, culminating in the imposition of Islamic Shari'a laws by presidential decrees in September 1983. When the judiciary apparently resisted such an abrupt and drastic legislative coup, Numeiri declared a state of emergency, suspended all constitutional rights and freedoms, and established parallel so-called "prompt justice" courts manned by lay magistrates who were willing to implement his decrees without questions (Mayer 1993: 136).

Thus, Sudan gained independence more than a year before Ghana, which is commonly regarded as the first sub-Saharan African country to become independent, in 1957. Sudan also has the dubious distinction of not only being the first in sub-Saharan Africa to suffer a military coup (in November 1958), but also of enduring the longest civil war on the continent. Moreover, Sudan has been ruled by military regimes and single party states since independence, except for four years in the 1960s and another four in the 1980s. In terms of constitutions, there was first the 1956 Transitional Constitution, which was suspended in 1958 and restored as Amended in 1964. Second was the Permanent Constitution of 1973 that established the first single party state until it was gradually repudiated by Numeiri himself in the early 1980s. The uprising of April 1984 re-introduced the Transitional Constitution, again as Amended, only to be suspended once more by the NIF military coup of 1989. This military regime also transformed itself into a single party state during the early 1990s, and then adopted the 1998 Constitution that has allowed for limited political liberalization. But the future of constitutionalism in Sudan is most critically tied to the prospects of sustainable peace and stability, which will remain elusive until the role of Islam in the government of the country is clarified and regulated.

Islam and Constitutional Stalemate

Constitutions are usually negotiated by politicians and drafted by lawyers, but they can only be successful to the extent that they respond to legitimate demands of various segments of the population for sustained self-determination within the framework of the territorial state (An-Na'im and Deng 1997). The most relevant issue in the case of Sudan for the purposes of this chapter is how to reconcile the claim of the Muslim majority that the constitutional and legal system of the country must express their Islamic identity with the demands of the non-Muslim minority for equal citizenship and an equitable share in the development of the country. While it is true that the underlying causes of the protracted civil war include a complex web of political, economic, ethnic, and other factors, a fundamental ambivalence about the role of Islam in the governance of the country clearly lies at the core of the problem. Various theories about the causes and approaches to the settlement of the civil war can be debated, but it is beyond dispute that sustainable peace, political stability, and development of the country are impossible to achieve without securing equal citizenship and full human rights for all Sudanese, Muslims and non-Muslims alike. This prerequisite condition is unattainable under a so-called Islamic state or any formal enforcement of Shari'a as the law of the land.

The question for our purposes here is whether it has been so difficult for the Muslim majority to acknowledge the legitimate demands of the minority, despite the horrendous human and material costs of a civil war that has raged for four decades What is driving the resistance of the Muslim majority to the obvious prerequisite conditions of peace, political stability, and economic development of the whole country? The basic answer to this question, it seems to me, is the ambivalence of all the political leaders of the Muslim majority on the role of Islam in the constitutional process. At first glance, it seems that the position of the various political parties in the Muslim north can be classified in terms of their commitment to the establishment of an Islamic state that will enforce Shari'a as the constitutional and legal system of the land, and those who oppose that model and favor a secular state. But this would be an oversimplification of a more complex situation. The two major political parties in the north, the Umma Party and Democratic Unionist Party (DUP), are too ambivalent on this fundamental question to permit a clear-cut classification. Moreover, even the NIF as the purported ideological proponent of the enforcement of Shari'a is quite vague and evasive about how that might be done in practice, and it has failed to implement this during the fifteen years it has been in complete and exclusive control of the state (since June 1989). If this characterization is true of the three major political forces in the Muslim northern part of the country, then that would not only support my general thesis about the contingent role of Islam, but also open possibilities of mediation among competing claims to self-determination.

The two other major Muslim political parties, the Umma and DUP, are even more ambivalent on the issue. The Umma Party, with the Ansar Islamic sect as its main political constituency, is nominally committed to an undefined form of an Islamic state and hold confused views on the application of Shari'a. Neither al-Saddiq al-Mahdi, the leader of the Umma party since 1964, nor any of his followers has ever produced a clear and comprehensive statement of the party's position on these issues. The DUP, with the Khatmyya Islamic sect as its main political constituency, is equally ambivalent and confused on the critical constitutional issues arising from the application of Shari'a. Although the Umma and DUP have governed Sudan during all democratic periods (1956–85, 1965–69, and 1986–89), either in coalition with each other or with other minority parties, they have never taken concrete steps to implement Shari'a. But when they ruled from 1986 to 1989, these parties were able neither to repeal the Shari'a statutes imposed by Numeiri in 1983, nor to enforce them in practice. The ambivalence and confusion of the leadership of the Umma and DUP persisted throughout the 1990s, when they continued their opposition to the NIF government of El-Bashir, mostly from exile in Egypt and Eritrea.

Despite their long history of extensive political rhetoric in favor of the application of Shari'a, the leaders of the NIF have never produced a definitive statement of their position or detailed in public the specific features of the model they hope to install in the Sudan (An-Na'im 1993: 102–3, 107–11). In particular, the leadership of the NIF has failed to develop a clear plan or consistent practice on this issue since they took exclusive control of the state after the coup of 1989. Indeed, as noted earlier, political disagreement among the leadership has resulted in the detention of al-Turabi and suppression of the PNC party, which he attempted to establish in opposition to the other leaders of the NIF who retained control over the NCP as the ruling party. It is also significant to note that this internal power struggle within the NIF was primarily about how to maintain commitment to Shari'a while negotiating a peaceful settlement of the civil war. These fundamental political realities of a postcolonial territorial state like Sudan are compelling reasons for ensuring the future of constitutionalism in Sudan.

This view is also confirmed by the same ambivalence about the role of Islam that we find in the positions of a variety of political parties and movements, such as the National Sudanese Party, the Sudanese Communist Party, and the Sudanese People's Liberation Movement. These parties have tended to support the separation of religion and the state, but are apparently unable to take that position to its logical conclusions openly and categorically for fear of its political consequences among their Muslim constituencies. Thus, the application of Shari'a seems to be the critical factor in Sudanese constitutional discourse: If or to the extent that a political party or organization is committed to the application of Shari'a, its position can be assessed in terms of the consistency or inconsistency between that position and modern constitutionalism, as discussed in Chapters 1 and 4 earlier. Conversely, if or to the extent that a party or organization is opposed to the application of Shari‘a, the question becomes how it deals with the aspirations of the Muslim majority in the country. None of the main political parties in the Muslim northern region, which constitutes at least two thirds of the country in size and population, seem to be able and willing to fully embrace either option, hence the need for the sort of mediation I believe the contingency thesis provides.

Since independence, the role of Islam in the state and the role of Shari‘a within the legal system has been a contentious issue (Mayer 1993: 133). The debates on whether Sudan should adopt an Islamic constitution and whether Shari‘a should replace the common law system were inconclusive and recurring. It has also been suggested that "The removal of Islam from public life in Sudan is not an option" (Salam 2001: 21). At the same time, it is also clear that the application of Shari‘a by the state is problematic for all religious traditions in the country, Muslim and non-Muslim, because it would inhibit debate about which interpretation of Islam is to be codified (Salam 2001: 22–23).

It is also reasonable to conclude that there is a clear correlation between the Shari‘a issue and the civil war in Sudan. The Shari‘a issue has apparently come to summarize and symbolize the totality of the grievances of the non-Muslim south against the Muslim north. This does not mean that the imposition of Shari‘a by former President Numeiri in 1983 was the sole cause of the resumption of civil war. As noted earlier, that arbitrary imposition of Shari‘a was the culmination of a series of violations of the Addis Ababa Agreement of 1972 which ended the first phase of the civil war. If peace and reconciliation are to be achieved, however, each side must appreciate the point of view of the other, and respond to it in a constructive manner.

For our purposes here, the constant constitutional transition and stalemate in Sudan revolve around the basic issue of how to conduct government in accordance with the will of the majority *without* violating the fundamental constitutional rights of the minority or other groups or individuals within the country. Since many aspects of Shari‘a are inherently inconsistent with the constitutional principle itself, as well as violating rights of non-Muslims and Muslim women, as outlined in chapters 1 and 4, the mediation of this tension cannot be achieved through direct application of Shari‘a by the state, which would mean the enforcement of legislation and implementation of official policies that are inherently unconstitutional. The contingency of the role of Islam thesis presented in the previous chapter may be helpful precisely because of the ambivalence of the major political parties on the issue. I will return to these issues in the last section of this chapter, following similar outlines and thematic discussion of the other two cases.

Nigeria: Pluralism and the Politics of Islamization

While there are many similarities between the cases of Sudan and Nigeria on issues of the contingent role of Islam in relation to constitutionalism, the Nigerian case has so far been on a more limited and less drastic scale than that of Sudan. One of the questions to be discussed in the last comparative section of this chapter is whether Nigeria can benefit from the experiences of Sudan in mediating the tensions of the politics of Islamization. But first, let us continue with a brief overview of background and context in Nigeria.

Like most African countries, present-day Nigeria was first unified under British colonial rule, and achieved full political independence in October 1960. With very little advance preparation, the British parliamentary model was abruptly and uncritically adopted by the Nigerian elite who took over power from the British colonial administration (Suberu 1995: 198). The constitution of 1954 divided Nigeria into ethnic regions, representing the ethnic majorities of the Hausa-Fulani, Yoruba, and Igbo. The division meant "an inequitable incorporation of more than two hundred ethnic minority groups into the tripartite regional structure" (199). The government responded to the urgent need for an adjustment of this unworkable structure during the first phase (1966–79) of military rule which implemented "the reorganization of the federal structure, the centralization of the political economy, and the reconstitution of critical political institutions. First, the lopsided regional system was transformed into a more institutionally balanced scheme of federalism through the establishment of twelve and subsequently nineteen states in 1967 and 1976" (199). It is therefore important to understand the role of the military in the constitutional development of Nigeria, like many other African countries, as discussed in chapter 3 earlier. The last phase of military rule in Nigeria lasted for nearly sixteen years, and ended in 1999, with the adoption of the current constitution.

The first period of military rule ended with the establishment of what is known as the Second Republic in October 1979, based on an "American-style presidential system, a uniform local government structure and police force, ingenious electoral provisions that required the president and all political parties to obtain broad inter-ethnic support, and a constitutional directive that enjoined the recognition of the country's 'federal character' of cultural diversity in the composition and conduct of key public institutions" (Suberu 1995: 200). Hence the Second Republic had a progressive, positive vision, for instance, in its emphasis on consensus across ethnic groups and its imperative for constitutional recognition of cultural plurality and diversity. However, in practice the Republic could not take root, and reflected similar patterns and failures of mismanagement of governance and corruption as the First Republic until it was removed by the military after four years.

The second period of military rule, from 1984 to 1999, was in turn marked by popular pressures for democratic renewal and politics and constant demands for return to democratic governance (Suberu 1995: 200). Despite the failure of the Second Republic and the ruthless efforts of the military to undermine democratic institutions, the popular democratic impulse has persisted. Indeed, ironically, successive military dictators offered this as the justification for military rule. This was the promise of the regime of General Ibrahim Babangida, and his failure to deliver became the justification for his overthrow. Thus, upon taking over the new military dictator, Sani Abacha proclaimed in his first broadcast to the nation on November 18, 1993, his strong determination to enthrone a true and lasting democracy, and announced the forthcoming national constitutional conference to determine Nigeria's political future (200). It took another 6 years for that promise to be fulfilled in 1999, after Abacha's sudden death.

It seems that ethnic pluralism provides an important basis for the commitment of Nigerians to democracy, since all groups strive for a system which can ensure equitable political representation. In this regard, "Nigeria's abiding commitment to the mediation of its ethnic fragmentation via federation has truly set the country's democratic ethos in the constitutional mold" (Suberu 1995: 209). Other sources of constitutionalism include the introduction and diffusion of British liberal institutions and values since the late colonial era and the impact of socioeconomic modernization and demography. This combination of factors has given rise to a healthy civil society dedicated to the establishment of democratic and constitutional principles, on the "premise that an inviolable body of fundamental human rights, coupled with the diffusion of power among different governmental arenas in the federal system would suffice to secure the most important group interests while preserving the overriding integrity of basic individual freedoms" (212). Another positive development is that constitutionalist culture has indeed inhibited the political role of the military, instead of being undermined by it. Nigeria's commitment to constitutionalism is seen as "a critical national project rather than an Anglo-Saxon ideal" (216). The restoration of civil democratic rule since 1999, especially the relatively successful critical second general elections of 2003, clearly supports this positive assessment in my view. As I am arguing in this book, however, should there be another setback or regression into undemocratic military rule or other dictatorial regime happen in the near future, that should be seen as only a phase in an ongoing process of constructing constitutionalism.

THE POLITICS OF ISLAMIZATION

For the purposes of this chapter, however, the most recent challenge that has to be taken into consideration in analysis of the incremental success of constitutionalism in Nigeria is what might be called the politics of Islamization, as played out in northern Nigerian states since 2000. Efforts by some twelve northern states within the Federation of Nigeria to enforce Shariʿa as positive state law have attracted a lot of international attention, often in terms of negative media reports and highly critical reaction from human rights organizations about stoning to death as punishment for adultery (*zina*). But the more serious crisis over this issue is internal to Nigeria itself. While it is not possible to examine the origins and dynamics of the multiple dimensions of this crisis here, I will attempt to highlight the most important contributing factors, analyze the competing claims for the proper interpretation of the Nigerian constitution and the possibility of religious and ethic reconciliation.

There seems to be a correlation between ethnic and religious diversity in Nigeria. The north is dominated by Hausa and Fulani ethnic groups, which are predominantly Muslim. In the middle belt states and in the urban centers of the north there are a significant number of Christians. In the southwest the Yoruba ethnic group constitutes the majority, but there is no dominant religion. In the east, the Igbo ethnic group dominates while the Catholics and Methodists are the majority, but many Igbos observe traditional rites and ceremonies. Rough estimates suggest that approximately 50 percent of the population are Muslim, 40 percent is Christian and 10 percent practice exclusively traditional indigenous religions or no religion.

Some observers suggest that the conflicts in Nigeria are artificially constructed or maintained by corrupt elites for selfish ends, and assert that the violence in Nigeria is politically orchestrated by politicians playing on religious fears of the population. Proponents of the political disorder theory claim that political actors in Africa seek to maximize their returns on the state of confusion, uncertainty and chaos (Chabal and Daloz 1999). Such theories do not, of course, explain why framing the issues in religious terms is a useful strategy for fermenting violence, confusion and chaos, or indicate strategies for mediating the conflict.

Another aspect of the causes or dynamics of the crisis over Shariʿa in northern Nigeria relates to competing claims of the various ethnic/religious groups in view of great disagreement over the interpretation of Article 10 of the Nigerian Constitution prohibiting the adoption of an official religion, and Article 38 guaranteeing freedom of religion (Ilesanmi 2001). One view is that the constitution creates a secular state that confines religion to the private realm by erecting a high and impermeable wall between religion and the state. Another view challenges secularism itself as a sort of religion that violates the neutrality of the state in matters of religion and limits the ability of Muslims to fully exercise their beliefs under Shari'a. There are also those who, while supporting the separation of state and religion, still argue that the government should allow religiously based arguments into politics on the same terms as they admit secularly based arguments (Gutman 1999: 907).

The Constitution of Nigeria provides that states may decide to implement Shari'a law and courts, though the issue of establishing a Federal Shari'a Court of Appeal was debated in the constitutional conferences of 1977, 1989, and 1995, without arriving at a clear resolution. Christian Nigerians opposed the Court as a first step toward the Islamization of the country and the repudiation of secularism. As one of the opponents argued, "to entrench the Shari'a court in the constitution is to legalize the inferiority of non-Muslims and the superiority of the Muslim" (Osaghae 2001: 191). The proponents of the Shari'a Court, on the other hand, asserted that "freedom of religion enshrined in the constitution would mean a truncated freedom for the Muslim who is denied Shari'a" (Osaghae 2001: 192).

While the debate continued, Ahmed Sani Yenma, the elected governor of the Zamfara state, declared in October 1999 that Shari'a law must govern personal and criminal issues in that state. The draft bill for the application of Shari'a was taken before the House of Assembly, passed into law, and returned to the governor within forty-eight hours. Yenma declared that Shari'a was adopted "to ensure justice, protection of peoples lives and property and sanctity which cannot be guaranteed without making the Shari'a our guide" (Osaghae 2001: 192). The law described its purpose as to curb high crime, moral decadence and anti-social behavior. Within two years, 12 states in northern Nigeria adopted Shari'a law: Zamfara, Sokoto, Kebbi, Niger, Kano, Katsina, Kaduna, Jigawa, Yobe, Bauchi, Borno and Gombe.

As to be expected, that development intensified the debate and raised the stakes for both sides. Proponents of the implementation of Shari'a viewed the law as an exercise of freedom of religion, federalism, and democracy, an assertion and realization of their full identity, while its opponents viewed it as a threat to religious freedom and an instigator of religious intolerance that undermines Nigeria's secularism. Ayo Adebanjo argued, for instance, "It is clear from what is happening that the North has an agenda to destabilize the nation. And they are doing so because President Olusegun Obasanjo is a southerner and a Christian (Osaghae 2001:191). Obasanjo himself expressed the view that the extended Shari'a provisions were unconstitutional, but the federal government did not intervene legally to annul the provisions. Conceding that the states have the ability to implement Shari'a criminal law under Nigerian federalism, the federal government appointed a committee to draft uniform Shari'a criminal and procedural law that could be adopted by all of the states. In March 2002, Justice Minister Kanu Agabi made public a letter written to northern governors, which provides that sentences under Shari'a law should not be harsher than those issued under the general secular law. But it is not clear how that sort of request can be taken seriously when Shari'a penalties are believed by Muslims to be divinely ordained, and not subject to judicial discretion in sentencing in individual cases.

Moreover, the conflict over the imposition of Shari'a laws has also led to grave violence in which thousands of Muslims and Christians have died in different parts of northern and central states. For example, it is reported that 2,300 people were killed in ethnoreligious violence in the city of Jos within one week in September 2001. Approximately 80 percent of the victims were Hausa Muslims, who constitute the minority in that city. That may indicate an underlying ethnic dimension of the violence emerging in the context of competition over economic resources and broader social tensions. While the advocates of Shari'a repeatedly promised that it would not be applied to non-Muslims, many of them have been subjected to its provisions and suffered discrimination from that. It is indeed difficult to imagine how such laws can in practice be enforced on Muslims alone when different religious communities are completely integrated, socially and economically, sharing the same services and public facilities, engaging in daily social interaction, and so forth.

For instance, the expansion of Shari'a in the northern states beyond the traditional field of family law and inheritance has also led to debate on whether punishments such as amputation for theft, stoning for adultery, and flogging for fornication and public drunkenness, constituted torture or inhuman or degrading punishment or treatment, which is prohibited by the Constitution of Nigeria. During 2002, seven men were convicted of stealing and burglary and sentenced to having their hands amputated while numerous criminals were sentenced to public caning for various minor offenses. There were also several sentences of stoning for women convicted of adultery that year. Moreover, private vigilante groups have sometimes received official state sanction to enforce Shari'a through extralegal means. It is reported, for instance, that Governor Ahmed Sani vested the local vigilante group with full powers of arrest and prosecution in Zamfara state because he believed that police were not enforcing the Shari'a laws, just like as Numeiri did in Sudan in 1983, as noted earlier. Governor Saminu Turaki of Jigawa state also mobilized a Shari'a enforcement committee to arrest, detain, and prosecute Muslim offenders. While these groups are still working to enforce Shari'a their activities have declined since 2002 (Report 2003).

Some commentators present the fundamental issue here in terms of competing rights: what is seen by Muslim supporters as an exercise of their right to self-determination and freedom of religion is perceived by opponents, including some Muslims, as a violation of these same rights (Osaghae 2001: 191). Others have emphasized the dangers of the manner in which Shari'a was enacted and implemented, especially the fact that these new laws and policies are being carried out by state-sponsored vigilante groups rather than officers of the state. In Kano city, for instance, vigilante groups were responsible for destroying drinking and night spots, and such groups were responsible for arresting individuals for playing music in Katsina state. This aspect of the process not only undermines the legitimacy of the application of Shari'a and makes objective monitoring and evaluation difficult, but also challenges the fundamental role of the state to ensure the rule of law and protect all citizens against arbitrary violence.

It is therefore remarkable that the federal government of Nigeria has not taken decisive action to settle the underlying constitutional issues raised by the implementation of Shari'a in the north, especially the prohibition of sponsorship of religion by the state under Article 10 and freedom of religion under Article 38 of the Federal Constitution. It is important to note that these constitutional provisions are critical for Muslims and non-Muslims alike, throughout the country and not only in the northern states, as members of both groups, and the groups in a collective sense, can suffer serious violation of their rights as equal citizens of their own country. Indeed, since Muslims are not united in their understanding of Shari'a, or on the question of whether it should be enforced by the state, Nigerian Muslims can also suffer serious violations of their constitutional rights under an Islamic state. This danger is probably greater in the predominantly Muslim northern states not only for the arbitrary nature of the enforcement of Shari'a by vigilante groups, but also because of the strong social pressure for conformity with the official position on the matter.

Moreover, and in view of the strong connection between religion and ethnicity in Nigeria noted earlier, it is critical for the governments of the northern states and the federal government as the ultimate constitutional authority throughout the country, to safeguard the fundamental rights of all citizens against private as well as official coercion and arbitrary violence. The ethnic dimension of violence over the enforcement of Shari'a raises the serious risk of civil war, which would undermine, if not totally destroy, the national unity and territorial integrity of the whole country. The economic and social underpinnings of ethnic conflict must be addressed in efforts to mediate the religious expression of those tensions (Falola 1988: 303). As Phillip Aka has argued, a well-tailored

program of reconciliation for past inequalities should redress the grievances and concerns of all ethnic groups (Aka 2000). The point I am
emphasizing in conclusion of this review of the case of Nigeria is the critical importance of securing the necessary space for debate over such
fundamental issues like the local and national consequences of the politics of Islamization in the states of northern Nigeria.

Senegal: Sustaining Secularism

The French colonized the region of West Africa now known as Senegal
from the mid-1600s until late 1958, when the country became an autonomous republic within the French Community. At the end of one year
of federation with Mali, Senegal became an independent state in 1960,
with political power divided fairly evenly between President Leopold
Senghor and Prime Minister Mamadou Dia. Following an unsuccessful
coup d'état by Dia in 1962, Senegal promulgated a new constitution that
gives the president more power than the previous constitution. This 1962
constitution has been revised, but retained by the National Assembly in
1991 and reconfirmed by national referendum in 2001.

In comparison to other African countries, Senegal has had a good
record of political stability and a relatively high degree of respect for
constitutional principles under the leadership of Senghor, a Catholic
who ruled a predominantly Muslim population from independence until
he retired in 1981. His political successor, Adbou Diouf, a Muslim, pre-
sided until 2001. Under these two long-term presidents, the executive
branch has retained most of the power in Senegal, with the legislative
and judicial branches as secondary institutions. However, the system has
been described as quasi-, partial, and semi-democratic (Schaffer 1998:
117). Its multi-party system is seen as nominal since The Parti Socialiste
(PS) actually exercised hegemonic control over the government from
independence until 2001.

President Diouf was defeated in 2000 by Abdoulaye Wade, his long-
time rival and leader of the Parti Démocratique (PD), but PS retained
control of the National Assembly. Wade's election was probably facilitated by the 1997 National Electoral Observatory which secured transparency in elections. Lacking the constitutional power to dissolve the
Assembly and call for new elections on his own, Wade organized a constitutional referendum in 2001, and by popular support amended the
constitution to allow for new elections. In the April 2001 elections, Wade's
party captured 89 of the 120 Assembly seats. The amended constitution
also grants more power to the legislature and less to the president than
used to be the case, though the judicial branch of government still remains rather ineffectual compared to the other two. With Wade's election

and subsequent constitutional reforms, constitutionalism in Senegal seems to be recovering from the legitimacy crisis of the late 1990s, when Diouf and the PS exercised excessively hegemonic control over both the executive and legislative branches of government (Villalon 1999: 132).

For the purposes of this chapter in particular, however, Senegal is also experiencing a surge in Islamic militancy against the secular constitution, and mounting claims for implementation of Shari'a law. This recent phenomenon appears to be associated with several factors. The economic crisis of the 1980s, with its particularly negative impact on agriculture, has severely affected the daily lives of many Senegalese (Coulon 1989: 157). The effects of the economic instability are compounded by social instability as Senegalese Muslims struggle to maintain a moral and social identity in the face of Western hegemony. This complex economic and social context has apparently affected the relationship between the state and the *marabout* Islamic leaders in Senegal, which is particularly important for the development of constitutionalism in the country, as explained below.

The broader question of how Senegal came to enjoy this relatively good degree of constitutional and democratic governance is beyond the scope of this book. What I am concerned with here is why and how Islam has played a positive role in Senegalese constitutionalism, where Muslims constitute more than 90 percent of the country's population, while it has been so problematic in the cases of Sudan and Nigeria. It is possible to approach this specific question in several ways or at different levels of analysis. For instance, one can begin by identifying apparently relevant factors in the local context and trying to understand their role in the constitutional development of the country. From this perspective, the next question would be whether it is possible to abstract broader theoretical implications from the empirical facts of a given situation that can be applied to understanding or influencing the role of Islam in other situations. Even to the extent that it is possible to identify the "correct" relevant factors and actors in Senegal, and accurately characterize their interaction with other factors and actors in that setting, it may still not follow that the same set of interactive factors and actors will operate in similar ways in countries like Sudan or Nigeria. Since no two situations are identical—indeed, the situation in the same setting can significantly change over time—it is simply impossible to completely isolate and examine one set of factors and actors for comparative analysis. Such comparisons depend not only on factor X being exactly the same in both Senegal and Sudan, for instance, but also on other factors being similar or different to some degree in both settings at a particular time.

Thus, the constitutional experiences of human societies cannot be subjected to supposedly precise analysis in a totally controlled environment that allows for the isolation and experimental mixing of various elements in the process. Still, some insights can be gained from comparative analysis for the purposes of the broader thesis of incremental success through process and the notion of the contingent role of Islam. Provided one is sensitive to the limitations of comparative analysis, understanding how the process works in each setting will enable those concerned to plan and implement strategies for facilitating the process through the internal dynamic of each situation. The more specific thesis of the contingent role of Islam can be applied by trying to identify relevant factors and actors, in order to promote those that are positive and discourage or minimize those that are negative from the point of view of constitutionalism.

From this perspective, it seems that the relevant factors and actors in the case of Senegal include the highly organized and centralized *marabout* brotherhoods and their relationships to the secular state in Senegal. Another factor, though harder to describe or identify, could be that Sufi Islam, to which many Senegalese subscribe, as cultivated by the French during colonialism, is highly conformist and open to the idea of a secular state. Whether or not these or some other set of factors and actors are relevant, another question is why Senegal has witnessed a recent rise in Islamic militancy and calls for the implementation of Shari'a. That question would then lead to an examination of the factors that may be associated with this recent negative development that can override the role of other factors in favor of a more positive role of Islam. One point to note here is that, whatever the precise factors and dynamics may be, the general analysis is one about the contingent role of Islam, how it has been shaped in a particular way and can change over time. Another point is that such contingency can be useful even when one disagrees about the relevance or role of one factor or another. It may therefore be useful to follow this line of analysis a bit farther to see whether it can yield some useful insights.

ISLAM AND SECULARISM

For the purposes of the following discussion, I take secularism to mean a principle of public policy for the institutional separation of religion and the state, while accounting for the fact that religion and politics cannot be separated. On the one hand, since historical experience has shown that the exclusivity of religion tends to undermine possibilities of peaceful coexistence and solidarity among different communities of believers, the state should not seek to enforce a particular doctrine of any religion (Islam here) as the official policy and law of the land. On the other hand, it is neither possible, nor desirable in my view, to prevent believers from acting politically in furtherance of their beliefs. In other words, I am defining secularism as a constant mediation between these two poles in the concrete context of each society over time, rather than a simplistic claim of relegating religion to the private domain. I will return to discussing this conception of secularism in relation to constitutionalism later in this chapter.

In Senegal, the mediation of the role of Islam in public life apparently involves the leaders of the three main sufi *tariqas* in the country, the Mouride, Tijaniyya, and Qadiriyya. Despite the fact that the French colonial administration increased the power of the Mouride brotherhoods to the detriment of the Tijaniyya brotherhoods, as explained below, in the mid-1960s the Tijaniyya Muslims outnumbered the Mouride Muslims by two to one (Creevey 1985: 716). But with fewer members than the Tijaniyya, the Mouride *tariqa* apparently enjoys stronger social, political, and economic influence in recent years, primarily because of its centralized, well-organized institutional structure (Ross 1995: 231). As can be seen in the city of Touba, the seat of the Mouride *tariqa*, this Sufi order has established a governmental system within a religious movement. The Mourides managed to translate their early economic success with cultivating peanuts in the agricultural basin into wider success in trading in urban and international markets.

The term *marabout* refers to those who enjoy religious authority and leadership because of their religious piety and superior knowledge of God. In the Sufi communities of Senegal, the marabout acts as an intermediary between God and the masses of their followers who are perceived to be dependant on the marabouts for spiritual development and well-being (Behrman 1970: 15–16). The allegiance of mass followers and their dependence on the marabouts have traditionally extended to worldly affairs as well as religious matters. Revered as "saints" who enjoy supernatural powers, marabouts were often rewarded materially by their followers. During French colonialism the marabouts cooperated with the French colonial administration, and the power and influence they cultivated in that way continued into the postcolonial era (Behrman 1970).

The consistent policy of French colonial administration of West Africa, including Senegal, consisted of several elements. First, where it had economic interests or prospects of future expansion, the French administration actively opposed the creation of an Islamic state. Another element of French colonial policy was to encourage "Senegalese Muslims to accept the compatibility of foreign rule and Islamic culture" (Robinson 1988: 416). Thus, the administration sought to contain and isolate the Tokolor and Tijaniyya religious leaders, who were deemed to be extremists or fanatical, especially in western Senegal, where peanut production was at its peak. Conversely, the French administration actively sought out Islamic leaders who opposed jihad and the idea of an Islamic state, and supported their efforts to expand their followings, especially in western Senegal. This aspect of the French colonial policy tended to favor the leaders of the Qadiriyya and the Mouride *tariqas.*

One reason for the stability in the relationship between the state and the marabouts (both past and present) might be "the highly conformist nature of the version of Sufi Islam which was carefully cultivated by colonial officials and further encouraged by the independent state" (Villalon 1995: 226). By heavily relying on and supporting specific conformist Islamic leaders, while openly exiling other more militant ones, the French colonial administration promoted the idea of secularism among the Muslim population of Senegal, and actively discouraged the notion of an Islamic government (Robinson 1988: 434–35). While this policy was of course intended to serve French colonial objectives, it also turned out to be conducive to the stable constitutional development of independent Senegal. In contrast, the British colonial administration was apparently too worried about Islamic resistance in Sudan and Northern Nigeria to attempt promoting a secular view of the state in those two situations. That concern is understandable in view of the precolonial history of both regions, but the post-independence consequence of that British colonial policy has been a continuation of precolonial notions of an Islamic state and the attempt to enforce Shariʿa in those two situations. The divergent impacts of British and French colonial policies confirm the theoretical point noted earlier that colonialism was critical in shaping the postcolonial state and influencing the political culture of the societies it dominated. This does not mean that local Muslim populations were completely passive subjects of colonial authorities. Rather, such external influences can contribute to internal transformation when they become ingrained in the consciousness of people who are receptive to such influences by virtue of their history or the influence of their own religious or cultural values and institutions.

Continuing with Senegal for now, it is important to note that the political leadership of the country had to continue to cooperate with the marabouts precisely because French colonial sponsorship has made them too powerful to ignore (Behrman 1970: 107). Already by the time of independence, the marabouts formed the Conseil Supérieur des Chefs Religieux du Senegal (Conseil) with the mandate to protect, watch over, and maintain the dogmas of Islam in their true sense; ensure that the new constitution would provide freedom for Islam; ensure that the constitution would conform to the interests of Islam and practicing Muslims and reject the constitution if it included any means of harming Islam, its practices, or the possibility of its expansion; mediate among different Islamic factions or between them and the state in order to achieve reconciliation and a cordial understanding for the common peace; defend the general and specific interests of Muslims in all domains—economic, political, social, cultural, and judicial—through advice and by presenting claims to the public and judicial authorities (Villalon 1995: 201).

Interestingly for our purposes, the Conseil did not actively or explicitly oppose adoption of the secular constitution in 1961, but it reconvened in 1970 under the new name of the Conseil Supérieur Islamique du Sénégal, as a united maraboutic organization to mobilize opposition to the draft Family Code on the grounds that the draft contradicted Shari'a, (Villalon 1995: 209, 227). The government succeeded in enacting the Family Code in 1972, presenting it as an affirmation of secularism and not a rejection of Islam (Creevey 1991: 361). The marabouts continued to actively encourage their followers to turn to them instead of the state in the area of family law. Exercising ability to adapt to changes around them that had ensured their economic and political success during the colonial period, the marabouts managed to retain their influence after independence, engaging the new modernizing forces and trends. In addition to representing the spiritual leadership of the country, the marabouts also tend to be the largest land owners and among the wealthiest citizens (Behrman 1970: 137). These factors forced the government to rely on them for tax revenues, investment decisions, debt repayment, and public acceptance of innovative technology in peanut farming.

Throughout the early years after independence, the marabouts were the commercial and agricultural elites of the country, exerting considerable pressure on the government in exchange for economic and political support (Behrman 1970: 138). But the country as a whole has also benefited from the leading role of the marabouts, who have actively supported the diversification of Senegal's crop, adoption of modern agricultural techniques, and generally helped in stimulating the economy and redistributing wealth (Behrman 1970: 142). They have also played a positive political role by mediating between the population and the government, sometimes questioning or actively opposing government policy, but often facilitating government efforts, especially with regard to economic reforms (154–55).

As to be expected, the dynamic of the relationship between the marabouts and the government is changing over time, as the two compete with each for status and popularity among the greater population (Villalon 1995: 201). The underlying nature of the relationship apparently continues to be one of cooperation and collaboration for the benefit of the country. The marabouts' support for the political regime legitimizes it in the eyes of the masses and helps the government to further its public policy goals. The state reciprocates by showing respect for the authority of the marabouts as well as advancing their material interests and providing public assistance for mosques and ritual celebrations (206). At the same time, "While the political elite finds itself regularly working through the marabouts, their ultimate goal is to be able to function without them. Marabouts, for their part, seek to ensure the state's dependence on them. They thus alternately have incentives to cooperate or defect depending on the situation" (201). Increasingly, therefore, the goals of the state and marabouts are growing apart, with the state trying to eliminate the need for the marabouts as their link to the population, while the marabous increase their appeal to disciples in order to demonstrate to the state their capacity to exert influence over the population (211). In trying to make this delicate relationship work, state officials also express concern that favoring the marabouts too much violates principles of secularization to which the state is committed (222).

Most recently, however, it seems that the power of the marabouts is decreasing as Senegal becomes more democratized at the local and national level, with more citizens seeking more accountability from their representatives, both religious and political (Beck 2001: 601). In Touba, for instance, the local political council is endorsed by the Khalife-General of Mouridism (the chief local religious leader), as in many Senegalese cities. In a recent unprecedented challenge, local merchants opposed a drastic tax increase imposed by the religiously endorsed political council, implicitly challenging the authority of the religious leaders. As to be expected, the Khalife was able to retain power and legitimacy by mediating the dispute, encouraging the council to enact a lower tax and the citizens to agree to a tax increase.

In a sense, this recent incident represents the traditional exchange and mediation between the marabouts and political leadership. However, it also indicates a shift whereby both sides to the state-marabout relationship are becoming more accountable to the mass constituency (621). Given the slow pace at which Senegal is decentralizing power, it is difficult to predict how far this process will democratize religious and as political power in the country, but that is certainly an interesting possibility that will be considered later in this chapter. Thus, the relationship between the marabouts and the state remains one of both stability and dynamism, of mutual dependence of the parties, though that continuously changing in response to shifting economic and social forces within the country and beyond. It is also interesting to note that this tension, cooperation and mutual dependence between religious and political leaders seem to operate as part of a constitutional system of checks and balances. Senegal does indeed have a secular constitution with three distinct branches of government, but the brotherhoods in Senegal function as a fourth, unofficial branch of government that operates as a political check on the government, while being checked by it as well. Because the brotherhoods attained and retain their power over their disciples through spiritual guidance as well as social and economic interests, they are also able to exercise significant influence on public policy.

Moreover, Senegal's economic and social crisis seems to have diminished the codependence between the state and the marabout (Coulon 1989: 152). Following Senghor's retirement, the country did become increasingly democratic under Diouf and Wade, but it has also been plagued by economic and social crises. This resulted in the decreasing power of the marabouts as the centralized economic, social, and spiritual leaders, and a consequent decline in their influence as the intermediaries between the state and the general population. Ironically, this transformation seems to widen and deepen the crisis, and to promote a rise in orthodox Islam as a counter to Western hegemony (Coulon 1989: 156). "As more Muslims went to the Middle East and North Africa for Islamic education and the Senegalese economy lost ground, Islamic fundamentalism has spread, attacking both lax politicians and the Islamic brotherhoods" (Creevey 1991: 360). However, as orthodox Islam increases, the marabouts use it as a means of increasing their power within the government, offering a more liberal form of Islam (Coulon 1989: 156).

There seem to be two main streams of Islamic ideology growing in Senegal, a radical orthodox movement in Southern Senegal and a reformist puritanical Wahaby movement coming from Saudi Arabia and the Middle East. Both trends threaten the state-marabout relationship, but the second trend is particularly hostile to Sufi Islam and the relatively more liberal interpretation and practice of brotherhoods (Gellar 1982: 109, 114, 143). Islamic reformist movements begin as religious movements, but often develop a political component (Villalon 1995: 230). Moreover, governmental efforts to contain such organizations by providing their members jobs in education or state institutions, for instance, seem to be counterproductive by enhancing the political and social influence of these movements and encouraging them to pursue their objectives. On the other hand, popular resistance to the "Arabization" of Senegalese Islam is apparently forcing these recent Islamic reformist groups to align themselves more closely with popular sentiment in order to survive, resulting in the groups becoming "intertwined with maraboutic organizations, and consequently with the state" (233, 236–37). But this can happen in ways that enable the reformist voice to be included without dominating local brotherhoods, or threaten to take over the marabout structure, as seems to have happened with the Tijaniyya brotherhood in Senegal (238).

While the situation continues to be volatile and uncertain, it seems that earlier predictions of the rise of a conservative Muslim political party that would undermine the delicate relationship between the marabouts and the state are not materializing (O'Brien 1986). "The rise of radical Islamic reform movements, anathema to the existing political and religious leadership, does not pose a serious or immediate thereat to either government or the traditional brotherhoods. The traditional ties of cooperation and interdependence will most likely be maintained." (Clark 1999: 165) Religious leaders in Senegal must be associated with economic and political power and change in order for them to maintain legitimacy. For instance, a reformist movement emerged from the Tijaniyya brotherhood, known as the Dahiratoul Moustarchidina wal Moustarchidaty (DMWM) (Villalon 1995: 238). The state attempted to contain this movement through official sponsorship, and the DMWM resisted. But as the members of this movement became disenchanted, the DMWM faded into the background. This episode seems to support the view that Senegalese Muslims tend to associate religious leadership with political power and economic resources, and to withdraw support for any new religious movement if it fails to associate itself with political power.

Nevertheless, while recent reformist Islamic trends have not revolutionized the state-marabout relationship, it may have evolutionized the relationship (Villalon 1999: 130). The evolution of the role of religion in the public sphere is shaped at least in part by the "generational pressures" of young urban intellectuals who are critical of the traditional state-marabout relationship, as well as the generational tensions within the powerful religious families themselves (131). As the relationship of the state and religious leaders continues to evolve, the threat of fundamentalist Islam may influence the direction of change. New political leaders, genuine democratic government, and a recent upturn in the economy will also influence the course and direction of the state-marabout relationship. Economic and social crisis is likely to reinforce the state-marabout interdependence, and provide both sides a good incentive to oppose more radical reformist Islamic movements.

Islam and Constitutionalism in African Contexts

In light of the preceding review of the postcolonial experiences of Sudan, Nigeria, and Senegal, with special attention to the most critical issues of Islam and constitutionalism in each case, I will now attempt a synthesis and some comparative analysis, subject to the caveat that the success or failure of constitutionalism will always be specific to each context, as no two countries are exactly alike. Another caveat to recall is that tensions and possibilities of mediation in the relationship between Islam and constitutionalism are only two among many factors and forces in this process. The basic point here is that the role of Islam in the development of constitutionalism in Islamic countries should be taken seriously, without either unduly exaggerating or belittling it, both as a general theoretical matter and in relation to the situation in any particular country. In terms of the subject of this chapter, the question is how to work with the notion of the contingent role of Islam in promoting constitutionalism in different contexts. In other words, granted that each society has to negotiate this relationship through practice and over time, is there some common theoretical framework that can inform and facilitate this essentially context-specific process?

My analysis of the relationship between Islam and constitutionalism is premised on the view that it is problematic when Islam is taken to be synonymous with historical understandings of Shari'a that are fundamentally incompatible with fundamental principles of constitutional governance. As I have explained earlier and elaborated elsewhere (An-Na'im 1990), the main concerns here include the lack of institutionalized accountability for the government, and serious discrimination against women and non-Muslims. For example, women and non-Muslims are deemed by traditional formulations of Shari'a to lack the capacity to hold certain types of public office, denied competence to testify in trials for capital offenses (*hudud*), and the monetary compensation to be paid for their homicide is less than that paid for Muslim men. While I believe these views of Shari'a to have been acceptable in the historical context of pre modern Islamic societies, and indeed represented significant improvements on political and legal systems that prevailed throughout the premodern world, they are totally unacceptable from a constitutional point of view today.

To mediate such tensions in the relationship between Islam and constitutionalism in Islamic societies, I am proposing a deeply contextual understanding of secularism that seeks to establish an institutional separation of Shari'a and the state, while addressing the unavoidable connections between Islam and politics. As discussed in Chapter 4, the first aspect of this view of secularism requires the categorical repudiation of the myth of an Islamic state that would enforce Shari'a as a matter of state policy and positive legislation. In my view, the notion of an Islamic state as a political institution is conceptually impossible, historically inaccurate, and practically not viable today (An-Na'im 2000). It is conceptually impossible because enforcement through the official institutions of the state is by definition the negation of the religious nature of Shari'a. In other words, the enactment of a purported Shari'a principle as positive law makes it applicable as the expression of the political will of the state, rather than by virtue of the religious beliefs of Muslims. The idea of an Islamic state in this sense also has no precedent in Islamic history and is practically untenable in the present context in which Muslims everywhere live today.

The repudiation of the idea of an Islamic state must nevertheless be reconciled with the unavoidable reality, and desirability in my view, of the political role of Islam in present Islamic societies. To begin with, the assertion of separation of Islam and the state can only be meaningful where it is widely perceived as legitimate from a religious and cultural point of view. Muslims will not observe the constitutional principle of the institutional separation of Islam and the state if it is believed to be inconsistent with their religious beliefs and cultural norms and institutions. In any case, how can one deny Muslims the right to make political choices according to their religious beliefs, and how can such a policy be implemented in practice? Moreover, Islam provides necessary moral depth for constitutional governance as the ethical resource for mediating disagreements over public policy in Islamic societies because the principle of separation of Islam and the state is incapable by itself of resolving such issues. That principle simply affirms that religious doctrine should not be enforced through state institutions, but does not provide a normative framework and content for public policy. For instance, the principle of separation does not determine how family relations are to be organized, what conduct should be penalized by criminal law and which punishments are appropriate, and the social justice objectives of economic development and allocation of public resources. Regarding family relations, for instance, should polygamy be recognized, which principles should govern decisions about custody of children, should abortion on demand by permitted or prohibited, is it good policy to impose the death penalty for aggravated murder? Religion, Islam for Muslims, is integral to the ethical and cultural debates and resolution of such practical matters for the daily administration of justice and many other issues of public policy.

But how can the institutional separation of Islam and the state be maintained in practice in view of this unavoidable and appropriate connection between Islam and politics? There are two aspects to my response to this question. First, this is a permanent dilemma facing all societies and religious traditions, whether Christianity in the United States or France, Hinduism in India, Judaism in Israel, or Islam in Sudan, Nigeria, and Senegal. All societies have to struggle with this dilemma constantly, shifting back and forth between a stronger or weaker influence of religion on public policy. I am not suggesting here that the issues are exactly the same for different societies or indeed for the same society at different times in its history. Catholic Christianity is being negotiated differently in France versus Poland, Spain, or Mexico. The role of Protestant Christianity in Germany is different from its role in the United States. But successful or sustainable mediation in each case requires certain understandings of the religious tradition, the second element of my response to the question. That is, some perceptions of each religious tradition are conducive to successful mediation of the dilemma of its relationship to the state and politics, while others are problematic in this regard. This is as true of Hinduism and Judaism, as it is of Islam, as discussed and illustrated earlier in this chapter.

If we consider the three countries in question from this perspective, the case of Sudan highlights the profound constitutional problems raised by attempts to create an Islamic state that enforces Shari'a as state policy and positive law. Nigeria illustrates the difficulties of accepting a political role for Islam while resisting the enforcement of Shari'a by the state. Finally, the post-independence experiences of Senegal demonstrate the complexity of establishing and sustaining a secular state that balances the separation of Islam and the state against the realities of a political (and economic in this case) role of Islam. Now let me elaborate on these three situations.

In relation to Sudan, I would first suggest that peace and national unity in Sudan cannot be achieved or maintained on the basis of the establishment of an Islamic state and application of Shari'a, simply because to do so is to repudiate any foundation for self-determination for women and non-Muslim citizens. The fundamental right of peoples to self-determination is the rationale and purpose of constitutional government and all its powers and functions. Self-determination is also the rationale and guide everywhere in the world today for setting and implementing public policy through the political process, regulation of economic activities, and provision of essential services like health and education,. If a people's right to self-determination cannot be achieved and maintained within an existing state, they should be entitled to secede and establish a separate state of their own. In practice, a choice between these options is conditioned by a wide and complex variety of factors and considerations, both internal and external to the situation. But from a constitutionalism perspective, all persons, men and women, Muslims and non-Muslims alike, must enjoy equal rights as citizens of their own country.

Moreover, since unity or separation are only means for the realization of the right to self-determination, rather than ends in themselves, any constitutional regime must always be judged by its ability to effectively realize this right for all segments of the population of the country. Self-determination must also be the guiding principle of the peace process in Sudan, whether the country remains united or the South becomes a separate state. An Islamic state enforcing Shari'a is simply incompatible with any possibility of self-determination and equal citizenship for all Sudanese. For instance, political opposition by a Muslim to an Islamic state and its mandate to apply Shari'a could be prosecuted as the capital offense of apostasy, punishable by death under section 126 of the 1992 Sudan Penal Code.

In my view, moreover, proposals to apply Shariʿa in the northern part of Sudan, while "exempting" the South, are still incompatible with self-determination within a united Sudan for two main reasons. First, applying Shariʿa in any part of the country will violate the basic citizenship rights of those non-Muslim Sudanese who live in that part of the country. What does unity mean if non-Muslim Sudanese cannot live in any part of the country they choose without losing their basic rights as citizens? Second, representing Shariʿa as the local state legal system in a federal regime like that of the United States does not resolve the question of what legal system applies at the national federal level. If Shariʿa is implemented at the national level, then non-Muslim Sudanese will not have equal citizenship rights at that level. If Shariʿa does not apply at the federal national level, then how can the Sudan as a whole be described as an "Islamic state" in any meaningful sense? Moreover, as shown in chapters 1 and 4, Muslim men as well as women will suffer grave violations of their human rights if Shariʿa is enforced against them.

As noted earlier, the case of Nigeria illustrates the difficulties of accepting a political role for Islam while resisting the enforcement of Shariʿa by the state. At one level, one can apply the preceding analysis in order to urge efforts to avoid the decline of the situation in Nigeria as a whole to the sort of multiple and persistent crises of Sudan. In other words, one can point to the drastic consequences for national unity and political stability of Nigeria as a whole of the official enforcement of Shariʿa by the Northern states. But that does not address the question of how to provide for a political role for Islam as part of a deeply contextual understanding of secularism in Nigeria, as I have suggested earlier, if that does not include the enforcement of Shariʿa by the state. In other words, the apparent quandary is that the enforcement of Shariʿa by the Northern states threatens the peace and unity of the country, while denying those states apparently violates their right to self-determination in terms of an Islamic identity. The way to mediate this quandary, it seems to me, would consist of two elements, namely, a strong political and legal commitment to the institutional separation of religion and the state, on the one hand, and the implementation of Islamic reforms to reconcile Muslims' understandings of Shariʿa with constitutional principles (An-Naʿim 1990). Such reforms would enable Muslims to act politically in accordance with their religious beliefs without undermining constitutional principles.

The first part will have to be implemented by the federal and state governments throughout the country, equally and consistently in relation to all religions, not only Islam. That is, the institutional separation of religion must be rigorously enforced by the federal government throughout the country, especially in relation to Christianity and Islam as the two competing religions. The same policy must be enforced by every state government within the Federation of Nigeria, again especially in relation to the two major religions. The second element in the proposed policy should be adopted by political parties and social movements throughout the country, especially in states and regions where the separation of religion and state is being challenged.

The experiences of Senegal in relation to Islam in particular could be instructive for the proposed process, in terms of the possibilities and risks of a political role for religion in Nigeria. First, it seems clear that a strict interpretation of religious texts tends to undermine constitutionalism, especially when that leads to the total conflation of religion and government. Second, Sufi Islam appears to be more open to diverse interpretations and therefore more adaptable to the separation of state and religion. Third, a mutual accommodation between state and religious authorities operates best as an informal, tacit understanding, rather than in official or institutional terms. Fourth, an economic and social role for religious authorities can facilitate the autonomy of religious communities, which will reduce the importance of direct control of the state apparatus. The more the state accepts and supports an independent economic and social role for religious leaders, the less interest or benefit will the latter see in attempting to control the state. In other words, there is a subtle distinction between the democratic value of seeking to influence government, on the one hand, and the authoritarian tendency to seek exclusive control of government to pursue the narrow interests of some segment of the population, on the other. The former is legitimate and constructive from a constitutional point of view, while the latter will probably lead to sharp confrontations with other constituencies, thereby undermining political stability and economic and social development for the country as a whole.

In concluding this chapter, I would emphasize that conflict over questions of public policy, allocation of resources, and so forth is a permanent feature of all human societies. The basic issue for constitutional resolution is how to mediate the variety of competing claims and interests in a given situation in a sustainable, peaceful, and orderly manner. A good constitution can be a useful framework for the transformation and mediation of conflict, but it cannot be a substitute for the political will and determination to achieve those essential objectives of coexistence. However perfect it may look on paper, no constitution can survive the absence of the political, institutional, and cultural conditions necessary for its successful application on the ground. But given the existence of the necessary degree of such conditions in a country like the Sudan,

Nigeria or Senegal, a good constitution can contribute to the promotion and consolidation of those conditions themselves, as well as support other initiatives for sustainable peace, national unity, political stability, and economic and social development. In other words, the proper functioning of a good constitution is contingent on the existence and sustainability of certain conditions, at the same time being a vital resource for realizing and sustaining those conditions in a given situation.

While there may be strong indications of the existence of those prerequisite conditions on the ground in any of these countries, it is difficult to verify and assess whether such conditions exist to the necessary minimal degree except through the practice of constitutionalism over time. In other words, it is not possible to ascertain conclusively the existence of the necessary minimal conditions for successful constitutional governance except in retrospect, reflecting back as the process continues. As such, constitutionalism is necessarily an act of faith — propelled by the strong realization that the present state of civil war, economic stagnation, and social collapse in the Sudan, or the risk of similar outcomes in Nigeria and Senegal, cannot be tolerated. Yet, it would be irresponsible and probably counterproductive to approach the matter in a spirit of naive optimism or with an inadequate appreciation of the difficulties facing this project in any Islamic society. Consequently, any viable proposal for mediation would need to strike a balance between assuming the existence of these conditions, on the one hand, and a clear appreciation of the hypothetical nature of this assumption. Given the difficulty of verifying the validity of that assumption, and the essentially incremental nature of the process of developing constitutionalism in each particular context, as emphasized throughout this book, I should not attempt to speculate here about precise constitutional and practical scenarios for each of these countries. Recalling my remarks about the role of human agency in chapter 4 it is up to Muslims in these societies to develop and implement the necessary strategies of mediation. Comparative analysis and assessment by observers can play a positive role in these processes, as discussed earlier, but should not attempt to formulate categorical judgments of success or failure, as the process continues.

Chapter 6
Conclusions: Sustainable Constitutionalism Through Practice

Constitutionalism can be viewed from a variety of perspectives, as a historical or sociological phenomenon, philosophical concept or desirable or practical political and legal system. It can be approached through the prism of certain core ideas such as the limitation of the powers of government, rule of law, or sovereignty. This concept can also be understood more broadly as an aspect of political culture that is related to a wider framework of political, social, and cultural processes, or normative and institutional development. I have attempted to draw on some of these perspectives and related ideas, without claiming to exhaustively apply any of them in particular. My purpose is more limited and specific, namely, to explore and clarify a *process-based approach* to the promotion and consolidation of constitutionalism in present African countries. In my view, the deeply contextual and evolutionary understanding of the concept presented in this book can be helpful in exploring possible strategies and policies for developing the concept and its institutions in African countries. This approach can also be useful for achieving similar objectives in relation to other parts of the world, provided it is applied in the same deeply contextual and evolutionary manner in each case.

Although this chapter is presented as a concluding chapter, I will begin with some reflections on the origins and evolutions of modern constitutionalism in Britain, the United States, and France, as countries where this concept is generally considered to be well established. This somewhat substantive discussion could have logically been presented in the first chapter of this book by way of definition of the concept. I have deliberately postponed this comparative review in order to emphasize that these experiences may be useful to consider as comparative, without taking them to as definitive of African constitutionalism. Accordingly, this review is not intended as a comprehensive or up-to-date statement of all relevant developments in those countries. The main point I am trying to make here is that the relevant philosophical underpinnings and political/legal institutions have emerged very gradually, and have been tested and adapted, through a concrete historical process that was highly specific to each setting. The apparent ultimate success of the concept in all three countries was neither immediate nor taken for granted at any point in that long process, indeed the outcome in each case was contingent on a variety of factors, both internal and external to those settings.

This emphasis on local context and possibilities of different "roads" to similar goals should not preclude comparative analysis and theoretical generalization about some of the basic themes and issues of constitutionalism and related concepts. This will be attempted in the last two sections of this chapter, where I offer some general reflections on different theoretical perspectives on the origins and development of constitutionalism, and then examine its symbiotic relationship to democracy.

Western Experiences in Constitutionalism

It is commonly asserted that Western constitutionalism as an intellectual discourse maintains important continuities with an old and rich tradition of thought all the way back to Athens. Billias, for instance, points out that American and European constitutionalism of the late eighteenth and nineteenth centuries drew inspiration from the same resources of western civilization and thought. This legacy is said to have comprised "religious ideas stemming from the Judeo-Christian tradition, ideas derived from the constitutions of classical antiquity in Greece and Rome, constitutional theories developed by thinkers in the medieval period, and ideas revived in the Renaissance by writers like Machiavelli" (Billias 1990: 14).

One may wonder about the so-called "Judeo-Christian tradition" when the exclusion and persecution of Jews was one of the shared features of Western constitutionalism until well into the twentieth century in some cases. It is also possible to question the distinctiveness of the purported constitutions of ancient Greece and Rome in contrast to their contemporaries in Persia and India, or how they somehow managed to reach Enlightenment Europe unadulterated by influences or experiences of the Islamic civilization which transmitted earlier legacies to medieval Europe. Moreover, such presumed continuities do not account for the social and economic conditions that probably provided a stronger impetus for the actual historical context in which modern Western constitutionalism first emerged and evolved. In any case, neither type of genesis precludes consideration of a different set of factors or characteristics as the basis of the emergence and development of the concept in other parts of the world.

It is also relevant to note for our purposes here that the contractual nature of European medieval law, with its origins in negotiated settlements between conflicting social classes, was an important factor in contributing to constitutionalism in that context. The idea of the law as an autonomous authority exclusive of control of royal power— a critical aspect of constitutionalism—was gradually consolidated during this period. Medieval European constitutionalism was by no means well-defined or consistent, but that idea did achieve sufficient legitimacy for a nascent system of rights and law, which was able to represent and negotiate the interests of different social groups. But it does not necessarily follow that the development of European constitutionalism was uniform, consistent or irreversible. There were always divergent experiences, as well as shifts back and forth, from positive development of constitutionalism to regression into autocratic rule, as happened in Spain, Germany, and Italy during the first half of the twentieth century. While examining the small sample of three leading Western experiences, each on its own terms, can yield some general features of the concept, the following review will also show the incremental and contingent nature of the process even in those so-called countries of origin.

BRITISH CONSTITUTIONALISM

The British constitutional tradition is commonly regarded as an anomalous and contrary to the standard conception of modern constitutionalism in other Western countries. In addition to being based on the only "unwritten" constitution in the region, British constitutionalism has had a relatively smooth transition into the age of modernity, with no significant upheaval since 1688 (Bromhead 1974: 13), in contrast to that of France and the United States, which emerged from revolutionary fervor in the late eighteenth century. Another distinctive feature of the British constitutional tradition is the doctrine of "parliamentary sovereignty," whereby Parliament, as representative of the people, is the sole source of legal authority, unfettered by the notion of the supremacy of a constitution. By the same token, however, each Parliament is supreme only during its own term, and cannot bind subsequent Parliaments as that would deny their sovereignty. However, at any given time, Parliament consists of the Crown, the House of Lords, and the House of Commons. While Parliament is supposed to be representative of the people, Britain remains a constitutional monarchy, where the Crown is somehow the official source of justice, and is above parliament. In other words, British sovereignty is vested in "The Crown in Parliament" (Pilkington 1999: 10).

British constitutionalism is closely intertwined with, and has been sustained by, the country's common law tradition, whereby a "substantial part of the law of the constitution is common law" (Turpin 1990: 86). There is no separate identifiable prior law that can be called "constitutional," but several seminal statutes have a kind of authority or de facto status that achieve that quality, though there have been some deliberate attempt to invest an Act of Parliament with a deliberate "constitutional character" (85).

Some scholars have argued that the written/unwritten distinction is exaggerated and misleading, and that the British constitutional tradition is better described as "un-entrenched" rather than unwritten because there are several written documents that clearly fall within the scope of British constitutional sources (McHugh 2002: 47). The term "unwritten" is misleading since the chief characteristic of British constitutionalism is not its lack of a single central written constitutional text. Rather, this tradition is distinguished by the "institutional means of identifying constitutional provisions and norms and the methods that have been recognized for establishing, modifying, and altering it" (47). These institutional means make the British constitution un-entrenched in the sense that any aspect of it can in theory be changed by a simple Act of Parliament. The interpretation and application of the British constitution depends on the ability to recognize it without the need for a formal document that defines it as such. It is grounded upon expectations that it is as powerful and binding as any formally entrenched constitutional legacy, despite its informal appearance.

Accordingly, what secures legitimacy for the viability of such an un-entrenched constitution is a kind of tacit agreement or consensus among those who exercise political and legal power to abide by the spirit of the principles that are embodied in the constitutional tradition. There is recognition across the political and legal spheres that violating the intrinsic tenets of constitutionality, even if in doing so one may technically be acting within the law, can risk putting the entire constitutional system in jeopardy. Such actions, therefore, are consensually reserved only for genuine exceptions when the situation might truly warrant it. The success of British constitutionalism is believed to derive from the notion of the spirit of the law as a living political, legal and historical force whose legitimacy does not need codification or enshrinement in a single document. From this perspective, even if the British constitution came to be written after all, that would be irrelevant to its underlying legitimacy. "An unentrenched system will succeed *only* within a society that is culturally attuned to this ideal" (McHugh 2002: 48, emphasis original).

This quality emerged from a long historical accumulation and consolidation of certain constitutional *practices* that may or may not hold legal status, which serve as an ongoing basis for the practice of government in the country. This form of "aggregative constitutionalism" (Turpin 1990: 13) can be viewed in terms of the emergence and evolution of both laws and conventions that are associated with British constitutionalism. "The *legal* rules that make up part of the constitution are either statutory rules or rules of common law. Many of the more important practices of the constitution also have the character of rules, and, like legal rules, are the source of obligations and entitlements. These non-legal rules are called conventions" (4, emphasis original).

The Magna Carta of 1215 was a foundational document in the history of British constitutionalism, "the most famous concession of legal rights made by the English king to his subjects" (Helmholz 1999: 297). Among its significant provisions was the rule that no freeman should be imprisoned or banished except by the law of the land. While affirming the critical principle of the rule of law, the text itself accepted the institution of slavery as a matter of course. It is also important to note for our purposes here that King John was pressured by Archbishop Langton and a group of barons to affix his seal to the Carta in order to enable a return to stability from the state of economic and political disarray, to avoid the imminent threat of rebellion. Thus, that document, which is commonly seen as important for the history of constitutionalism in general, was in fact the product of a negotiated compromise for retaining authority and reestablishing control over the kingdom, rather than any noble sentiment on the part of the king. I would also note in relation to the role of Islam discussed earlier, the political power of Christianity was the midwife at the birth of one of the foundational documents of modern constitutionalism.

While accepting the seminal importance of the Magna Carta, Schwartz challenges the assumption that it marks the beginning of British constitutionalism. In his view, the foundations of English law and political institutions are to be seen in the political and social changes following the Norman Conquest in 1066, especially the continuity in English law and institutions (Schwartz 1967: 3). The roots of this continuity were planted through two transformative changes that were introduced into Anglo-Saxon government after the Norman Conquest, namely, "the establishment of a strong monarchy and the introduction of political feudalism" (4). The contractual nature of the land-sharing agreements between feudal lords and tenants, and of the political equation between the sovereign and his subjects, involved "rights and obligations on both sides" (6–7). This equation prevented the strong centralized monarchy implemented by William the Conqueror from lapsing into an exercise of untrammeled power. It was during that formative period that the "vital notion was developed that the obligations of the tenant were limited by the feudal contract to those stated and could not be increased by unilateral action by the lord" (7). The same notion of a constraint on power also dominated the public law of England after the Norman Conquest (8). Thus, a contractual relationship was translated into a framework for the limitation of sovereign power and operated as a legal as well as polit-ical principle in regulating relations in feudal society.

McIlwan also argued that constitutionalism, as the limitation of power and guarantee of rights in Britain, was preserved by the common law tra-dition, though the line between legal jurisdiction and governance was often fuzzy and the mandate of the former was severely limited. In his view, however, the great defect of medieval constitutionalism was "its fail-ure to enforce any penalty, except the threat or the exercise of revolu-tionary force, against a prince who actually trampled under foot those rights which undoubtedly lay beyond the scope of his legitimate author-ity" (McIlwan 1940: 95). As noted in chapter 1, this fault was also true of traditional Islamic constitutional theory at that time. In the case of Britain, legal jurisdiction survived during the earlier half of the sixteenth century, as "one outpost of law after another fell before the new forces of despotic will" (96). That survival was due to two factors: "the unex-ampled toughness of the ancient English common law and the ultimate emergence of new and radical religious differences among the subjects of the king" (97). The problem posed by religious difference for the king was that, being sworn by duty to maintain the Church, he had to protect and enforce religious uniformity at a time when there was no longer even a semblance of actual unity. If any religious group were punished for nonconformity, they could "regard the ruler not as a true king but as a tyrant who by fighting against God had abdicated his lawful authority" (99). The fact that each religious group could legitimately claim royal support effectively limited the powers of government.

These factors contributed to the turning point for the history of mod-ern British constitutionalism, namely, the Revolution of 1688, when the *legal* sovereignty of Parliament was firmly established with the forced abdi-cation of James II on the grounds that he had violated it. While Parlia-ment as the core element of government evolved in the course of British political history, it could not be called sovereign over royal power till the seventeenth century. With the Revolution of 1688, "the king himself came to owe his title to parliament, and parliament's complete political con-trol of administration made further legal limitation of it unnecessary" (McIlwan 1940: 138). The principle of parliamentary sovereignty that ensued in the wake of the events of 1688 was

at once historical reality, theory of the constitution, and a fundamental principle of the common law. In accordance with this principle the courts hold that statutes enacted by Parliament must be enforced and given priority over rules of com-mon law, international law binding upon the United Kingdom, the enactments of subordinate legislative authority, and earlier enactments of Parliament itself. (Turpin 1990: 24; emphasis added).

Schwartz points out that the "fundamental importance" of these events for constitutional development was that "they settled the essential nature of the English polity and, as such, were the constitutional culmination of the struggle between prerogative and law which is the great theme of the seventeenth century" (Schwartz 1967: 197). However, the distinctive constitutional significance of the Revolution of 1688 for British constitutionalism was in that "the idea prevailed that the best guarantee of a just political order was the supremacy of Parliament over the monarch and not a law antecedent to and constituting both. . . . The Glorious Revolution marks the beginning of an era in which parliamentary sovereignty supplanted for good the idea of a paramount law" (Preuss 1995: 28). Thus, paradoxically, British constitutionalism evolved on the basis of the displacement of the notion of a paramount law from the country's political practice and culture.

The relationship between democracy and constitutionalism, discussed later in this chapter, also evolved over the centuries in British political culture, despite the fact that individual civil rights were not expressly documented or protected in constitutional terms as such. While British constitutional documents since the Magna Carta speak of "the ancient rights and liberties of England," these rights are not positively articulated in any document. As framed in such instruments as the Bill of Rights of 1689, for instance, these rights "are expressed in the negative sense of English subjects being entitled to do anything they are not actually forbidden to do. . . . [There is] no constitutional protection of an individual's rights other than the common law of the country" (Pilkington 1999: 21). The current validity of this principle is illustrated by the fact that, although Britain ratified the European Convention of Human Rights in 1950, the process of incorporating these rights as part of the domestic law of the country did not begin until the parliamentary session of 1997–98. As a matter of present British constitutional doctrine, this incorporation remains a matter of ordinary legislation, rather than an "entrenched" bill of rights, as in other constitutions.

Similarly, democracy as the term is commonly understood today came to be incorporated in the British constitutional system through various and gradual developments. "Britain is by no means the 'mother of modern democracy,' since the principle of 'one person, one vote' was not institutionalized there till the middle of the nineteenth century" (Franklin and Baun 1995: 11). It was only with the achievement of universal suffrage through the enactment of the Representation of the People Acts of 1918 and 1928 that it can be claimed that the British Constitution has finally embodied the principle of democracy (Turpin 1990: 19).

British constitutionalism may indeed be undergoing drastic changes that were unimaginable a few years ago, as membership of the Council of Europe and the European Union, among many other factors, may lead to the adoption of a written constitution and an entrenched bill of rights. While it is too early to speculate about such possibilities, even that apparently new direction will still confirm the main point I am trying to make here, namely, that constitutionalism is always the product of local and regional context, even when it appears to depart from a long-established tradition. British constitutionalism as the product of its own history has so far evolved into particular forms and institutions as a result of the practical experiences of the people of Britain, and will continue to evolve as a result of that experience. Whatever new or different directions it may evolve into, British constitutionalism is sustained by the country's political culture and political and legal institutions, which have evolved through a practical process of trial and error over centuries. There is nothing predetermined or given about this process, which is simply a matter of actual practice and real experience.

American Constitutionalism

The United States of America is credited with the establishment of the modern idea of the constitution as a central, single document that operates as a paramount law representing the fundamental compact between people and their government, with popular sovereignty being expressed and preserved by the paramount status of the constitution. The principle of limitation of government power is realized in this tradition through such principles as the separation of powers, also known as the doctrine of "checks and balances," whereby the lawmaking power is vested in the Legislature, the Executive implements the decisions of the legislature, and the Judiciary is charged with adjudication disputes about the interpretation and application of all public law, including constitutional law. Another characteristic feature is federalism as a principle of limitation of power, whereby the power of the federal government is limited in favor of state power that is supposed to better reflect the direct democratic local voice of the people. Maintaining constitutional limitations on governmental power through judicial review by the courts is another key American contribution to modern constitutional doctrine. The constitution of the United States is also noted for its strong commitment to the protection of citizens' rights and liberties. I will now attempt to briefly show that all these features were the product of the deeply contextual evolution of constitutionalism in the history of the country. As with the case of Britain earlier and France next, what follows are reflections on this process, and not an exhaustive or up-to-date discussion of all relevant developments.

While the Constitution of the United States, drafted in 1787 and ratified the following year, came to represent the core of this constitutional tradition, one should take account of "the complex of political concepts observable in certain documents, procedures, and institutions that came into being within the United States during the founding period from 1776 to 1791" (Billias 1990: 2). These include six documents which represent, though do not exhaust, the significant constitutional texts of the time: "the Declaration of Independence, the first state constitutions, the Articles of Confederation, the Federal Constitution, the Federalist Papers, and the Federal Bill of Rights" (2). Note should also be taken of the embryonic expression of this constitutional tradition in several colonial documents, such as the Pilgrim Code of Law and the Mayflower Compact. Other influences that have contributed to shaping the American constitutional tradition are said to include "the Judeo-Christian tradition as interpreted by the radical protestant sects to which belonged so many of the original European settlers in British North America . . . modified, enriched, and differentiated as a result of shared colonial experiences, the influence of English Whigs, the European Enlightenment, and English common law, as well as political events and problems after independence" (Lutz 1988: 7).

The constitutional experience of the United States was also shaped by the struggle of the colonies for independence from British imperial power, which apparently caused the American constitution-makers to be particularly concerned with certain specific features of their project: "First and foremost, a constitution must list the fundamental principles and individual rights which lawmakers were bound to respect because they were, in the words of the American Declaration of Independence of 1776, 'truths' held to be 'self evident'" (Preuss 1995: 30). The practical legal consequence of this idea was that the power of lawmakers must be limited since the lawmaking assembly itself was created on the basis of the constitution. That conception represented "the truly revolutionary idea that political sovereignty is first created by a constitution and is not a preexisting entity whose powers a constitution merely limits" (30). The notion that constitutions constitute government in the first place was an evident truth to people of the American colonies, since it was the constitution that would settle and regulate the kind of government they had in mind.

The second fundamental attribute of American constitutionalism, according to Preuss, was that it had to have a normative character. Precisely because they had to contest the absolute power of the British Parliament, the framers of the American constitution were determined to have a constitution that would have "the binding force of a higher law whose infringement would give people the right to rebel" (Preuss 1995: 31). The ultimate source of authority regarding the legal exercise of power had to rest in clearly defined principles whose authority exceeded that of men. The normative status of constitutional dictates would mean that any particular government could not conveniently interpret the constitution to suit its own purposes.

Another reflection of the normative character of a constitution related to its codification in a single written document, which is to be viewed as "sacred." To secure legitimacy as a foundational statement of paramount law, a constitution had to be a categorical, unambiguous statement of principles, which is best achieved by stating them in a single document. As written law, the constitution had to be presented like a sacred document, in order to have "the same status for American settlers and their political intentions that Luther's translation of the Bible had for the German Protestants" (Preuss 1995: 32). Still, it should be emphasized, the written constitution was only a stage in a long process, part of subsequent as well as earlier developments rather than an autonomous, self-contained, and conclusive "event."

A third key feature of American constitutionalism is the manner in which the principle of the sovereignty of the people is organized. "The Constitution set up a system of government based on the idea, however circumscribed in its application, that sovereignty ultimately resided not with 'the nation' (as the French would have it) but with 'the people'" (Keller 1987: 678). The reason for this difference may have been that the citizens of the United States did not see themselves as a nation, with a national culture and history, as those of France perceived themselves at the time. "Prior to the 1760s, there was no 'people' that could be properly called American. The colonies were really a collection of peoples, each one engaged in a separate process of self-definition" (Lutz 1988: 7). Although a common culture was emerging and a sense of national identity was taking root, constitutionalism did not have an established "Americanness" to work with, whether in positive or negative ways. To the contrary, constitutionalism appears to have been integrated into the meaning of being American, where the constitution itself became part of the emerging nationalist mythology of the new nation:

American constitutionalism was fed as well by the swelling popular nationalism of nineteenth century American culture. Like its European counterparts, American nationalism required legends, heroes, totems; unlike them, it had no deep traditions of an American *volk* on which to draw. The sanctification of the Constitution (like tales of valor in the Revolution and the War of 1812, the popular hagiography of the lives of Benjamin Franklin, George Washington and other founders, and the veneration of the Declaration of Independence) helped meet that need. (Keller 1987: 680)

These associations may well have helped to create or sustain the resonance of the constitution as sacred among American settlers. Another reason for the initial success of American constitutionalism was that, in contrast to France at the time, there was no support for any kind of monarchy in competition with the republic (Keller 1987: 680). But the point to emphasize for my purposes here is that there are different ideas of sovereignty in the British, American, and French histories of constitutionalism. This is true for the manner in which popular sovereignty is authorized as political power, as well as for the manner in which the people are defined. Moreover, whatever notion of the "people" was dominant in early America and reflected in the constitution, that has in turn reinforced that idea and helped strengthen it in American political and public life.

In Keller's view (1987), Power and Rights are the two major themes in American constitutionalism. The first century of American constitutionalism (late eighteenth and nineteenth centuries) reveals a focus on control and demarcation of power; the second century (twentieth century) on civil liberties, and the rights of individuals and groups. For my part, it is important to note that the constitutional protection of rights in the American constitution refers to a particular societal conception of liberties. On the one hand, the American constitution "has come to stand for individual rights, protected even against legitimate authority, even against the elected representatives of the people, and in large measure, even when they act in good faith and the public interest" (Henkin 1990: 1). On the other hand, "The idea of rights is not explicit in the U.S. Constitution. . . . The individual's rights then do not derive from the Constitution. They are not, strictly, 'constitutional rights.' But they are *protected* by the Constitution" (3). Thus, as in the British case noted earlier, rights in the American setting are also understood in terms of a wider notion of liberties. The vital difference between these two traditions is that these liberties are positively protected in the American constitution as opposed to the British model, where they are upheld in the negative sense of not prohibiting them.

American constitutionalism is credited with exceptional influence not only on the constitutions of many other countries, but on the concept of constitutionalism itself. Thomas Paine's analysis of the American constitution, often called the first clear elaboration of the modern sense of the term (Sartori 2003), include the following key points (McIlwan 1940: 11):

- There is a fundamental difference between a people's government and that people's constitution, whether the government happens to be entrusted to a king or to a representative assembly.
- The constitution is antecedent to the government.
- The constitution defines the authority which the people commit to their government, and in doing so they thereby limit it.
- If the distinction is not actually observed between the constitution and

the government, the state will in fact be despotic because the will of the government has no check upon it.

The preceding brief review confirms the view that American constitutionalism is first and foremost a product of its own history, process and context; constantly evolving and adapting in response to its own challenges, internal and external. Secondly, American constitutionalism is sustained by its own culture, institutions, and nationalist mythology. All these underlying factors evolved in dynamic interaction with each other over several centuries, rather than being a given state of affairs from the start. The following reflections on the French experience, without attempting a detailed discussion of all relevant developments, suggest similar conclusions in that case as well.

French Constitutionalism

Since the French Revolution in 1789, France has had at least 12 constitutions, whereby the ideals that inspired the Revolution and the radically new notion of political order it generated were translated into a stable constitutional framework over a long period and through many stages. In fact, however, only the last 5 constitutions are classified as "republican," though that idea was one of the main objectives of the Revolution. The French constitution operates in the context of a civil law system, which has a different conception of how government power is limited and rights protected from that of the British and American systems.

The conception of political authority changed with the Revolution to be seen as no longer flowing from God to the king, but instead "surging from below, from the people themselves, who conferred legitimate authority upon their duly elected representatives in parliament" (Rohr 1995: 11). The Revolution also created "a solidly democratic basis for the rule of law in France, but the law that ruled was *statutory* law, that is, laws passed by the sovereign parliament in the name of the people" (11; emphasis original). The laws passed by parliament could not be challenged, since "(1) as a practical matter, there has been no Supreme Court in France empowered to strike down unconstitutional laws passed by Parliament; and (2) as a matter of principle, there is no logical basis to challenge a legislative enactment duly authorized by the Parliament" (11). Hence, although the constitution might technically speaking have had paramount status in France, in practice it did not have the power to check the action of political power in the same way this is done in the United States. The French answer to this question remained different from the American approach even after the introduction of the Constitutional Council under the Fifth Republic to "adjudicate" such matters, as noted below.

While the rule of law may have been given a democratic foundation with the Revolution, the relationship between democracy and the functioning and limitation of political power seems to have been a problematical one in the history of French constitutionalism. To some extent this is also true of the American experience. Writing of the French and American Revolutions, Bukanovsky states that

Democratic legitimacy did not emerge victorious from the eighteenth century revolutions, but neither was dynastic legitimacy reasserted in its traditional form. Rather, it was the idea of *popular sovereignty*—the notion that legitimacy must come from the will of the people—that proved the most potent, immediate legacy of the revolutionary wars and domestic struggles. Closely linked to this development was the idea that the people, rather than the monarch, constituted —and ought to constitute—the nation. Popular sovereignty and nationalism were *not* inextricably linked to the notions of democratic rule or even the rule of law. (Bukanovsky 2002: 6, emphasis added)

In the case of France, it appears that translating the rather abstract association of the "people" with the "nation" into actual political practice required a series of experiments with different constitutional forms and systems. In contrast, the definition of the "people" who could actually benefit from the constitution was limited and exclusionary in the American experience. After all, "the original document [the Constitution of the United States] recognized slavery and permitted states to restrict the voting franchise to only a very limited population of propertied, white males" (Franklin 1995: 11). Nevertheless, the *idea* that the link between people and constitution is prior to any functioning of government, which is the doctrine of constitutional supremacy, distinguishes the American from the French experience.

Constitutional development in France can be viewed in terms of three repeated cycles of "the assertion of sovereign control from the monarchy, different elite sources, and the democratic polity" (McHugh 2002: 149). However, while the term "republican" in the French context seems to refer to the establishment of democratic practice, its true meaning would be "closer to some of the French experiments with limited oligarchy, since that sort of government would seek to accommodate the interests of various classes, groups and regions" (150). The idea of constitutional monarchy survived the Revolution, and "was revived under the First and Second Empires, and briefly, under the Vichy government that ruled France, under Nazi auspices, during World War II" (149). The democratic imperative was represented in particular by the constitutions of the First, Second, and Fourth Republics, while the Fifth Republic is more genuinely republican since it represents the objective of combining the various cycles of French constitutional history.

The Fifth Republic, established in 1958 under the leadership of Charles de Gaulle, signified radical transformations in the French Constitution. The presidency was invested with real powers, but parliament was not divested of all its powers. Indeed, "the most distinctive feature of the Constitution of the Fifth Republic is the division of executive power between the president and the government headed by the prime minister" (Rohr 1995: 51). It should also be noted that the Declaration of the Rights of Man and of the Citizen of 1789 is a part of the Constitution of the Fifth Republic. However, a crucial innovation in this current phase is the establishment of the Constitutional Council, which has autonomy from government power, to "police the constitutional boundary erected between the spheres of law and regulation" (139). Rohr suggests that "it is no exaggeration to say that the Constitutional Council has totally transformed French constitutional law and has provided France for the first time with the institutional capacity to impose constitutional discipline upon an errant parliament" (139).

A brief note on the notion of law may be helpful at this stage. The sanctity of the law is a culturally established aspect of French society. The Napoleonic Code, adopted in 1804, replaced the courts and the king with a concise body of rules and principles determined by the "representative assembly of the people, thus reflecting a new relationship between legislators and those governed by the law (Dadamo and Farran 1993: 10). The French tradition has

a rather more conceptual and abstract approach to the law, preferring to see it in terms of fundamental principles rather than as a means of providing remedies for specific cases . . . it is not just the preserve of lawyers and the courts, but permeates and concerns the whole of society. . . . Emphasis is therefore placed on the importance of the rule of law, the safeguards of individual rights, and the accessibility of the law to non-lawyers. (Dadamo and Farran 1993: 12)

To conclude these brief comments on a comparative note for our purposes here, the notion of the constitution as paramount law is totally absent in the British tradition; it is present in the French and American experiences, but in two different forms. In the American case, the constitution as paramount law both guides the functioning of the judiciary and is enforced by it. In France, the constitution is paramount because it is an integral part of the law which is paramount. A second critical distinction is that in the United States of America, the courts can interpret the constitution but in France this is outside the province of the jurists. I will now draw on the preceding remarks and earlier discussion for some general theoretical reflections on the nature and evolution of modern constitutionalism as a matter of gradual consensus among various experiences.

Nature and Evolution of Modern Constitutionalism

According to Ackerman (1997), until the late 1930s, constitutionalism did not necessarily seem empowering or attractive to many nations. While the British example provided some hope, the notion of constitutionalism it represented was ambiguous, for example, with its lack of a formal constitution. Such a relatively positive view of British constitutionalism at that time would have to overlook, of course, the fact that the hope it offered did not include the "native subjects" of the Empire in Africa and Asia. Still, I agree with Ackerman that what seemed to characterize the success of the British political example, for its own citizens, was "their culture of self-government, their common sense and decency, that distinguished their evolving commitment to democratic principles—not paper constitutions and institutional gimmicks like judicial review" (771–72). In his view, many Americans believed this British cultural heritage, as opposed to their own constitution, to be primarily responsible for American democracy. By the 1990s, Ackerman suggests that it has become possible to speak of "world constitutionalism" (772).

Constitutions and constitutionalism can be viewed descriptively, as "the laws, customs and conventions which define the composition and powers of organs of the state and regulate the relations of various state organs to one another and to the private citizen" (Bromhead 1974: 13). A constitution can also be seen as "the framework of norms and practices which define and regularise the management of political relationships. . . . The absence of a [written] "constitution" need not be very significant; in any case the whole body of norms and practices is only one aspect of the political system, which is a much wider concept" (7).

The core idea of modern constitutionalism is commonly taken to be a framework for the limitation of political power by law. As McIlwan states, "in all its successive phases, constitutionalism has one essential quality: it is a legal limitation on government; it is the antithesis of arbitrary rule; its opposite is despotic government, the government of will instead of law" (McIlwan 1940: 24). It is also said that "The dominant theme of Western constitutional thought has traditionally been the design of political institutions to limit the exercise of power" (Elkin and Soltan 1993: 21). But the notion of limiting political power by law is not necessarily a modern invention. For example, Islamic political philosophy evolved around the idea of subordinating the political authority of the Caliph (Khalipha) to Shari'a as the ultimate normative system of Islam. As noted in chapter 1, however, the Islamic principle of the supremacy of Shari'a was negated in practice by the failure to develop institutional arrangements for its effective implementation and enforcement when necessary (An-Na'im 1990: 91–94).

The more significant feature of modern constitutionalism, in my view, is the combination of a new definition of political power with clearer and more effective normative and institutional limitations of power. Both elements are intended to effectuate the revolutionary notion articulated in Western Enlightenment thought, and historically associated with the American and French Revolutions of the late eighteenth century, namely, that sovereignty ultimately derives its authority from the people. Indeed, constitutionalism can be conceptualized as the legal recognition and enforcement of the idea of vesting sovereignty in the people. The core idea from this perspective becomes one of determining and regulating the relationship between the limitation of political power and the location of sovereignty in the people.

It is also important, however, to perceive the concept more widely than as the strictly *legal* limitation of government. Doing so does not necessarily contradict or rule out the limitation doctrine, but anchors this central proposition in broader political processes. From this perspective, constitutionalism can be defined as "a method of organizing government that depends on and adheres to a set of fundamental guiding principles and laws" (Holmes 1995: 299). Moreover, the definition can also be further expanded beyond the legal and non-legal operations of government to relate it to the substratum of values on which the concept is founded. "The ultimate role a constitution plays depends upon the sovereign source of the fundamental values upon which it is based and, indeed, the very identity (more importantly, the *self*-identity) of each source of sovereign authority" (McHugh 2002: 1; emphasis in original). The issue can be seen in this light as a matter of the adequacy or legitimacy of constitutional values, whereby the effectiveness of the concept depends on the extent to which the constitution is recognized and endorsed by the people as a genuine expression of the values, norms, and customs of their society.

To follow such basic ideas into related concepts, if sovereignty is ultimately located in the people, then the political framework based on such authority must effectively enable the people to develop and express their will. In other words, the principle of democracy is the necessary implication of the notion of popular sovereignty, as the latter finds its practical expression in the former. Similarly, if government power is to be limited, that should happen in terms of some fundamental quality that people rightfully possess, which we can understand as rights, liberties, or freedoms. If the purpose of constitutionalism is the protection of rights and application of the principle of popular sovereignty, then it must enjoy a foundational status in the legal and political structure of any society. But its precise relationship with democracy, sovereignty, and rights can take a wide variety of forms among different models, and even within the same national experience over time.

Constitutionalism and African Constitutionalism

Taking some of the preceding general remarks as my point of departure, I will now offer some reflections in relation to African constitutional experiences. These reflections are premised on the following propositions that have been discussed at various stages of this book. First, all human societies strive to implement their own mechanisms for the mediation of conflict over political power, economic resources, and social justice. Since the choice of one mechanism over another can have a significant impact on the outcome of such mediation, this choice is also the subject of contestation among competing perceptions of justice, order, and morality within the same society. It would therefore follow that such choices can change, or be modified over time, in response to changing circumstances. Second, the appropriateness and efficacy of those mechanisms is conditioned by the nature and dynamics of political, economic, and social relationships and processes within each society. However, the reality and permanence of conflict mean that the prevalence of certain mechanisms of mediation is contested by those who feel oppressed or aggrieved by their outcome.

The third proposition on which this part of my discussion is premised is the view that, while a prevailing framework would primarily be the product of internal factors and processes, no society is immune from external influences through a variety of channels ranging from the borrowing and adaptation through peaceful relations with other societies, to violent conquest and imposition by external forces. An acknowledgment of the extent and consequences of external influence, regardless of its sources and manner, is necessary for a clear understanding of the nature and operation of the prevailing system, rather than a negation of the role of internal factors and processes. From this point of view one can appreciate the special role of the Enlightenment, and developments associated with the French and the American Revolutions, in locating constitutionalism in formally articulated philosophical system for those societies. Other societies may benefit from but cannot be limited to those philosophies.

Moreover, the fact that what is commonly referred to as the "Western tradition" shares some common philosophical resources does not mean that the experiences of different societies within that tradition were either homogeneous or consistent, as they varied not only from one society to another, and over time, but also from one class or group of people to another within the same society. Mamdani clarifies this point by a brief discussion of the contrast between democracy as a stabilizing and conservative force in the United States, and a revolutionary and destabilizing force in France. A central concern of Republican thought and practice in the United States at the inception of constitutionalism there, he argues, was to set parameters on popular sovereignty by the rule of law that was expressed in terms of the inviolable rights of the minority against the majority, or of the individual in relation to the political power of the state. That conception of the rule of law forbids the majority from appropriating the property of the minority, hence the contradiction between "natural rights" to transform society and "vested rights" that remain judicially enforceable, and between the public rights of citizens and the private rights of property. "Whereas in Western Europe the rule of law was seen as a check on an arbitrary and capricious royal power, in the American tradition it emerged really as a limitation on popular sovereignty. The general point is that the historical routes to the rule of law and the concept of constitutionalism are several and contradictory" (Mamdani 1990: 361).

From my perspective, though internally differentiated and contradictory, Western models of the nation-state ("territorial" states in the case of Africa as explained in chapter 1) and conceptions of constitutionalism have been effectively universalized, including dominant liberal models as well as their critiques and proposed alternatives. Thus, as indicated earlier, newly independent African states have "inherited" the models of their respective colonial powers. Even the "alternative models" some nationalist leaders subsequently attempted to implement, as happened in Egypt, Ghana, and Tanzania in the 1960s, were based on Western critique of liberalism, whether on the socialist or nationalist single party state model. More recently, some African states have returned to the liberal fold, with countries like Ghana and Zambia attempting to revive a revised version of their independence constitutions and others, like Ethiopia and Uganda, launching new experiments in constitution-making.

Without going into a discussion or evaluation of the variety of these postcolonial experiences, I wish to emphasize that internal African perceptions and experiences have been too much conditioned by external visions to permit an independent starting point or clear break at a subsequent stage of development. In light of the framing propositions above, this sort of influence and interaction is both to be expected and useful for African countries. After all, these are the ideological orientations and political realities of the world African societies have to live in. Moreover, the above-noted internal variety and contradictions among Western models provide African societies with a range of options and possibilities. My primary concern is that indigenous African perspectives are to be taken seriously on their own terms, as part of the process of promoting and legitimating constitutionalism in Africa, without claiming that such perspectives are somehow unadulterated by external influences, or that they should have an exclusive monopoly on the process.

To contribute to this balancing process, of being open to external, primarily Western, influence, while keeping the final word for African experiences, I will now present some critical reflections on Western conceptions of constitutionalism.

One of the main theoretical themes of liberal constitutionalism is the notion of a social contract between the state as the apparatus of government, on the one hand, and civil society as social and economic institutions and processes autonomous of the state, on the other (Rawls 1971; Held 1984). From this widely accepted perspective, the primary role of a constitution is to limit the scope of governmental power, and to prescribe the method for its exercise, in order to preserve the autonomy of civil society (Shils 1991). A constitution is to perform these functions through separation of legislative, executive, and judicial powers, the incorporation of principles of a representative government that is accountable to the will of the governed, protection of individual civil liberties, and some form of judicial review. The values traditionally associated with this model, as they have evolved especially during the twentieth century, emphasize individual civil, political, and property rights based on the equality of all citizens under the law. Earlier tensions between the competing values a constitution is supposed to embody and mediate have been mitigated by a broad agreement on these values, especially with the acceptance of social welfare to moderate the rigors of the market. Yash Ghai sees this as a kind of a "class compromise" that facilitated liberal constitutionalism (Ghai 1993: 54–55); hence there is a strong connection between the emergence of liberal constitutionalism and the needs of capitalism.

> Important roots of constitutionalism lie in the need of capitalism for predictability, calculability and security of property rights and transactions . . . The generality of rules prevented both discrimination and arbitrary action (important for competitive capitalism); it prevented the subordination of the judge to the legislature in specific disputes, while at the same time it put a curb on judicial adventurism; and generality, with its rules for the future, ruled out the retroactivity of law. . . . There is considerable tension between the needs of capitalism in general and the desires of individual enterprises or sections of industry, which different modern states resolve in different ways. (Ghai 1993: 54)

Ghai also emphasizes the ideological function of liberal constitutionalism, in that it hides the way in which power is exercised by giving the impression of pluralistic, competitive, and responsive political systems. By emphasizing the primacy of state representative and judicial institutions, constitutionalism mitigates the appeal of radical politics. "The appearance of the neutral autonomy [of the law] is possible because the primary form of subordination or unequal relations is not the law but social and economic forces which rely upon equal and neutral legal concepts and rules to achieve that effect" (55). Yet, he concludes that this ideology has broadened over time to encompass democracy, political freedoms, and social justice, especially by the extension of the franchise and the recognition of certain social and collective rights. "An essential basis of contemporary western constitutionalism is a social compact between capital and labour under which the market system is accepted within the context of a welfare state" (56). Accordingly, I understand Ghai to be suggesting that Western constitutionalism seems to be designed to mitigate the worst social consequences of the market and to ensure a reasonable standard of living.

The general social theoretical critique of bourgeois constitutionalism is that it is a means of domination of society by capitalists who control the apparatus of the state through advantages such as ownership of the press, access to education, and greater resources for political organization. The separation of powers and institutions of government is negated by class solidarity (protecting vested interests through the various organs), while the narrow scope of state power also enables capitalists to dominate civil society through the economy and other private institutions. To rectify these defects, socialist theory proposes that since law and constitutions are instruments of class rule, the transformation of society into a truly egalitarian society requires the dictatorship of the proletariat to break the economic, social, and political power of the bourgeois.

From a theoretical socialist perspective, the proletariat should resist bourgeoisie domination of the state, and take over the state in order to use it to change society. In this way, a model Marxist constitution is supposed to become an overtly authoritarian instrument of the working class, to enable it to dominate the state and transform civil society. Liberal constitutionalism emphasizes permanence, though not immutability, seeks to maintain order and stability, gives primacy to the individual and protection of civil society, and reflects distrust of power and belief in pluralism as enshrined in freedoms of expression and association and the right to political opposition. In contrast, Marxist constitutions are based on the notion of change, seek to uproot old values and social structures in order to transform society, give primacy to the state and cooperatives as representing the community, seek to dominate civil society in order to transform it through political control and the development of a new economic order, acknowledge the supremacy of and usually the monopoly of power by the Communist Party, and reject separation of powers to facilitate the transformative potential of political power (Ghai 1993: 57–59). Separation of powers is replaced by centralization of power in the state, subject only to the supervisory role of the Communist Party, "which owes its existence and powers to a mandate higher than the constitution, to history itself" (57). However, none of the states that attempted to implement this model (primarily in the Soviet Union and East and Central Europe, but also in Africa, Asia and Latin America) have succeeded in moderating "the extra-constitutional status of the Communist Party, its leading role, or the absence of its legal accountability" (58).

This brief comparison of liberal and socialist theories of constitutionalism is useful because both models have had significant influence on constitutionalism in Africa, though the former has had a more formative and continuing impact than the latter. For the same reason, it is instructive to note here the similarities between the rationale and claims of some Islamic political movements and those of Marxist socialists. First, the leaders of Islamic movements tend to subscribe to a critique of liberal constitutionalism similar to that launched earlier by socialists, albeit presented in Islamic terminology. Second, they profess a similar utopian vision and corresponding authoritarian approach to power and politics in order to achieve their objectives in social transformation. In this regard, Islamic political movements tend to endow their own cadre with the same leading and ultraconstitutional role that Marxist socialists have envisaged for the Communist Party. Third, some Islamic political movements have also adopted Marxist political strategies of building temporary alliances and seeking exclusive political power by any means possible, whether through popular mobilization in Iran, tactical use of democratic means in Algeria, or military coups in Pakistan and Sudan. The following remarks on the liberal/socialist debate may also be applicable to the liberal/Islamic debate.

In my view, the above-noted Marxist critique of liberal constitutionalism is basically valid on its own terms, but the socialist theory and practice are not the answer. From a constitutional perspective in particular, socialist theory seem to suffer from a fundamental ambiguity regarding the notion of popular sovereignty. Seeking to rule in the name of the working classes, Marxist socialists were still unable to trust the political judgment and action of their own purported constituencies. Instead, they sought to enthrone the Communist Party as the guardian of the working classes, without providing any effective safeguards against the abuse of power, mismanagement, and corruption of Party officials and cadre. The same is true, I believe, of the role of elites and cadres in Islamist political organizations, like the National Islamic Front of Sudan.

Despite its problems and limitations, liberal constitutionalism clearly has the ability to incorporate the insights of its critics, and is more open to adaptation to effective efforts to resolve the paradox of popular sovereignty than other models. The way forward, in my view, is to take socialist and other critiques of liberal constitutionalism seriously, and incorporate them into a liberal approach to theory and practice in each country. The challenge is therefore to ensure that popular sovereignty will not be abused or manipulated when exercised by the public at large, rather than pursue the illusion of elite leadership in the name of ideological purity, social justice, or national or Islamic self-determination. This can only be achieved through the actual practice of constitutional governance over time, hence the idea of incremental success presented in this book.

Constitutionalism and Democracy

In light of the preceding reflections, I agree with the view that constitutionalism "includes the doctrine of official accountability to the people or to its legitimate representatives within the framework of fundamental law for better securing citizens' rights. Behind the doctrine lies the axiom that the people as a whole are the best judges about what is (not) in their own interest" (Rosenbaum 1988: 4). Thus, the modern concept is supposed to be fundamentally related to notions of rights, democracy, and popular sovereignty. But as the earlier review of the actual historical constitutional experiences of Britain, the United States, and France indicates, there was no neat correlation with democracy as commonly understood today. In France, for instance, constitutionalism did not immediately and completely dislodge monarchical authority from participating in the exercise of power, despite its emphasis on the idea that political authority derived from the people.

Moreover, the democratic ideals that the concept was supposed to represent in each case did not extend to all citizens in practice. Indeed, the history of citizens' rights in each case can be seen as following a different trajectory, according to a different contextual meaning for each society. On the one hand, constitutional ideals permitted the persistence of slavery and its aftermath for nearly two centuries after the bill of rights was adopted in the United States, and the exclusion of women and the poor classes from political participation in all three countries until the early twentieth century. Yet, each of the three countries negotiated its own way out of those undemocratic limitations, according to its own internal context and sociopolitical dynamics. In the final analysis, however, there was nothing predestined or irreversible about these developments in each case, only specific outcomes of political struggles, a civil war in the case of the United States, and social transformation over time in all three countries.

It is therefore important to affirm the need to invest in democracy and protection of rights, while realizing that the association between constitutionalism and democracy is part of a progressive evolution in each specific context. It is from this perspective that I will now approach the relationship between the two. While specific strategies should be developed and implemented to promote and secure the relationship, one should neither despair if the desired outcome is not immediately realized, even after several attempts, nor become complacent when the relationship appears to be established and secured.

Although the functioning of both presume the same basis or idea of political authority, namely, that governance is legitimized by the will of the people, "the relationship between constitutionalism and democracy, that is, between limited government and self-government, remains one of the most important but least understood subjects in political theory" (Holmes 1995: 299). Indeed, there is an obvious tension between constitutional limitations of the powers of government, on the one hand, and the implementation of the will of the majority of the population, on the other. This tension or paradox was apparent in the American and French constitutional experiences, reviewed earlier. "During the revolutions, the 'people' appeared as direct participants on the political stage, giving tangible expression to the principle of democracy. A constitution, on the other hand, acts as an intermediary between the people and the exercise of power; all political authority derives from it, and as a fundamental law it expressly limits the power of the popularly elected assembly" (Preuss 1995: 34).

Murphy attempts to mediate this tension by emphasizing human dignity as the unifying principle of both democracy and constitutionalism, the basis of both principles. In his view, however, democratic theory adopts a more positive view of human nature in the belief that people will make rational decisions that are genuinely in their best interest, and "will not tyrannize themselves" (Murphy 1993: 4). Moreover, the practical working of democracy tends to develop checks and balances against the possibility of majoritarian misuse of democratic power. Such checks and balances might include formations of temporary alliances based on strategic interests, the pressure on particular parties in government not to alienate support by oppressing any group, and a culture of mediation among public officials. Murphy also points out that the functioning of democracy may help establish the idea that competing interests is "itself a form of justice" (5).

In contrast, Murphy suggests, constitutionalism adopts a more skeptical view of human nature, and does not accept that such organic checks and balances are sufficient to prevent the abuses of power. Constitutionalists "want *institutional* restraints on substantive matters to prevent lapses into an authoritarian or even totalitarian system cloaked with populist trappings" (1993: 6; emphasis added). From the constitutionalist perspective, legitimacy for policy is guaranteed not just by faith in the decision-makers' credibility but "also on substantive criteria" (6). Thus, Murphy maintains that both democracy and constitutionalism "accept the centrality of human dignity; they differ on how best to protect that value" (8). He argues that both need each other and that many of the societies commonly described as having democratic systems, such as Australia, India, and the United States, are more appropriately termed constitutional democracies. In Murphy's view, constitutionalism is consistent with the fundamental democratic principle, except that it requires a pragmatic check on undesirable consequences that may occur when the "people" grant a government power to act in their name. Constitutionalism, from this point of view, is a set of measures and safeguards to ensure governance in accord with the spirit of democracy.

Holmes, on the other hand, challenges the idea of any intrinsic contradiction between constitutionalism and democracy as "empirically unconfirmed and theoretically inadequate" (Holmes 1995: 300). For him, "the primary function of a liberal constitution—as this novel political form emerged in the United States at the end of the eighteenth century—is to constitute democracy, that is, to put democracy into effect." Like Murphy, he understands self-government and limited government as "mutually supportive", but he views constitutionalism as a more foundational doctrine, indeed, as the very substratum of democracy. To him, the relationship between the democratic electorate and their representatives can be conceived of as a principal-agent relationship. While decision-making power rests with the people, public officials operate as their "proxies" (301). In democracies, typically elections are the means by which the principals can monitor or check their proxies to ensure that the latter are doing their job. However, elections are essentially inadequate as a check because proxies often justify their actions in the name of the people or public good, whatever the real intent and consequences of those actions might be.

It may seem that constitutionalism is an inherently undemocratic means of constraining the will of the people, but if one understands that these checks on the people's proxies as being authorized by democracy itself, on a broader understanding of the term, then there is no inherent conflict. Constitutional safeguards against the abuse of vested power can be understood in terms of "plural agency" (Holmes 1995: 300), authorized by the people themselves. In other words, "constitutionalism attempts to solve the principal-agent problem not only by institutionalizing periodic elections but also by appointing multiple agents who can monitor each other" (301). This is what the separation of powers is supposed to achieve in the American constitutional system. The common sense of democratic citizens, it is said, recognizes "the need for a variety of indirect techniques for enforcing their will on public officials."

Holmes also argues that the entrenchment of rights "beyond the reach of ordinary democratic processes" (1995: 303) is not antidemocratic.

Since rights are essential for deliberative democracy, their constitutional protection is a democratic safeguard against, for instance, abridging the right to vote or freedom of the press, by the people's representatives. Constitutional rights that are unrelated to the issue of representative government, such as freedom of religion and the right to fair trial are also necessary for securing deliberative democratic functioning in the larger sense. In other words, the protection of all these rights is essential for the survival and effective operation of democracy itself, and therefore integral to its proper understanding.

For our purposes here, one may wonder about the best participatory framework for identifying and securing the basis for such essential democratic rights. If these rights are to be enshrined constitutionally as non-negotiable and immune from fundamental alteration by any government, the practical question is how can that be achieved in practice? More broadly speaking, the success of constitutionalism apparently lies in its grounding in some idea, phenomenon, or practice that already possesses national or societal legitimacy. In other words, for constitutionalism to become a self-perpetuating phenomenon by developing a history of success that is evident proof of its value, it must be fundamentally connected to some such aspect of social or cultural existence whose legitimacy has already been assured. For the purposes of constitutionalism in present African societies, as discussed throughout this book, the question is what sources of legitimacy can sustain constitutionalism until it becomes culturally or socially legitimate in and of itself?

Concluding Remarks

As I have repeatedly emphasized throughout this book, each society must answer these questions for itself in light of its own history and context. By the same token, I have also stressed that comparative analysis should not mean taking European and North American models as definitive, or expecting other societies to simply copy those successful models. Thus, the concept of constitutionalism can be expanded and positively universalized, provided the idea it represents can include different histories, without necessarily privileging any one. In contrasting different trajectories of constitutional development in Western Europe and the Ottoman Empire, Spivak observes:

If we take the Conquest of Istanbul (1453) as a dividing line, we can see parallel but highly differentiated formations developing in Mediterranean and Western Europe on the one hand and the Ottoman Empire on the other. What characterizes the latter is the extraordinarily active and vastly heterogeneous diasporic activity that is constantly afoot on its terrain. . . . [If] Western Europe is not taken as a norm, the successes and vicissitudes of the Ottoman Empire can be seen as an extraordinary series of experiments to negotiate questions of ethnicity, religion, and "national" identity upon a model rather different from the emergence of nationalism in the former space. (Spivak 1993: 175–76)

Accordingly, I believe, associating modern constitutionalism with certain basic principles but not limiting their meaning to the history of their so-called "countries of origin" can provide a wider set of historical resources as well as conceptual tools for sustaining the principle itself. Moreover, constitutionalism can also be seen as constantly concerned with issues of mediating power, the progressive securing of power by the people and the process by which the agency of the people is institutionalized within structures of power that obtain in any society. The focus should therefore be on the de facto power that was (is) available to the people, whatever mechanisms and processes they were (are) able to actually use in realizing and sustaining that power. The implication of this is that the events by which the power of the people was historically secured in any Western context need not be seen as a necessary prerequisite for the establishment of a successful constitutionalism in other societies.

However, as illustrated with reference to the American constitution earlier, a key attribute of the modern notion of a constitution is its prescriptive and normative character, beyond its function of describing political organization in any particular society. In this modern sense, a constitution "becomes a legally binding blueprint for constructing rational society; rather than reflecting social conditions, it proposes to model them on its own image" (Preuss, 1995: 31). This dimension of constitutionalism encompasses both the process of constitution-making and the idea of shaping a society along certain lines. The earlier discussion of the contingent role of Islam in either promoting or obstructing the development and legitimization of constitutionalism in Islamic African societies is an effort to address this prescriptive and normative dimension of the subject.

To the extent that the vision reflected in any constitution is idealistic, there will necessarily be some gap between the defining ideals and the mechanisms for the actual operations of government, preservation and protection of sovereignty, or protection of rights. But there should also be some coherent relationship between the ideals sought to be achieved, such as equality, liberty or sovereignty of the people, and the processes that are guided or regulated by these ideals. In the case of Western constitutionalism, the ideals themselves can clearly be seen as part of a legacy of Enlightenment thought. At the same time, that legacy has been reflected and shaped in actual historical events such as the French Revolution of 1789 which sought to translate those ideals into practice.

In my view, the lasting value of such ideals rests in the synergy between the ideal and its practice or history. For instance, if civil rights as an ideal are constitutionally articulated and protected, they would be available to citizens as an enabling resource. The practice of various groups in using this ideal or mobilizing for their rights, in turn, expands and further entrenches the ideal in more institutional and practical terms. That practice reaffirms the value of the ideal while demonstrating its practical applicability. The point here is that if we view a constitution as a legally binding blueprint for constructing rational society (Preuss, 1995: 31), that rationality must have the necessary degree of concrete relationship with the rationality of social and cultural life. The two must fall within some common framework, whether the reference points are historical events, or current conditions and challenges facing the particular society.

This does not mean that these ideals do not have value beyond their contexts of origin or do not have any intrinsic rationality. But for the rationality of the social vision of a constitution to be effective, it must be understood and appreciated by citizens from their own frames of reference. How constitutional ideals are articulated and protected, as well as the manner and degree of their practice that is necessary for rationality to be appreciated by the citizens of a country, are the product of the historical experience of each society. As the earlier review illustrates, the political ideals of equality, liberty or sovereignty are neither interpreted in identical fashion in the American, French, and British constitutional systems, nor have they been practiced in the same way by those societies at different stages of their development. Thus, the intrinsic rationality of these concepts is linked in contextually-specific ways to the rationality (or rationalities) of the social and political fabric of each of these societies.

In the final analysis, the question is how to communicate and link the rationality of constitutional ideals with the economic, social or cultural contextual rationalities of the people concerned. With regard to African constitutionalism, this question and others raised earlier are significantly conditioned by the historical experience of colonialism and the dynamics of global political and economic power differential among different regions or countries of the world. The ultimate conclusion of the analysis presented in this book, I hope, is that constitutionalism is succeeding in African counties, each on its own terms. Since that process is necessarily contextual and its outcome contingent on a variety of factors, this book is a call for action to consolidate and promote constitutional governance in all African countries, and not for accepting the status quo as an inevitable or final situation.

References

Abraham, W. E. 1962. *The Mind of Africa.* London: Weidenfeld and Nicolson.

Ackerman, B. 1997. "The Rise of World Constitutionalism." *Virginia Law Review* 83 (4): 771–97.

Ahluwalia, D. Pal S. 2001. *Politics and Post-Colonial Theory: African Inflections.* New York: Routledge.

Aka, P. 2000. "Nigeria: The Need for an Effective Policy of Ethic Reconciliation in the New Century." *Temple International and Comparative Law Journal* 14: 328–61.

Anderson, J. N. D. 1976. *Law Reform in the Muslim World.* London: University of London, Athlone Press.

Anderson, L. 1997. "Fulfilling Prophesies: State Policy and Islamist Radicalism." In J. Esposito, ed., *Political Islam: Revolution, Radicalism, or Reform?* Boulder, Colo.: Lynne Rienner. 17–32.

Anderson, W. T. 1990. *Reality Isn't What It Used to Be.* San Francisco: Harper.

An-Na'im, A. A. 1990. *Toward an Islamic Reformation: Civil Liberties, Human Rights and International Law.* Syracuse, N.Y.: Syracuse University Press.

———, ed. 1992. *Human Rights in Cross-Cultural Perspectives: Quest for Consensus.* Philadelphia: University of Pennsylvania Press.

———. 1993. "Constitutional Discourse and the Civil War in the Sudan." In M. W. Daly and A. Sikainga, eds., *Civil War in the Sudan.* London: British Academic Press. 102–11.

———. 2000. "Shari'a and Positive Legislation: Is an Islamic State Possible or Viable?" In E. Cotran et al., eds., *Yearbook of Islamic and Middle Eastern Law.* The Hague: Kluwer Law. 29–42.

———. 2002a. "Religion and Global Civil Society: Inherent Incompatibility or Synergy and Interdependence." In M. Glasius et al., eds., *Global Civil Society 2002.* Oxford: Oxford University Press. 55–73.

———. 2002b. *Cultural Transformation and Human Rights in Africa.* London: Zed Books.

———, ed. 2003. *Human Rights Under African Constitutions: Realizing the Promise for Ourselves.* Philadelphia: University of Pennsylvania Press.

An-Na'im, A. A. and F. Deng. 1997. "Self Determination and Unity: The Case of Sudan." *Law and Society* 18: 199–223.

Appiah, K. A. 1992. *In My Father's House: Africa in the Philosophy of Culture.* New York: Oxford University Press.

Ashenafi, M. 2003. "Ethiopia: Processes of Democratization and Development." In Abdullahi Ahmed An-Na'im, ed., *Human Rights Under African Constitutions: Realizing the Promise for Ourselves*. Philadelphia: University of Pennsylvania Press. 29–51.

Assensoh, A. B. and Yvette Alex-Assensoh. 2001. *African Military History and Politics: Ideological Coups and Incursions, 1900–Present*. New York: Palgrave.

Beck, L. 2001. "Reining in the Marabouts? Democratization and Local Governance in Senegal." *African Affairs* 100: 601–21.

Behrman, L. 1970. *Muslim Brotherhoods and Politics in Senegal*. London: Oxford University Press.

Bhargava, R. 1999. "Introduction." In R. Bhargava, ed., *Secularism and Its Critics*. New Delhi: Oxford University Press. 1–28.

Bilgrami, A. 1999. "Secularism, Nationalism, and Modernity." In R. Bhargava, ed., *Secularism and Its Critics*. New Delhi: Oxford University Press. 380–417.

Billias, G. 1990. "Introduction." In G. Billias, ed., *American Constitutionalism Abroad: Selected Essays in Comparative Constitutional History*. New York: Greenwood Press.

Binsbergen, W. van. 1990. "Islam as a Constitutive Factor in African 'Traditional' Religion: The Evidence from Geomantic Divination." In A. Breedveld, J. van Santen, and W. M. J. van Binsbergen, eds., *Islam and Transformations in Africa*. <http://www.shikanda.net/african_religion/islampaper_def_2003_RTF.pdf>

Blaut, J. M. 1993. *The Colonizer's Model of the World: Geographical Diffusionism and Eurocentric History*. New York: Guilford Press.

Boahen, A. 1987. *African Perspectives on Colonialism*. Baltimore: Johns Hopkins University Press.

Brenner, L. 1988 "Concepts of Tariqa in West Africa: The Case of the Qadiriyya." In C. O'Brien and C. Coulon, eds., *Charisma and Brotherhood in African Islam*. Oxford: Clarendon Press. 33–52.

Bromhead, P. 1974. *Britain's Developing Constitution*. New York: St. Martin's Press.

Bukovansky, M. 2002. *Legitimacy and Power Politics: the American and French Revolutions in International Political Culture*. Princeton, N.J.: Princeton University Press.

Busia, N. K. A. 2003. "Ghana: Competing Visions of Liberal Democracy and Socialism." In A. A. An-Na'im, ed., *Human Rights Under African Constitutions: Realizing the Promise for Ourselves*. Philadelphia: University of Pennsylvania Press. 52–96.

Camilleri, J. 1990. "Rethinking Sovereignty in a Shrinking, Fragmented World." In R. B. J. Walker and Saul Mendlovitz, eds., *Contending Sovereignties: Redefining Political Community*. Boulder, Colo.: Lynne Rienner. 35–36.

Chabal, P. and J. Daloz. 1999. *Africa Works: Disorder as Political Instrument*. Bloomington: Indiana University Press.

Chakrabarty, D. 1992. "Trafficking in History and Theory: Subaltern Studies." In K. K. Ruthven, ed., *Beyond the Disciplines: The New Humanities*. Canberra: Australian Academy of the Humanities. 101–8.

Chazan, N., R. Mortimer, J. Ravenhill, and D. Rothschild. 1992. *Politics and Society in Contemporary Africa*. 2nd ed. Boulder, Colo.: Lynne Rienner.

Cheru, F. 2002. *African Renaissance: Roadmaps to the Challenge of Globalization*. London: Zed Books.

Clark, A. 1999. "Imperialism, Independence, and Islam in Senegal and Mali." *Africa Today* 46: 148–67.

Collins, R., ed. 1994. *Historical Problems of Imperial Africa*. Princeton, N.J.: Marcus Weiner.

Cooper, F. 1994. "Conflict and Connection: Rethinking Colonial African History." *American Historical Review* 99: 1516–45.

Coulon, C. and D. O'Brien. 1989. "Senegal." In D. O'Brien, J. Dunn, and R. Rathbone, eds., *Contemporary West African States*. Cambridge: Cambridge University Press. 145–64.

Coulson, N. J. (1957), "The State and the Individual in Islamic Law." *International and Comparative Law Quarterly* 6: 49–60.

Creevey, L. E. 1985. "Muslim Brotherhoods and Politics in Senegal in 1985." *Journal of Modern African Studies* 23: 715–21.

———. 1991. "The Impact of Islam on Women in Senegal." *Journal of Developing Areas* 25: 347–68.

Dadamo, C. and S. Farran. 1993. *The French Legal System*. London: Sweet and Maxwell.

Davis, G. et al., eds. 2004. *Towards a Transcultural Future: Literature and Society in a "Post"-Colonial World*. Amsterdam: Rodopi.

Dworkin, R. 1977. *Taking Rights Seriously*. Cambridge, Mass.: Harvard University Press.

———. 1996. *Freedom's Law: The Moral Reading of the American Constitution*. Cambridge, Mass.: Harvard University Press.

———. 2000. *Sovereign Virtue: The Theory and Practice of Equality*. Cambridge, Mass.: Harvard University Press.

Elkin, S. and K. E. Soltan, eds. 1993. *A New Constitutionalism*. Chicago: University of Chicago Press.

Eltringham, N. 2004. *Accounting for Horror: Post-Genocide Debates in Rwanda*. London: Sterling.

Erlich, H. and I. Gershoni, eds. 1999. *The Nile: History, Conflict, Myths*. Boulder, Colo.: Lynne Rienner.

Eze, E. 1997. "Democracy or Consensus? A Response to Wiredu." In E. Eze, ed., *Postcolonial African Philosophy: A Critical Reader*. Cambridge, Mass.: Blackwell. 303–10.

Fage, J. D. with William Tordoff. 2002. *A History of Africa*. 3rd ed. London: Routledge.

Falk, R. 1992. *Explorations at the End of Time*. Philadelphia: Temple University Press.

Falola, T. 1988. "Violence in Nigeria: The Crisis of Religious Politics and Secular Ideologies." Book Review. *Journal of Religion in Africa* 18: 243.

Falola, T. and C. Jennings, eds. 2002. *Africanizing Knowledge: African Studies Across the Disciplines*. New Brunswick, N.J.: Transaction Publishers.

Fegley, R.A. 2005. "Mobutu Sese Seko." *Microsoft® Encarta® Online Encyclopedia 2005*. http://encarta.msn.com

Franklin, D. and M. Baun, eds. 1995. *Political Culture and Constitutionalism: A Comparative Approach*. Armonk, N.Y.: M.E. Sharpe.

Gahamanyi, B. 2003. "Rwanda: Building Constitutional Order in the Aftermath of Genocide." In A. A. An-Na'im, ed., *Human Rights Under African Constitutions: Realizing the Promise for Ourselves*. Philadelphia: University of Pennsylvania Press. 251–94.

Gellar, S. 1982. *Senegal: An African Nation Between Islam and the West*. Boulder, Colo.: Westview Press.

Gellner, E. 1983. *Nations and Nationalism*. Ithaca, N.Y.: Cornell University Press.

Ghai, Y. 1993. "Constitutions and Governance in Africa: A Prolegomenon." In S. Adelman and A. Paliwala, eds., *Law and Crisis in the Third World.* London: Hans Zell. 52–75.

Giddens, A. 1990. *The Consequences of Modernity.* Stanford, Calif.: Stanford University Press.

Gordon, S. 1999. *Controlling the State: Constitutionalism from Ancient Athens to Today* Cambridge: Harvard University Press.

Griffiths, I. 1995. *The African Inheritance.* New York: Routledge.

Gurevitch, P. 1998. *We Wish to Inform You That Tomorrow We Will Be Killed with Our Families: Stories from Rwanda.* New York: Farrar, Straus and Giroux.

Gutman, A. 1999. "Law and Responsibility Lecture Series: Religious Freedom and Civic Responsibility.' *Washington and Lee Law Review* 56: 907–22.

Gyekye K. 1997. *Tradition and Modernity: Philosophical Reflections on the African Experience.* New York: Oxford University Press.

Haile, M. 1996. "The New Ethiopian Constitution: Its Impact upon Unity, Human Rights and Development." *Suffolk Transnational Law Review* 20: 1–84.

Held, V. 1984. *Rights and Goods: Justifying Social Action.* New York: Collier Macmillan.

Helmholz, R. H. 1999. "Magna Carta and the *ius commune,*" *University of Chicago Law Review* 66.

Henkin, L. 1990. "Introduction." In L. Henkin and A. Rosenthal, eds., *Constitutionalism and Rights.* New York: Columbia University Press. 1–15.

Hinsley, F. 1986. *Sovereignty.* New York: Cambridge University Press.

Hiskett M. 1984. *The Development of Islam in West Africa.* New York: Longman.

Hodder-Williams, R. 1984. *An Introduction to the Politics of Tropical Africa.* London: Allen and Urwin.

Holmes, S. 1995. "Constitutionalism." In S. M. Lipset, ed., *Encyclopedia of Democracy.* 4 vols. Washington D.C.: *Congressional Quarterly* 1: 299–306.

Howard R. E. 1995. *Human Rights and the Search for Community.* Boulder, Colo.: Westview Press.

Huband, M. 2001. *The Skull Beneath the Skin: Africa After the Cold War.* Boulder, Colo.: Westview Press

Hunwick, J. O. 1997. "Sub-Saharan Africa and the Wider World of Islam: Historical and Contemporary Perspectives." In E. E. Rosanders and D. Westerlund, eds., *African Islam and Islam in Africa: Encounters Between Sufis and Islamists.* Athens: Ohio University Press, 28–54.

Ibiranga, G. 1973. *The Forging of an African Nation: The Political and Constitutional Evolution of Uganda from Colonial Rule to Independence.* New York: Viking Press.

Ibrahim, J. 2003. *Democratic Transition in Anglophone West Africa.* CODESRIA Monograph Series. Dakar: CODESRIA.

Ilesanmi, S. 2001. "Constitutional Treatment of Religion and Politics of Human Rights in Nigeria." *African Affairs*: 529–54.

Isaacman, A. 1990. "Peasants and Rural Social Protest in Africa." *African Studies Review* 33 (2): 1–120.

Jackson, R. H. and Carl G. Rosberg. 1984. "Pax African and Its Problems." In R. Bissell and M. Radu, eds., *Africa in the Post-Decolonization Era.* New Brunswick, N.J.: Transaction Books. 157–82.

———. 1986. "Sovereigty and Undevelopment: Juridical Statehood in the African Crisis." *Journal of Modern African Studies* 24: 1–31.

Kane, I. 2003. "Guinea: Building the Rule of Law for Social Development." In A. A. An-Na'im, ed., *Human Rights Under African Constitutions: Realizing the Promise for Ourselves.* Philadelphia: University of Pennsylvania Press. 97–151.

Karugire, S. 1980. *A Political History of Uganda.* Nairobi: Heinemann Educational Books.

Keller, M. 1987. "Powers and Rights: Two Centuries of American Constitutionalism." *Journal of American History* 74: 675–94.

Kloppenberg, L. A. 1999. Review of E. D. Smith and P. Fitzpatrick, eds., *Laws of the Postcolonial, Law and Politics Book Review* 10, 5 (May 2000): 330–32.

Lattimer M. and Philippe Sands, eds. 2003. *Justice for Crimes Against Humanity.* Oxford: Hart.

Levtzion, N. 1994. *Islam in West Africa.* Hampshire, UK: Variorum.

Lewis, I. M. 1980. *Islam in Tropical Africa.* Bloomington: Indiana University Press.

Low, D. 1960. *Buganda and British Overrule, 1900–1955: Two Studies.* London: Oxford University Press.

Lutz, D. S. 1988. *The Origins of American Constitutionalism.* Baton Rouge: Louisiana State University Press.

Mamdani, M. 1990. "The Social Basis of Constitutionalism in Africa." *Journal of Modern African Studies* 28: 359–74.

———. 1991. "Social Movements and Constitutionalism in the African Context." In Issa G. Shivji, ed., *State and Constitutionalism: An African Debate on Democracy.* Harare: Southern Africa Political Series (SAPES) Trust. 237–50.

Mathews J. T. 1989. "Redefining Security," *Foreign Affairs* 68: 168.

Mazrui, A. 2003. "Afrennaissance: Struggles of Hope in Post-Colonial Africa." In E. Onwudiwe and M. Ibelema, eds., *Afro-Optimism: Perspectives on Africa's Advances.* Westport, Conn.: Praeger. 63–176.

Mayer A. E. 1993. "The Fundamentalist Impact on Law, Politics, and Constitutions in Iran, Pakistan, and the Sudan." In M. Marty and R. Appleby, eds., *Fundamentalisms and the State.* Chicago: University of Chicago Press. 110–51.

McHugh, J. T. 2002. *Comparative Constitutional Traditions.* New York: Peter Lang.

McIlwan C. 1940. *Constitutionalism Ancient and Modern.* Ithaca, N.Y.: Cornell University Press.

Mudimbe, V. Y. 1994. *The Idea of Africa.* Bloomington: Indiana University Press.

Mukholi, D. 1995. *A Complete Guide to Uganda's Fourth Constitution: History, Politics and the Law.* Kampala: Fountain Publishers.

Muriuki, G. 1974. *A History of the Gikuyu 1500–1900.* London: Oxford University Press

Murphy W. 1993. "Constitutions, Constitutionalism, and Democracy." In Douglas Greenberg et al., eds., *Constitutionalism and Democracy: Transitions in the Contemporary World.* New York: Oxford University Press, 1993. 3–25.

Mutua, M. 2000. "The Tutsi and Hutu Need a Partition." *New York Times,* August 30.

Negash, T. and K. Tronvoll. 2000. *Brothers at War: Making Sense of the Eritrean-Ethiopian War.* London: James Currey

O'Brien, D. 1986. "Wails and Whispers: the People's Voice in West African Muslim Politics." In P. Chabal, ed., *Political Domination in Africa.* Cambridge: Cambridge University Press. 71–191.

Osaghae, E. 2001. *The Management of the National Question in Nigeria.* Idaban: University of Ibadan.

Pilkington, C. 1999. *The Politics Today Companion to the British Constitution.* New York: Manchester University Press.

Pouwel, R. 1987. *Horn and Crescent: Cultural Change and Traditional Islam on the East African Coast.* London: Cambridge University Press.

Prakash, G. 1994. "Subaltern Studies as Postcolonial Criticism." *American Historical Review* 99 (5): 1475–90.

Preuss, U. 1995. *Constitutional Revolution: The Link Between Constitutionalism and Progress.* Atlantic Highlands, N.J.: Humanities Press.

Quinn, C. and F. Quinn. 2003. *Pride, Faith, and Fear: Islam in Sub-Saharan Africa.* New York: Oxford University Press.

Ranger, T. O. 1967. *Revolt in Southern Rhodesia, 1896–7: A Study in African Resistance.* London: Heinemann.

———. 1994. "African Reaction to the Imposition of Colonial Rule in East and Central Africa." In R. Collins, ed., *Historical Problems of Imperial Africa.* Princeton, N.J.: Marcus Weiner. 74–83.

Rawls, J. 1971. *A Theory of Justice.* Cambridge, Mass.: Harvard University Press.

Report 2003. U.S. Department of State Bureau of Democracy, Human Rights and Labor, *International Religious Freedom Report 2002, Nigeria* (released on October 7, 2002) <http://www.state.gov/g/drl/rls/irf/2002/14073.htm>.

Robinson, D. 1988. "French 'Islamic' Policy and Practice in Late Nineteenth Century Senegal." *Journal of African History* 29 (3): 415–35.

Rohr, J. 1995. *Founding Republics in France and America: A Study in Constitutional Governance.* Lawrence: University Press of Kansas.

Rosenau, P. 1992. *Postmodernism and the Social Sciences: Insights, Inroads, and Intrusions.* Princeton, N.J.: Princeton University Press.

Rosenbaum, A., ed. 1988. *Constitutionalism: The Philosophical Dimension.* New York: Greenwood Press.

Rosenfeld, M. 1994. *Constitutionalism, Identity, Difference, and Legitimacy.* Durham, N.C.: Duke University Press.

Ross, E. 1995. "Touba: A Spiritual Metropolis in the Modern World." *Canadian Journal of African Studies* 29 (2): 222–59.

Salam, A. and A. de Waal, eds. 2001. *The Phoenix State: Civil Society and the Future of Sudan.* Trenton, N.J.: Red Sea Press.

Sanneh, L. 1997. *The Crown and the Turban: Muslims and West African Pluralism.* Boulder, Colo.: Westview Press.

Sartori, G. 2003. "Constitutionalism: A Preliminary Discussion." *American Political Science Review* 56 (4): 853–64.

Schachter, O. 1983. "Editorial Comment: Human Dignity as a Normative Concept." *American Journal of International Law* 77 (4): 848–54.

Schaffer, F. 1998. *Democracy in Translation: Understanding Politics in an Unfamiliar Culture.* Ithaca, N.Y.: Cornell University Press.

Schwartz, B. 1967. *The Roots of Freedom: A Constitutional History of England.* New York: Hill and Wang.

Selassie, B. 1997. "Self-Determination in Principle and Practice: The Ethiopia-Eritrean Experience." *Columbia Human Rights Law Review* 29(1): 91–142.

Serequeberhan, T. 1994. *The Hermeneutics of African Philosophy: Horizons and Discourse.* New York: Routledge.

———. 2000. *Our Heritage: The Past in the Present of African-American and African Existence.* Lanham, Md.: Rowman and Littlefield.

Shahin, E. 1997. *Political Ascent: Contemporary Islamic Movements in North Africa.* Boulder, Colo.: Westview Press.

Shils, E. 1991. "The Virtue of Civil Society." *Government and Opposition* 26: 3–20.

Shivji, I. 1998. "Problems of Constitution-Making as Consensus-Building: The Tanzania experience." In O. Sichone, ed., *The State and Constitutionalism in Southern Africa*. Harare: SAPES Books. 23–50.

Slater, D. 2004. *Geopolitics and the Post-Colonial: Rethinking North-South Relations*. Malden, Mass.: Blackwell.

Smith, A. 1991. *National Identity*. London: Penguin

———. 2000. *Nationalism: Theory, Ideology, History*. Cambridge: Polity Press.

Spivak, G. 1993. "Scattered Speculations on the Question of Cultural Studies." In S. During, ed., *The Cultural Studies Reader*. London: Routledge. 169–88.

Stewart C. C. 1990. "Islam." In A. D. Roberts, ed., *The Colonial Moment in Africa: Essays on the Movement of Minds and Materials*. New York: Cambridge University Press. 191–222.

Sztompka, P. 2002. "Civilizational Competence: A Prerequisite of Post-Communist Transition." http://www.ces.uj.edu.pl/sztompka/competence.htm

Suberu, R. T. 1995. "Institutions, Political Culture, and Constitutionalism in Nigeria. In D. Franklin and M. Baun, eds., *Political Culture and Constitutionalism: A Comparative Approach*. Armonk, N.Y.: M.E. Sharpe. 197–218.

Thieme, J. 2003. *Post-Colonial Studies: The Essential Glossary*. London: Arnold.

Thorpe, N. F., ed. 1909: *The Federal and State Constitutions, Colonial Charters, and Other Organic Laws of the States, Territories, and Colonies Now or Heretofore Forming the United States*. 7 vols. Washington, D.C.: Government Printing Office. 7: 3812.

Tignor, R. 1971. "Colonial Chiefs in Chiefless Societies." *Journal of Modern African Studies* 9 (3): 339–59.

Triaud, J. L. 2000. "Islam in Africa Under French Colonial Rule." In Nehemia Levtzion and Randall L. Pouwells, eds., *History of Islam in Africa*. Athens: Ohio University Press. 169–87.

Trimingham, J. S. 1970. *A History of Islam in West Africa*. London: Oxford University Press, 1970.

———. 1980. *The Influence of Islam upon Africa*, 2nd ed. London: Longman, 1980.

Turpin, C. 1990. *British Government and the Constitution: Text, Cases, Materials*. 2nd ed. London: Weidenfield and Nicolson.

Twibell, T. 1999. "Ethiopian Constitutional Law: The Structure of the Ethiopian Government and the New Constitution's Ability to Overcome Ethiopia's Problems." *Loyola of Los Angeles International and Comparative Law Journal* 21 (2): 399–465.

Villalón, L. 1995. *Islamic Society and State Power in Senegal*. Cambridge: Cambridge University Press.

———. 1999 "Generational Changes, Political Stagnation, and the Evolving Dynamics of Religion and Politics in Senegal." *Africa Today* 46: 129–47.

Voll, J. 1982. *Islam, Continuity and Change in the Modern World*. Boulder, Colo.: Westview.

Wagaw, T. 1997. "Education and Language Policy in a Divided Ethiopia: Reversing the Quest of the Centuries and Pressing Toward the Uncharter Future." In K. Fukui, E. Kurimoto, and M. Shigeta., eds., *Ethiopia in Broader Perspective: Papers of the XIIIth International Conference of Ethiopian Studies*, vol. 3. Kyoto: Shokado Book.

Winchester, B. N 1995. "African Politics Since Independence." In Phyllis M. Martin and Patrick O'Meara, eds., *Africa*. 3rd ed. Bloomington: Indiana University Press.

Wiredu, K. 1997. "Democracy and Consensus in African Traditional Politics: A Plea for a Non-Party Polity." In E. Eze, ed., *Postcolonial African Philosophy: A Critical Reader*. Cambridge, Mass.: Blackwell. 303–12.

Woody, H. 2005. An "Excess of Democracy"—Or a Shortage? Federalists' Earliest Adversaries." *Journal of the Early Republic* 25 (3).

Wriston, W. 1992. *The Twilight of Sovereignty: How the Information Revolution Is Transforming Our World*. New York: Maxwell Macmillan.

Young, C. 2002. "Itineraries of Ideas of Freedom in Africa: Precolonial to Postcolonial." In R. H. Taylor, ed., *The Idea of Freedom in Asia and Africa*. Stanford, Calif.: Stanford University Press, 2002. 9–39.

———. 1994. *The African Colonial State in Comparative Perspective*. New Haven, Conn.: Yale University Press.

Zacher, Mark W. 1992. "The Decaying Pillars of the Westphalian Temple: Implications for International Order and Governance." In J. N. Rosenau and E.-O. Czempiel, eds., *Governance Without Government: Order and Change in World Politics*. Cambridge: Cambridge University Press. 60.

Index

Abacha, Sani, 91, 140
Aboud, Ibrahim, 133
Abbasid monarchy, 11; empire, 12
Abu Bakr, first Caliph, 11
Acholi, 83
Addis Ababa Agreement, 134, 138
Agabi, Kanu, 143
Afrennaisance, 30
African Charter on Human and Peoples'
  Rights, 73, 77, 89
African Union, 50, 52. *See also*
  Organization for African Unity
Ahidjo, Ahmadou, 93
Ahmed, Mohammed, 133
Akan, 36, 37–38
al-Banna, Hasan, 119
al-Mahdi, Saddiq, 133, 136
al-Turabi, Hassan, 134
Ali, fourth Caliph, 10, 11
Almoravid Islamic sect, 110
Alur, 83
American Declaration of Independence
  (1776), 168, 169
American Revolution, 169, 175, 176
Amhara, 64
Amin, Idi, 86, 92, 93
Ankole, 83–85
Apartheid regime, 92
Arab/Palestinian conflict, 114
Armed Forces Revolutionary Council
  (AFRC), 69
Articles of Confederation, 168
Arusha Peace Agreement of 1992–93, 77
Asante, 92
Ashanti, 36–37, 45

"Assimiliation," 44, 45, 92. *See also*
  Colonialism
"Association," 44, 45. *See also* Colonialism
Association Malienne pour l'Unité et le
  Progrès de l'Islam (AMUPI), 117
Association for the Social Progress of the
  Masses (APROSOMA), 76

Babangida, Ibrahim, 140
Baganda, 39, 83
Bakiga, 83
Banda, Kamuzu, 93
Banjul Charter. *See* African Charter
Banyankole, 83
Banyoro, 83
Batoro, 83
Bay'a, 11, 15
Berbers, 107
Besigye, Kizza, 87
Bill of Rights (1689), 4, 166
Black Islam, 114–15
British Commonwealth, 91
Buganda, 83–86
Bunyoro, 83–85

Cairo Declaration of Border Disputes, 89
Caliphs, 9–10, 11, 12; political authority
  of, 174; "rightly guided," 9–10
Capitalism, 178; European, 40; global, 32,
  90, 92
Chama cha Mapinduzi (CCM), 80–82
Chernobyl, 57
Civic engagement, 5, 6
Civil society, 28, 49, 57, 140, 178
Cold war, 90, 92